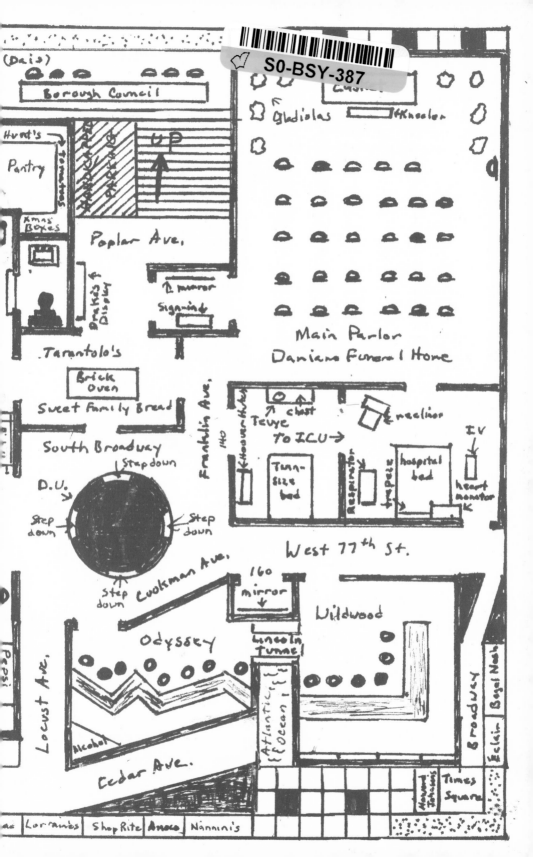

LUNCHEON
ETTE

LUNCHEON-
ETTE

A MEMOIR

STEVEN SORRENTINO

10 ReganBooks
Celebrating Ten Bestselling Years
An Imprint of HarperCollins*Publishers*

*Luncheonette is a memoir about my family and particularly about my father and his restaurant, Clint's Cor-
ner. However, some of the names of employees and patrons of the restaurant have been changed, and some of the
details about these characters and others involved in my personal life have been changed.*

HarperCollins books may be purchased for educational, business, or sales promotional use. For information please write: Special Markets Department, HarperCollins Publishers Inc., 10 East 53rd Street,
New York, NY 10022.

FIRST EDITION

Designed by Kris Tobiassen

Printed on acid-free paper

Library of Congress Cataloging-in-Publication Data

Sorrentino, Steven, 1957–
   Luncheonette : a memoir / Steven Sorrentino.
      p. cm.
   ISBN 0-06-072892-2
      1. Clint's Corner (Restaurant) 2. Restaurants—New Jersey—West Long Branch. 3. Sorrentino,
Steven, 1957– 4. Fathers and sons. I. Title.

TX945.5.C55S67 2005
647.95749'46—dc22

                                                                                        2004051462

05   06   07   08   09   RRD   10   9   8   7   6   5   4   3   2   1

TO
FRANK "CLINT" SORRENTINO
MY FATHER, FOR FILLING MY LIFE WITH SONG

AND
DEL GORDON
MY FRIEND AND SPIRITUAL GUIDE, FOR HELPING ME FACE THE MUSIC.

FOR BOTH OF THESE MEN,
I AM ETERNALLY GRATEFUL....

CONTENTS

PART II

PART III

LUNCHEON-ETTE

PROLOGUE
CLINT'S CORNER

Not one of the old prophets was waiting to greet me the day after Christmas at five-fucking-freezing-thirty in the morning. Instead, sad sacks of bread huddled outside the front door: the seeded Knipp's rolls, a dozen of Eli's water bagels, and crusty submarines from Nino's. And smack up against the step, a small bundle of the *New York Times* lay crushed beneath the much larger stacks of the *Asbury Park Press*—the *real* paper of record if you lived in West Long Branch, New Jersey.

I'd been coming to this luncheonette since I was a kid, way before Dad bought it a year ago. The old regulars still spun around on the turquoise stools, predicting the outcome of the local elections or extolling the promises of life in general. But none of them could have foreseen what happened to my father on Christmas Eve—or that I was about to experience life from *behind* the counter for the first time.

I clutched the bankroll (actually fifty bucks stuffed into a Dutch Masters cigar box) and fumbled with my keys to unlock the door. Once I had transferred all the deliveries from the sidewalk into the warmth of the luncheonette,

TABLE	GUESTS	SERVER
	2	PROLOGUE

I pulled out my spiral notebook to review the copious notes I'd taken last night at the hospital.

Okay, what did Dad say to do next? Oh yes, turn on the lights—with the switch!

The first customer of the morning came tripping through the front door, regained his footing, then scuffed over to the counter in his unbuckled galoshes.

"Howdy, Mr. Steve. Givin' the ole man a break?" Stanley was an employee of the roads department, but his plaid hat with the flaps made him look more like a duck hunter.

"Well, not exactly, Stanley. We had to rush him to the hospital on Christmas Eve."

"What the heck?" He pulled the hat from his head as if he hadn't heard right, then hopped up onto the spinning-stool center counter, where he'd be afforded the best view of the grill.

"Coffee?" I asked.

"Yep." He scractched his head, waiting for more details.

"Well, his leg started going numb on him like he was having a stroke or something. Milk?"

"Yep."

I walked down to the dispenser and filled one of those old-fashioned, single-portion glass creamers. Dad didn't use pitchers. It may have required a little extra effort, but these vintage little throwbacks to the golden age of diners and luncheonettes went a long way in adding charm and atmosphere to the joint.

To-do list: Get rid of those goddamn creamers.

Stanley emptied his little plop of milk into his coffee.

"Is Pop gonna be okay?" He talked into his cup like it was one of those Magic 8 Balls with the free-floating stock answers.

Outlook not so good.

"They don't know what's wrong with him, Stanley. All we know is that he can't walk. He's paralyzed."

Even on a good day, Stanley's style was more deadpan than one of the refrigerated stiffs over at the Damiano Funeral Home, so it was difficult to gauge his reaction to the news. "Shit," he said drily, "I'll have a porkroll-egg-and-cheese."

"Coming right up."

The Bay Marie was just beyond the grill, situated between the Corey coffee machine and the electric meat slicer. The large aluminum hood opened like a convertible car roof. I stared for a few seconds at the chilled bins of mayonnaise, tomatoes, tuna salad, shredded lettuce, and cold cuts. *Hmmm.*

I needed to refer to my spiral notebook again. But I neglected to lower the hood when I walked away. My heart skipped a beat when the warped metal came thundering down.

Stanley immediately looked up at the ceiling and began whistling a random tune to spare me the embarrassment.

I retrieved my notebook from under the counter, did a quick review of *porkroll-egg-and-cheese,* and finally returned to the Bay Marie to start my order.

The three porkroll slices curled up when I tossed them onto the hot grill until I remembered that Dad had told me to score them around the edges. I made little cuts into them with the spatula, allowing them to relax flat and brown properly just like he said they would.

But he left out one little detail about the egg.

I slathered the cooler part of the grill surface with an oozy yellowish product called Kaola Gold, named as if it were some precious natural resource when in fact it was just lard and additives. I cracked open an egg and emptied its contents onto the slick of golden fat, thinking I had everything under control until Stanley offered a little tip.

"Uh, maybe you could break the yoke to harden it up," he hinted. "I'm wearin' m'good shirt today," he indicated, miming a bite into the imaginary sandwich and egg leaking onto his flannel as he flinched for effect.

Getting the point, I popped the egg yoke with the spatula and let it cook for about thirty seconds, flipped it, and topped it with a slice of American cheese that immediately began to melt. Finally, I stacked the egg and cheese onto the porkroll slices and transferred the greasy delicacy onto a buttered Knipp's roll. I delivered the small blue plate to Stanley with just enough of a thud on the counter to punctuate the first porkroll-egg-and-cheese sandwich of my career.

"There."

"Yep," he mumbled through his first bite. "It's good that you're helpin' out your dad."

"Yeah," I acknowledged, pulling a Knipp's roll from the bag and biting into it.

Cold air rushed in through the back door along with Googie the Gizmo. "Buuurrr!" He rubbed his arms up and down and shook his head, all the folds and excess flesh on his face shifting and jiggling like a Hanna-Barbera creation.

"Hey there, Mr. New York." Googie the Gizmo blew into his hands then rubbed them for friction. "What'd you do with the boss?"

"Mmm," I responded through a mouthful, "I'm afraid I have shum bad newsh."

His jowls dropped below chin line, the skin on his forehead bunching up like a wad of Silly Putty. He saw Stanley put his head down. "What the hell's goin' on here? Where's Clint?"

I told Googie what happened to his old high school buddy, adding a graphic description of the leg spasms I'd witnessed in the emergency room. As disturbed as I was by what I'd seen, I felt robotic telling the story and ending with a rigid hand gesture to demonstrate. "He's paralyzed up to *here*."

"Well, I'll be goddamned!" Googie tried to be tough like the leather jackets he and Dad and the other Gizmos had worn back in high school, no doubt feeling vulnerable in that moment—but nothing that a little porkroll-egg-and-cheese couldn't fix. "I'll have coffee with mine," he said.

I poured a round of refills as the three of us washed down the fresh Knipp's rolls, savoring the gentle numbing effect like they were St. Joseph's baby aspirins.

The shock was still lingering over the speckled Formica counter at about seven-thirty when we all heard the heavy slam of a car door and looked up to see Dad's head waitress storm the back entrance like a buxom paratrooper, her bosom crossing the threshold just slightly ahead of her Coke-bottle glasses. She spotted me behind the counter.

"Oh, Jesus Christ, if it isn't Mr. Long Black Coat from New York finally comin' in to do some work! How you doin', bay-bay?" she graveled in a voice that made Tallulah Bankhead sound like a coloratura. "Hey bay-bay, hey bay-bay," one each for Stanley and Googie, her lips flapping with each *b* as she unzipped her Poly-Fil parka, pulling it from her shoulders to reveal an apron already in place.

"Jesus Christ, I'm freezin' my tits off!" She pulled at her pilly Banlon shell and did a quick bra adjustment. "Turn up the goddamn heat and lower that goddamn radio. Everybody had a merry Christmas? Where's Clint?" Before anyone could respond, she disappeared into the back to hang up her coat.

"Dolores's here," Googie noted.

"Yep," Stanley droned.

"Dolores!" I tried to get her attention when she emerged from the kitchen.

"Hey, Steven, it's about time you gave your father a break. He's been workin' too goddamn hard. You know, I been in this business twenty-three years—twenty-three years!—and I know what it's like for your father to just be starting out. He's on that learning curb, ya know. I remember when my Vern—God rest his goddamn soul—and I opened the Pickle Place—ain't that a clever name?—we *never* took a break. Once he dropped dead, it was too late!" She was heading west toward the coffee station when her frosted bubble-cut wig began to inch up as if its elastic base would propel it from her head at any moment. She gave it a good yank down and swiftly tucked some errant hair back under. "You're a good son to be giving him some time off for the holidays—ya-know-wadda-mean? Good for you!"

"Dolores, I'm going to be running the business for a while, I think. You see—"

"Ohhh, brother, here we go!" she ranted while pouring herself a cup of coffee. "Sure, I remember when you came in here a few weeks ago with your long black coat from New York and sat your ass on one of those stools and got waited on like you were Billy Jean Queen. I'm tellin' you, hon, I been in this business for thirty years—thirty years!—ya-know-wadda-mean? And you don't just march in here and know what the fuck you're doing just because you come from New York!" She brushed by me again, though her synthetic fibers clung temporarily to my T-shirt as if her breasts were emitting a powerful magnetic field. I was practically pulled down the end of the counter after her.

"Dolores!" I finally got her attention. "We had to rush my father to the hospital on Christmas Eve." I began to recount the story to her, complete with my little hand gesture. "He's paralyzed up to *here*." Even Stanley, who sat for the encore, shook his head as if hearing it for the first time. I, on the other hand, was growing more numb with each telling, but couldn't seem to get enough of others' reactions.

"*Rrranny bozke!*" Dolores did the sign of the cross and finally came in for a landing on the end stool. I assume that the color had drained from her face, but I would have needed a spatula to scrape off the layers of pancake to be sure. "Holy *goovno*! It's just not fair, bay-bay. What happened, he have a stroke?"

"No, Dolores. They're not sure yet."

"Oh Jesus, I bet he's got that mutable sclerosis."

"Dolores, it's *multiple* sclerosis."

"Oh my Christ, what a shame!"

"No, he doesn't have multiple sclerosis. I was correcting you. You said *mutable* sclerosis."

"As they say in Polish, hon—*yebotch yeh!*" She raised the accompanying hand gesture then popped up from the stool and jumped right back into service. "Now come on, hon, we got a lotta work to do!" She hoisted up her stretch pants. "Clint's countin' on us to keep this business goin', now move your ass!" She gave her own a little slap.

"Dolores—" I stood in front of the Bay Marie frozen in my tracks, my head beginning to ache with stress.

"Oh, *boychick*." She slowed down on her way to the sink. "I know, I know. Your father's a very sick man—but these people still gotta eat, ya-know-wadda-mean?"

"Yeah," I agreed, pulling a selection from the Drake's counter display, tearing open the cellophane wrapper, and popping a crumb cake into my mouth like it was an extra-strength Tylenol. "I know whatcha mean."

Guest Check

TABLE	SERVER	240128	GUESTS

PART 1

TAX

I.
MR. LONG BLACK COAT FROM NEW YORK

The only thing I loved more than going home for Christmas was turning around a day or two later and getting back to New York City. It wasn't that I didn't love my liberal little family, or my conservative little hometown down the shore. But moving to the Big City at the age of nineteen had offered greater hope for love and splendor, and artistic success—everything that had seemed elusive in West Long Branch, New Jersey. *And* I had a much better shot at getting laid.

All this was especially true on Christmas Eve 1980, two days before my impromptu grand opening at the luncheonette. I stood at the mirror, wrapped in my vintage, hand-me-down black cashmere coat—scarved just so—and imagined how it transformed me from Jersey Boy to Nouveau Yorker. Even my thinning hair blossomed with new volume, reproportioning my face as if I'd gotten a nose job—just one of the benefits of a salon perm. I pivoted in front of the full-length mirror like I was modeling Sasson jeans, sniggering over my shoulder at my own reflection.

Okay, so the transformation was not yet complete. But at least I was having fun trying to become a star. For me, every day in New York City was like Christmas Eve, filled with the anticipation of gifts waiting to be opened and a feast to be consumed. I still loved my visits home, but West Long Branch was more like Christmas Day, when there were no more surprises left—only the feeling that I'd had too much to eat.

But sometimes, you just have to go home.

One-sixty West Seventy-seventh Street was also home. I could hear the traffic that vroomed and honked up Amsterdam Avenue, and snippets of street conversations from below my ninth-story window. Some called it noise, but I loved it.

As a singer, I heard the city sounds as chords in an orchestration marked *vamp till ready,* like the strains that once guided me into "If I Were a Rich Man" on the hallowed stage of my high school. A statuette of Tevye the Dairyman, frozen in his *deedle, daidle, dum* pose, stood on the dresser, a gift from my parents when I played the lead in *Fiddler on the Roof.* I hoped that my teen glory days were a portent of things to come. But until such day when the stretch limo pulled up to whisk me away to some stage door, I still had to straighten up my own room.

I gathered up the spread of eight-by-ten head shots and the scattered sheet music from my recent frenzy to choose an audition piece for the *Grease* open call, and packed them away in the middle desk drawer. Then I opened the top one and rummaged through my collection of matchbooks from the Wildwood Bar at Seventy-fifth and Columbus. First names and telephone numbers were scribbled on the inside flaps with little monikers to jog my memory of each prospective soul mate, like *great teeth* or *contortionist.* I suppose it was about time I transferred Parris—or as I had so spiritually described him on his flap: *dancer with the thighs*—into my Filofax. I shut the drawer, hiked up my coat, and slid his matchbook into my pants pocket.

Ah, yes. Parris. I'll call him before I get on the train.

I opened the valet on top of the dresser, and there among the string ties, gold chains, a roach clip, and a tuning fork (so I could always find an A-natural)— was my pick comb. I used it quickly to pull at my (unnaturally) curly hair until it was expanded to full volume like a Jackson.

Finally, I hitched my canvas sack onto my shoulder and picked up the Big Brown Bag from Bloomingdale's and the red one from Macy's where I had stuffed all my family's Christmas presents. Key ring suspended from my finger, bags in hand, Afro picked out to full capacity, black cashmere coat—scarved just so, I took one last backward glance at myself in the mirror. Satisfied with the big picture, I left the apartment and scurried down Seventy-seventh Street to Columbus Avenue. I must admit that I relished my role as twenty-three-year-old artiste as I scooped the tails of the long black coat into the Yellow Cab after me and directed the driver to Penn Station.

"I'm going home for Christmas!"

I think Dad was secretly delighted that I wanted a career in musical theater. After all, he was the one who had fostered my love of the arts—especially music. But like everything else, we never talked about it directly. Fortunately, we had a twenty-seven-inch Magnavox as a go-between. For years, we shared a sofa and gabbed through every episode of *The Dean Martin Show* and all the Perry Como specials. It was like having my own personal tour guide through the golden age of television variety shows.

"Hear that?" he said one Saturday night as we watched Jackie Gleason introduce the Sammy Spear Orchestra.

"Hear what?" I was puzzled, the musical piece had barely begun.

"It's 'Skylark'—Gene Krupa's big hit in 1941," he announced proudly. "Anita O'Day could really sing this one!"

I knew he wasn't finished.

"And of course Krupa was on the drums and Roy Eldredge played trumpet. I think Musky Ruffo was on alto sax. Yeah, Musky Ruffo."

Musky Ruffo?! Dad was in his glory in those moments.

And when he wasn't wowing me with his encyclopedic knowledge of everything big band, I loved listening to him sing.

Every day, during his morning shave, he'd perform his velvet-voiced repertoire of forties standards straight off the airwaves of the *Make Believe Ballroom* or the *Milkman's Matinee*. Apparently, my father had always been a singer. He told me that it had been crushing enough when his oldest brother, Alphonso, died of leukemia in 1938, but his mother's decision to turn off the radio in the house for a full year of mourning was unbearable. Music had entered the swing era and—at nine years old—little Sorrentino had already begun testing his own pipes against the new breed of crooners he heard on the airwaves.

Dad sang at every opportunity and even got to perform on the local radio station once, mimicking one of his idols singing "Goodbye Sue" and "Till the End of Time." I heard that he sounded so much like Perry Como that anyone who tuned in that day thought they were actually listening to the man who invented casual.

And somewhere along the line, it rubbed off on me—though I had a different style.

At the age of eight, I borrowed a brown dress from Aunt Rosie and an Easter hat from my sister, and sauntered onstage for the annual Cub Scout variety show at the Old First Methodist Church hall. I had methodically rehearsed a lip sync to Mrs. Miller singing "Sweet Pea" in her wobbly soprano—much the way Dad and I had seen her perform it on *The Merv Griffin Show*. A few jaws dropped in Pack 145 that night but the final ovation was thunderous. I discovered that if I could really give 'em a great show, they didn't seem to notice that the Sorrentino boy was having a little *too* much fun in his mother's sling-backs.

Much of my family was there cheering me on, but I wondered what Dad was thinking. (The *Official Scout Manual* didn't mention anything about a special merit badge for drag.) Being gay was not something you advertised in a small town back in the sixties. But while I was dropping hints like an old lady's hairpins at the jamboree that night, my love affair with the stage began.

I couldn't wait to get to Shore Regional High School and try out for the spring musicals so I could perform roles that would be perceived as a little more, uh, masculine. Dad was there for my freshman-year debut in the chorus of *Camelot,* but I remember him best right after the final ovation I received senior year for *Fiddler*. His reaction was understated and ambiguous as usual, his eyes glistening with tears, arms rigidly at his sides as if waiting for permission to hug the star. "That was really something," he crackled before I reached for him in a rare show of physical affection.

I tried out college for a year, but felt as miscast in that role as I did playing a Nazi with big brown hair and a Roman nose in the campus production of *The Sound of Music*. Some of my performances were subtler than others. I have no idea if the man in my life had any idea how much I desired men in my life, but by the time I was nineteen, I didn't want to hide anymore. I quit college to seek out the spotlight, convinced that New York City was the place where my dreams could come true—onstage and off.

Dad was right there with me. He had already filled my head (and heart) with music, but on January 22, 1977, he helped load up the trunk with my things and drove me to New York City, my passion for the performing arts burning as hot as my hormones!

And by Christmas Eve 1980, Dad and I were both happy to have found our paths.

I was heading toward what I thought would be my glory days, while my father stationed himself center counter at his newly acquired luncheonette, beaming like he'd launched a stage career. A little daunted by New York, I occasionally looked over my shoulder to make sure Dad was watching. And he always was. You'd think he'd found his dream job by the way he slipped in tunes between porkroll-egg-and-cheese sandwiches. The only thing vicarious about that existence was the dream or two he may have been living through me. Ask any of the old regulars and they'd probably say Dad loved that lunch-eonette like one of his sons.

After four years in the Big City, there were still stars in my eyes and—I must admit—something similar twinkling in my groin. Maybe it was the change jingling in my pants pocket, next to the Wildwood Bar matchbook, as I gathered up my things, slammed the taxi door, and ran into Penn Station to look for a phone booth.

"Hi, it's me."

"Hello, lover!" Parris was happy that I had called.

"I'm not your lover." I blushed. "We're just friends!"

"Hello, liker!"

"That's better, thank you. I just wanted to call you. Merry Christmas. That's all."

"The merrier when you get back from that dreadful place! And don't forget our big audition coming up at the Ansonia—we can practice on my casting couch!"

"Shut up, you!" I loved when Parris teased me, though I was intimidated by his utter confidence in his sexuality. Like I said, my transformation was not yet complete.

"What song are you going to sing?" he pushed.

"I don't know. They want something with a swing. I'll ask my father, that's his specialty."

"NEW JERSEY TRANSIT 2:40 TRAIN TO LONG BRANCH. NOW BOARDING ON TRACK NUMBER 2."

"And when do I get to meet this singing Dad of yours?"

"I gotta run. I'll see you when I get back."

"Love you—oh sorry. Like you!"

"Have a merry." *Like you, too.* I hung up the phone, gathered up my bags once again, and ran down the stairs to track number 2.

I slid my Christmas presents onto the overhead rack and settled down into my window seat, luxuriating in the feel of the cashmere coat as the train began to pull out of the station, another journey about to begin.

As much as I had come to love New York, I still loved my periodic jaunts down to the Jersey shore, unable to resist each triumphant homecoming. Even when I had attended a wake two weeks earlier at the Damiano Funeral Home in Long Branch, I was reminded that for some of the folks back home, I was the portal to a romanticized world beyond their scope of experience. When it was my turn to swing by the casket and express my sympathy to Great-aunt Fanny, she temporarily ignored her dead husband. "How's that New York goin', dear?" she sniffed while wiping her nose with a handkerchief. The late Great-uncle Freddy was one of the few who didn't crane his neck that night to hear the update.

And the next day, when I had stopped by the counter at Clint's Corner, Dad's best friend, Angelo Valenzano, puffed his unlit cigar like George Burns and patted me on the back. "I heard you worked with Stallone!" I spun around on my stool, throwing Dad a look over at the grill and feigning anger that he had misrepresented my recent catering gig on a Manhattan film set. Maybe I wasn't quite ready to let go of New Jersey, but I always returned to New York after those weekends, satisfied that I was on my way to—wherever!

I leaned my head against the train window, feeling a sudden craving for *baccalà* as northern Jersey blurred by. As a kid, I never knew that I was eating old salted codfish, though I think I would have eaten an old salted shoe as long as it was cooked in tomato sauce. My mouth watered as I imagined the traditional Christmas Eve feast that awaited me upon my homecoming.

Our untamed black Lab mutt would rush to me like Dino on the *Flintstones* the second I set foot in the back door. "Down, Reggie!" I'd scream while he nosed his way into my armpits and crotch.

John, the fourteen-year-old, would be distracted by the overflowing shopping bags, though my nineteen-year-old brother, Michael, would go straight for the perm. "Nice hair!" he'd snip.

Mom wouldn't leave her post at the stove to meet me at the door. She'd be too busy stirring the clam sauce with a wooden spoon, the smell of garlic and tomato mingling with the scent of vanilla candles wafting from the windowsill. "You're just in time! You and your brothers can clean the shrimp!" She would turn her head so I could plant a kiss on her cheek. "Hello, love," she'd say.

But nothing would match the sight (and sound) of Dad crooning along with Bing Crosby's "White Christmas"—spinning no doubt for the second or fifth time on the hi-fi. *"Brrruta!"* he'd slip in before the refrain, though the term of endearment would be lost in translation since it actually referred to my ugly face. I'd smile. Of all the welcoming faces in the kitchen, Dad's eyes would brighten the most at the homecoming of the family's (self-appointed) rising star.

Well, that isn't exactly how it happened on Christmas Eve 1980.

Mom was the first to go off script, delivering her line in a stage whisper, her face inches from mine the second I set foot in the door. There were no savory smells to taunt my appetite or scented candles to warm my spirit. Dad never even chimed in with a *Brrruta!* All I heard was the immediacy to my mother's plain English when she met me at the back door.

"There's something wrong with your father."

2.
BACCALA-LA-LA, LA-LA-LA-LA

"What?" I asked her to repeat it, even though I'd heard her the first time.

"There's something wrong with your father."

Mom's words didn't make sense to me as I looked over her shoulder to Dad, who was standing at the far end of the room talking calmly on the kitchen telephone. (But then again—he was *always* calm.)

She stepped aside and let me in. Eyes fixed on our father, John barely noticed my shopping bags or that I had even entered the kitchen at all. Michael watched Dad, too, no wisecracks about my hairdo, though Reggie stared me down as he paced like an agitated guard dog between Dad and the lazy Susan.

My father continued talking on the telephone. "It's nothing, I'm sure. You have a Merry Christmas now!" He mouthed *Hi, Steve!* and waved at me.

"He's been like this for about ten minutes," Michael whispered while punching his right fist into his left palm. John nodded in agreement.

What the hell are my brothers looking at? What's happening?

Then I saw it. Every few seconds, Dad listed slightly to one side as if someone had snuck up from behind and kicked him in the left leg. Each time his knee unlocked, he grabbed for the refrigerator door handle or a chair back to keep from falling over, though his voice was solid and clear when he hung up the phone and lurched dangerously to the left. "Hi, Steve, you just get home?"

New York is my home now. Remember?

"What's wrong, Dad?"

"Ah, nothing. Just going a little numb. I'll be all right." Dad shrugged off the rubber leg as if it were nothing more serious than a little agita, nothing a little burp or an Alka-Seltzer couldn't fix. But as usual I could depend upon my mother to fill in the emotional blanks. "Your father!"

And then it worsened. When he staggered into the living room like a drunk and finally collapsed onto the carpet in front of the Christmas tree, he never broke character. "I'm not going to the hospital!" he protested while Mom frantically dialed the local emergency number.

And even though his motor skills were rapidly disappearing by the time the first paramedic arrived, his social skills never wavered. "Hey sweetheart!" Dad greeted Joyce like she had just entered Clint's Corner for her morning decaf. "What the hell are *you* doing here?"

"I just happened to be in the neighborhood, honey. Merry Christmas!" Then she kidded him like usual. "And what the hell are *you* doing on the floor?"

That's when Sonny and Jimmy rushed in with the stretcher, expecting the worst—only to find Dad lying on the rug, basking in his local popularity. "I hope you guys aren't looking for a fresh pot!"

The luncheonette regulars chuckled as the numbness in Dad's lower body progressed upward.

"Are you in any pain, Clint?"

"Naaah."

Within minutes, Dad was ferried out the door, down the porch steps, and across the lawn. Mom followed close behind, clutching her pocketbook, waiting her turn to step up into the ambulance that had been backed into the driveway.

"I'll call Judy and tell her not to hold dinner!" I yelled from the porch. "Then I'll follow you to the hospital!" My mother turned around and frowned at me like I was speaking old Sicilian as Dad's head perked up from the stretcher, seemingly struck by the harsh reality that he'd be missing that night's *baccalà* and scampi.

I made the call to my sister. Then—even though my appetite for fish and pastas and sweets had been replaced by a feeling of dread—I turned to reassure my younger brothers. "Everything will be all right." I'm not sure if Michael bought it, but I had to turn away when I saw that John was starting to cry.

The tails of my long black coat flapped behind me like the cape of a superhero as I rushed out the door to the car, but I couldn't seem to move fast enough. The ambulance was already pulling out of the driveway as I fumbled to get my key into the ignition. In one twisted shot of reality, the upbeat homecoming I had envisioned seemed to be transformed into grainy slow motion like the Zapruder film. My hands were shaking when the engine finally turned over in a rage. I pressed the pedal to the floor and skidded away from the curb.

As I chased the ambulance toward the intersection where Monmouth Road converged crookedly with Cedar and Locust, the borough Christmas tree sparkled as tall as a flagpole in the small park to the right, just across from Borough Chemical and Truck Company Number One and a nineteenth-century landmark building to my left. The view in my windshield's frame was like a perfect Currier and Ives greeting card—with one major disturbance: At the far side of the intersection, I could see the flashing lights of the ambulance whipping relentlessly across the quaint facade of Dad's luncheonette.

The ambulance slipped through the yellow signal, leaving me behind in Dad's blue Pontiac as the traffic light shifted to red.

Shit!

While waiting for the light to change, I was struck by the oddest fantasy: *If I were to fly down Monmouth Road at full speed and jettison straight into this crooked intersection—without braking—I could ram this car right through that front window and kill myself at the luncheonette.*

But there would be plenty of time for that later.

The green light and a toot from the car behind pulled me out of the imaginary wreckage as I made the turn onto Locust Avenue and chased the ambulance the rest of the way to the hospital.

★   ★   ★

I had to argue my way past the woman at the emergency-room desk before locating the area in the back where they had brought my father. I didn't know what the hell to expect.

Dad's legs had gone into spasms like he was being electrocuted. But even then, he seemed unfazed. "Can you believe this?" Dad sounded more like someone had just told him they were canceling *M*A*S*H* as we watched his power fade away slowly yet violently.

My stomach was turning but Mom was steadfast as ever, resting her hand like a healer on Dad's body just above the waist, as a team of neurologists and infectious-diseases experts and whoever else took their turns poking and prodding, concluding nothing except that it was imperative Dad undergo a type of spinal tap, called a myelogram, that night.

At one point, I ducked out into the waiting area to start calling some of the family with an update. While talking on the phone, I watched the television set bracketed to the ceiling in the far corner of the room, distracted by the strains of a familiar song: *You may saaaay I'm a dreamer, but I'm not the only one.* Coverage of a candlelight vigil for the recently slain John Lennon was followed by familiar documentary footage of the blindfolded hostages in Iran being paraded for the cameras. Dan Rather reminded his viewers that it was Day 417 of the crisis that seemed to have rendered all of us powerless.

How will we ever get out of this? I thought.

The spasms in Dad's legs were winding down when I rejoined my parents. It was approaching midnight. Christmas. In true yuletide tradition, it was a silent night. Beatles fans mournfully lit candles, and the frightened hostages weren't going anywhere. And just as I had watched the television with empathy that night, my own knees went weak when Dad's legs finally came to a dead halt.

It had always seemed to me that at any time, Dad could close his eyes and free-fall backward and there would always be someone there to catch him. Right from day one, when his mother's frail health had prevented her from breast-feeding her new son, the infant never lacked for mother's milk. The only group of willing volunteers bigger than the Long Branch Fire Department was the lactating women in the old neighborhood. If Mrs. Sestito wasn't available for the afternoon feeding, then any number of the other surrogates would answer the knock at the door, take the baby from his sister Rosie's arms, and open her blouse to serve up the daily special.

Not much had changed since then.

"They're bringing Mr. Sorrentino up for his test now, in the other wing of the hospital," the intern said when he found Mom and me waiting out by the television. "We've made arrangements to open a little office nearby for the family so you can see him as soon as they're finished—follow me, please."

But Mom and I weren't the only ones who stood up.

The intern did a double take when nearly everyone in the waiting room began putting down magazines and gathering up pocketbooks and coats. Some of them hadn't even made it to the coffee and Sambuca before they'd slipped the leftovers into the fridge, unplugged their Christmas trees, and rushed on over to Monmouth Medical Center. Members of *la famiglia* weren't worth their weight in powdered sugar if they didn't make every wedding and birthday and wake, so they certainly weren't going to miss out on a midnight myelogram.

The intern's eyes widened as he took a quick head count.

"You said *family*," I reminded him.

"Uh, uh, just one moment please." His tone sharpened before he rushed away and everyone sat back down grumbling until he returned a few minutes later with a new plan.

"Okay, everybody, let's try this again—follow me, please." One, two, and three at a time, aunts, uncles, cousins, and grandparents slowly fell into procession behind the intern and Mom and me as we snaked down two long hallways to a bank of elevators.

"Uhhh!" Uncle Tony groaned while limping along, his gut more ballooned than usual from the meal he had just consumed. He had driven his wife and Dad's two other sisters in the Impala, and probably toyed with the idea of parking in a handicapped space. (The bad leg was legitimate, but it was doubtful that a belly swelled from fried smelts and too much linguine *aglio e olio* was considered a disability.)

"Can you believe this?" Aunt Angie mused while clinging to her husband, her height enhanced by silvery blue hair sculpted and glistening like their aluminum Christmas tree. She began to cough loosely, a pack of Salems no doubt beckoning her from her purse as they passed the "No Smoking" sign.

Aunt Rosie's even tinier frame would have been lost among the crowd had it not been for her running commentary. "Right on the holiday!" she groused, legitimately concerned for her baby brother, her sourness well within the license our family afforded its old maid. "What's that smell?" She sniffed.

Aunt Mary rolled her eyes then smiled at me, perhaps in acknowledgment of our matching perms. I estimated that the three sisters had all peaked in height back around 1967 when osteoporosis began to devour their bone mass, but Aunt Mary was still arguably the "tall" one at a robust five-foot-one. "Oh, Rosie!" She prodded her sister along.

Just behind the shrinking Sorrentino sisters, Mom's father walked tall, despite the slightly hunched back of his eighty-three years. His hook nose, held high, seemed to navigate him forward like a divining rod. The fluorescent lighting reflected off Poppy's high waxy forehead as he moved along in slow deliberate strides while my diminutive grandmother waddled at his side in an agitated double time to keep up.

"Oh, sweet Jesus," Nonny prayed while taking her usual two steps to Poppy's one. She was only trying to relieve the pressure on her bunions, though it looked more like she was scampering over hot coals.

The caravan of curved spines, bad feet, topiary hair, and swelled guts limped, waddled, smiled, and complained all the way to the elevator. The red "up" arrow lit simultaneously with the *ding* as the doors opened. It took two runs to reunite everyone on the third floor, where the intern waited before leading us down another hallway.

"Mr. Sorrentino has just been brought into *there* for the myelogram." He pointed to the room on our left. "You can all wait across the hall in *here*—it shouldn't be more than a half hour or so."

He held the door open like a bellhop showing us our accommodations, though the women seemed to hesitate, as the makeshift waiting area turned out to be the mammography room. But it may as well have been someone's paneled den or backyard or finished basement as everyone began to chatter and interrupt one another like any family gathering.

"I just talked to Clint yesterday and he seemed fine," one of the blur of uncles said, checking his watch while one of my cousins eyed the metal panel with dials on the wall.

I don't remember which one of them snapped something about that "goddamn Reagan" getting elected. It could have been any of them. They were all Democrats and they all groaned at the mention of his name as if he might somehow be responsible for what was happening to Dad.

There was certainly an underlying concern for my father, but it was easier to focus on things like politics and pastry. "Did I cover the cannolis?" one of my aunts mused, nudging her husband like he might actually need to run home and check.

Great-aunt Fanny was *not* there grasping nervously for topics of conversation, though I imagined what she'd have brought up. *How's that New York goin', dear?* I waited to hear those words from anyone as I leaned on an apparatus meant for a woman's breast.

But the group's volume and attention were suddenly focused in one direction when *the* topic came up: "Who's gonna run the luncheonette?"

There was an obvious lull in conversation when Uncle Tony posed the question to no one in particular, though he and Aunt Angie led the synchronized turning of heads toward the eldest son. "You're a good kid," Uncle Tony declared while nodding his head up and down. He had a laugh that rolled out in slow distinctive breaths, roping me in with each monosyllabic stamp of approval. "Heh . . . heh . . . heh . . . heh."

Poppy smiled at me, his gold tooth glistening like the Star of Bethlehem as he pointed his Sicilian finger and offered grandfatherly advice: "Don't letta nobody butta *you* toucha da money!"

I wanted to run away. I imagined the tail of my long coat flapping in my wake as I rushed to the Long Branch Passenger Station and hopped the next train back to my New York life before it had a chance to change or unravel.

I'll show Great-aunt Fanny how that New York is goin', dear!

I could still feel that rush I got every time the new edition of *Back Stage* hit the newsstands, and how Parris and I would head straight to the Bagel

Nosh on Broadway at Seventy-first to comb the trade for the next week's adventures. When I had circled the open call for *Grease,* I underscored the requirement to prepare an up-tempo and a ballad. *What's that song Dad used to sing? "Love Me Forever." Yes. Perfect!* Dad always had the answer; he had given me the gift of music in the first place—*Shit!*

I knew that I had no choice but to trade in my cushy black cashmere for a greasy red apron. Dad was doing one of his free falls, and maybe this time, it was my turn to catch.

"They're bringing him out now," one of the nurses stuck her head into the mammography room and said. "Everything went well." Dad would be lucid since no anesthesia had been required—the paralysis had sufficiently numbed him all the way up to his nipple line.

The family poured out into the hallway like excited old bobby-soxers just as the orderlies were wheeling Dad out on a gurney. They slowed down as my father, still flat on his back, rolled his eyes to the right and strained to see everyone. He smiled—no doubt pleased with the size of the crowd—and raised his right forearm, the elbow anchored to the gurney as he gave a candidate's wave. "Merry Christmas, everyone!" I think he really meant it.

"How are you feeling, Dad?" I asked after the crowd had dispersed.

"Good," Dad piped like he was getting over a damn cold.

"Good." I sighed while walking alongside the gurney on the way to the intensive care unit. "Dad, I want to talk to you. I have some questions I need to ask you about Clint's Corner."

"Ah, jeez," he said as Mom and the orderlies looked at me.

"No, I didn't mean *now*—I'll talk to you tomorrow!"

"Steve, you don't have to—"

"I'll talk to you about it tomorrow!" I'm sure my father really needed me yelling at him right after they had taken spinal fluid, but he didn't seem to mind. "Merry Christmas, Dad."

"Merry Christmas." He smiled.

"Yeah," Mom chimed in. "Merry Christmas." Her eyes rolled up to heaven.

There was nothing else I could do once Dad was situated in the ICU and hooked up to an IV and some monitors. But at least I had made a decision.

If I couldn't save the man, maybe I could save his luncheonette.

3.
THE BURBS AND THE BEES

Dad's brown eyes lit up behind his gold wire frames when I showed up at the ICU late on Christmas night. He was a handsome man, but I always thought there was something innately comical about his face, as if he were always one beat away from delivering a wisecrack or a punch line. And he didn't just have teeth. He had a set of choppers that filled the biggest smile—that is, until he saw me pull out a spiral notebook and a Bic pen.

"Okay, so how many slices of porkroll go on a porkroll-egg-and-cheese sandwich?" I asked.

"Ah, jeez." Dad's head fidgeted against the pillow, causing his glasses to bob up toward his forehead.

He never actually said *Jesus*. I don't think it was a taking-the-Lord's-name-in-vain issue since he had always been more than generous with *goddammit!*

But I thought that my questions were perfectly legitimate considering I had never run a luncheonette before, like "How do you turn on the lights?"

I should have seen it coming when Dad pushed his glasses back onto the bridge of his nose and replied, "With the switch."

But the porkroll issue was serious, maybe even one of state pride. I had heard that this product was indigenous to New Jersey, though I wouldn't compare the gritty pinkish mystery meat to Hawaiian pineapples or Maryland crabs. I just knew that I had to get it right.

"Come on, Dad. I'm serious! How many slices of porkroll go on a porkroll-egg-and-cheese sandwich?" I tapped my pen against the open page, a little nauseated from both the prospect of that sandwich and the smell of hospital coming at me.

"Steven, you don't have to do this. What about New York?" The blips on the heart monitor seemed to pick up their pace. "And besides, you've never done this before."

"Dad, they don't know what's wrong with you or if—or how long it will take for you to get better. Until then, what are we supposed to do, just close up shop? I'll figure it out—now come on!"

I hated being a bully in the ICU but I almost forgot that anything was wrong. Dad looked so normal—well, normal for Dad. He always made efficient use of his thin dark hair, swept around the top of his head so it didn't look quite like a comb-over. And not everyone noticed, but on close inspection, his left ear was slightly higher than the right, a theme carried through to sideburns that only appeared even when he cocked his head to one side.

Hmmm. He looked like Dad. He sounded like Dad.

"I wish they had a TV in this place."

"You're in the ICU," I said impatiently. "They don't have televisions, they have heart monitors!"

I wished we could have been somewhere else, watching television, like the Sunday night when he'd turned to me during *The Ed Sullivan Show* as Pearl Bailey performed "You're Nobody Till Somebody Loves You." Pearlie Mae was strutting around the soundstage, the camera barely keeping up with her movements as she deftly maneuvered the long wire to her microphone. "See how she makes it part of the act?" Dad had never bothered to explain the birds and the bees to me but he did make sure that I observed the craftsmanship of the entertainer.

"Try changing the channel." Dad looked up at the screen displaying his heartbeats.

"Now come on, Dad! How many slices of porkroll go on a porkroll-egg-and-cheese sandwich?"

"Okay. Okay. Well, first you should know that sometimes customers want a plain porkroll sandwich, in which case you use four slices. Oh, and use the number-five setting on the electric slicer to get the right thickness—ah, jeez." He waited as I furiously scribbled down the information like it was a state secret. "Now if you are adding the egg and cheese, then you only use three slices of porkroll. And always serve the sandwich on a Knipp's." The way Dad pronounced the *K* made the bakery's name sound more like a hiccup. "They deliver the rolls fresh every day; you'll find them at the front door in the morning."

"Okay. I got it. Now—"

"Wait! There's one more thing you have to know." Dad was about to tell me something even more important than the Pearl Bailey microphone thing. I could tell by his tone. If he hadn't been so paralyzed, this is the part where he would have leaned in and put his hand on my shoulder, like we were about to have that *father–son* talk I had heard so much about, but never got.

"What is it, Dad?" My Bic was poised.

"Before cooking the porkroll, you have to score it."

"What do you mean—*score it?*"

"You have to cut into each slice three or four times around the edge so it has some flexibility. Otherwise she'll just curl up on you when you throw it on the hot grill. You got that?"

Wow! Other than one of his tangents about Glenn Miller's orchestra or Robert Goulet's vocal technique, I hadn't gotten this much information out of my father since I was nine years old and my mother had prodded him to talk to me about male hygiene. He had come into my room that night unexpectedly. "Uh, Steve, I wanted to catch you before you go *shake a tower.*" (Dad sometimes spoke in spoonerisms to mask his discomfort.) "Uh, uh, make sure you peel it back and wash underneath. You got that?"

Peel *it* back?! One of the things I had come to love about my New York life all these years later was the fact that "it" was in a much freer state. But I hadn't expected to find myself in New Jersey again, refocusing my attention back from penis to porkroll.

"Great, Dad. So I score the porkroll before throwing it on the hot grill. But I just realized that I need to know one more thing."

"Okay. But then I—" His sentence was cut short by a strange, aspirated and unfinished cough. It frightened me, not in its power, but rather in its softness. It sounded hollow and unsatisfying, as if there weren't enough breath to complete it.

"Are you all right, Dad?" I could see his choppers again, but this time they were gritted in discomfort.

"Yeah. I'm fine. You said you had one last question?"

"Yes. And then I'll leave you alone. I swear."

"What'd I tell you?" He smirked. "Don't swear."

"Okay, okay—so how do I light the grill?"

"Ah, jeez."

He started to cough again, but it was even weaker this time. I don't know why, but it scared the shit out of me.

"Get some rest, Dad."

He nodded.

"And don't worry about the luncheonette."

I recapped the pen, closed my notebook, and kissed him on the forehead. I stopped in the doorway on the way out and saw that he had fallen asleep with his glasses on. He looked so normal.

I'm sure this is only temporary, I told myself.

I left the ICU that Christmas night with my detailed instructions on how to operate the lights in the luncheonette, but there was nothing in that notebook about a switch somewhere to turn off whatever the hell was happening.

4.
EATING ALL THE PROPHETS

Joe and Dickie Gallo first opened the luncheonette in 1960, at the intersection where Monmouth Road converged crookedly with Cedar and Locust. It was barely a mile away from our house on Girard Avenue, but, for a kid, it seemed like an exotic destination where grilled cheese sandwiches and double-decker dreams were served up in no short order.

I would pedal my stingray bicycle there after school or on Saturdays to meet friends for hamburgers or Ring Dings. Sometimes I mingled with the adults who knew me through Dad or their kids, or from my paper route. They always seemed to have special messages for me. "You're going places, son!" Googie the Gizmo prophesied after spinning halfway round on his turquoise stool and patting me on the back like he knew something.

"That's right," Harold the banker concurred. He had somehow recognized my potential the first time I knocked on his door to collect sixty cents for a week's worth of the *Asbury Park Press.* "You're going to be a big success at whatever you do." He raised his half cup of coffee like he was toasting Fate.

"Thanks!" I'd beam, waving my sky blue Popsicle and Hershey bars at the owner, charging them to some mythical tab that I'm not sure Mr. Gallo ever remembered to collect from my father. Then my friends and I would hop back on our bicycles and take off down Monmouth Road or Locust Avenue, grinning at one another with some psychic knowledge that there was a great future waiting for us.

Dad probably stopped at Gallo's more than I did, maybe twice a day to drink coffee and smoke Camels at the speckled Formica counter, though it's a wonder he found the time between all his jobs and civic duties.

Dad had always been self-reliant and worked steadily since returning from service in Korea in 1952, the same year he married Mom. His three older brothers had mentored him in all the skills of carpentry and masonry, providing him with gainful employment until 1957, the year I was born, when Poppy set him up in the bread-baking business.

But by 1966, he'd traded in his work shoes and khaki pants for a pin-striped suit. He got certified as a stockbroker and was soon made branch manager at a local firm called Dempsey-Tegler. In the years that followed, he began to ensconce himself in public service, volunteering at the local community center, getting elected to the board of education in 1970, and running as a Democrat and winning a seat in 1976 on what had traditionally been an all-Republican borough council. Simultaneous to his stint at the brokerage, Dad opened the Towne Arte and Book Shoppe right next to Valenzano's Office Supplies, around the corner from Gallo's luncheonette. That business didn't last but the friendship with his neighbor continued at the speckled Formica counter.

Angelo Valenzano and Dad didn't always make it on time for lunch. If Joe Gallo was in one of his grumpy moods, he'd shut down the sandwich station early. "I'm outta bread," he'd grumble at some disappointed kid, then wink at Dad and Angelo, who were eyeing the subs sitting in plain view right next to the Bay Marie.

My father would have a good laugh over that, though Angelo still wanted to get him going. Dad was a real sucker when his best friend prodded him with lyrical cues, knowing his propensity to break into impromptu song.

"I'm a little down today, Clint." Angelo Valenzano would tap his unlit cigar over Dad's coffee and grin, knowing damn well that his crony would launch into a chorus or two of "Melancholy Baby" or "Am I Blue?"

Dad's career as a stockbroker ended when his firm fell victim to the weak economy of the late seventies. He scrambled to find another job, landing one with a home-security-systems business. But a year later, in 1979, he found himself financially crippled and without a pension after losing that job as well. It was the first time Dad seemed to be on shaky ground, his self-confidence eroded away with the job market.

Until—that is—Joe Gallo told him that the luncheonette was up for sale.

My father couldn't afford the down payment, but Angelo Valenzano lent his best friend half the cash. And nearly as broken as his father-in-law's English, Dad went to Poppy for the rest. "No you worry, Clint. I'ma getta you da money!"

Trading in his pinstripe suit for an apron might have appeared to some to be an act of desperation, but for my father, it was a joyous return to his workingman's roots—and an opportunity to shore up his rattled self-esteem right along with the new sign hoisted up over the front door of the luncheonette: CLINT'S CORNER.

But Dad still needed help getting back on his feet. The business was new to him, so he started asking around for experienced counter help.

"Oh, Clint, have I got a girl for you!" said Nettie Tupperton from Garden Street. She may have been in her seventies, but she could still run from her volunteer post at the community center over to the activity room at Peter Cooper Village, where she helped out "those old people" as the almost-octogenarian called them.

"Really, who?" Dad asked.

"My baby sister!" She sprang into action like she'd found a new cause.

"Wait, I mean, thank you, but is she experienced?"

"Experienced? Why she and her Vern ran the Pickle Place for years!"

"The Pickle Place?"

"Just the biggest luncheonette in Asbury Park! You know—*before* the riots."

"She didn't start them, did she?"

"Oh!" Nettie threw her head back and opened her arms in a wide gesture to God. "Why didn't I think of this sooner!"

"I'm just not sure—"

"I'm runnin' home to tell her right now." She hopped off her stool. "You know she lives right next door to me. Oh, this is perfect!"

"Well, I guess that would be okay—"

Nettie pulled the keys from her pocketbook then hesitated.

"What?" Dad sensed an ominous change of tone.

"Just one more thing, Clint." She climbed onto the footrest and leaned across the counter. "You don't have to keep her." With that, she jumped off the little ledge and sped toward the back door. "Oh, this is perfect!"

"Wait!" Dad stopped her. "What's your baby sister's name?"

"Dolores!" she yelled as the door slammed behind her.

Dad's new counter girl started that Monday. And so did the stories, like the one where Dad (half-jokingly) laid down a line of red tape behind the counter that she was forbidden to cross. It was the only way he could keep her away from the cold cuts and out of his thinning hair.

And weeks later, he arrived home after an exhausting day at the luncheonette and (half-jokingly) whined to my mother, "I have to get rid of her— she's driving me nuts."

I'm not sure that I fared much better on my first day at the helm of Clint's Corner.

I was gobbling down my second Drake's crumb cake of the morning when Dolores raised the hood of the Bay Marie. "What the hell you been doin' all morning besides eatin'?" She put her hands on her hips and inspected the contents. "You haven't sliced up enough porkroll for the rush! That's a big seller, ya know!"

"Dolores, I don't think there is going to be much of a rush today. It's the day after Christmas, people are resting up from the holiday—"

"Listen, bay-bay, I've been in this business for thirty-five years—thirty-five years!—and one thing I learned is even the day after doomsday, people still want a nice sandwich." The metal hood crashed back down.

"Wait a second. How many years? You keep changing the number: twenty-three, thirty, thirty-five—"

"Hike!" Googie the Gizmo never looked up from his *Asbury Park Press*.

"Oh, what can I tell you," Dolores dismissed me. "Sometimes I flunktuate."

"Fluctuate."

"That's what I said."

"No, you said *flunktuate*."

"What are you, a fuckin' grammararian?"

"I'll slice the porkroll." I knew when to quit.

Dolores gave her wig another quick tug before placing a hand alongside her mouth to whisper to Googie, "Isn't he a doll?"

"A living one!" Googie lowered the sports page and winked at me.

"Yep," Stanley concurred.

I opened the refrigerator below the Bay Marie to look for the porkroll.

"You'd better pull out the ham while you're down there. Carmen will be comin' in for his ham and eggs, ya know."

"Yes, sir!" I pulled out the square of processed ham that had already been opened. Saran Wrap had replaced the original packaging.

"Oh Christ, look at that! I told your father not to wrap the ham in cellophane. It gets all slimy that way. You have to use alyoominum!"

"Okay, Dolores," I spoke deliberately. "After I finish slicing the ham, I'll be sure and wrap it in al-um-in-um."

I think she was onto me. "Quit talkin' funny and slice the fuckin' ham!"

Admittedly, the ham was a little slimy, but it smelled fine. I wiped the outer surface with a cloth and placed the fleshy block on the electric slicer and flipped the switch. Dad had said to try to get it as thin as possible, so I turned the setting to "1" and began guiding the square piece of meat back and forth across the round spinning blade.

"What the hell you doin', Steven? You're slicin' that ham too thin!"

"Dolores, it makes a better sandwich."

"Ohhh, brother. I bet you're a goddamn ham shaker like your father."

"A what?"

"The first time I saw your father make a ham-and-cheese sandwich, he picks up a slice of ham and gives it a shake. I says, 'Clint, what the hell you doin' shakin' that ham?' and he tells me, 'You gotta shake it like that so it bunches up on the sandwich to make it bulkylike,' and I say to him, 'Your customers want *ham* in their sandwich—not air!' Then he tells me to 'Stay behind the red line and mind your own business, Dolores,' and I says, 'Now listen here, Clint—' "

"I know! Then you tell him, 'I been in this business eighty-five years and I know how to make a ham sandwich!' "

"You sonovabitch."

Dolores had been right about one thing: People still gotta eat!

As the familiar parade of hometown faces marched through the luncheon-ette that morning, the news was spreading about my father, though not all of it was accurate. It took me several tries to get Dolores to drop the mutable-sclerosis diagnosis. Later on, she overheard me telling Al from the Amoco sta-tion that one of the doctors had suspected temporary paralysis as a result of Guillain-Barré syndrome. Dolores really ran with that one when Lorraine from the beauty parlor next door came in to pick up a toasted bran muffin, rushing down to the cash register with a news flash: "Lorraine, hon, did you hear? Clint's got the syndrome!"

But again and again, I stepped in and replayed my rendition of the events of Christmas Eve, hitting each chord perfectly on cue, before bringing in the hand gesture for maximum effect. "He's paralyzed up to *here.*" I'd hold for the shattered looks on their faces—reliant on the old regulars to react on my behalf—before plopping down a porkroll-egg-and-cheese sandwich in front of the shocked patron like I was a bartender delivering a stiff drink.

The routine began to wear thin, leaving me high and dry, until, that is, about eleven, when a sculpted vision of testosterone (if not a missing link) walked in the front door. I watched Pepsi Man squat down at the showcase to restock the Mountain Dew, his blue poly uniform hugging a pair of legs more developed than some nations. Even Dolores got off my back long enough to run over to table one with her spray bottle, not so much to clean the table as for a better angle on the simian soda guy.

When Pepsi Man finished, he lumbered over to the cash register like an ape.

"Where's de uddah guy?" he grunted at me.

Not wanting to be the bearer of bad news, my mood finally beginning to elevate, I gave him the watered-down version.

"He's not here. How do you do? I'm Steven." I extended my hand, hoping to cop a little shake.

"Dat'll be twenty-faw bucks—Steven." He handed me an invoice instead.

As Pepsi Man walked out the front door, I found myself grabbing another package off the Drake's display and tearing off the wrapper while watching him clamber up into the cab of his truck and drive away.

"Just how much *cheska* do you intend to stuff in that face of yours this morning?" Dolores asked when she rejoined me behind the counter.

"*Cheshhhka?*" I mumbled with a mouthful of Yodel.

"Christ! Try to save some for my customers!" Dolores put her spray bottle back on the shelf as one of the two Anitas from the dry cleaners across the street came in for a late breakfast and an update.

"He's paralyzed up to *here*," I informed her right on cue.

Her audible gasp was followed predictably by an order for two porkroll-egg-and-cheese sandwiches—to go.

I couldn't understand the hold this mystery meat had over the town nor was I ready to share in the sadness. I packed up the order for the two Anitas then shoved the rest of the *cheska* into my mouth—thankful that I didn't have a full-blown porkroll habit.

That's when I got the phone call that Dad had stopped breathing.

5.
WHEN YOU WHOOSH UPON A STAR

The automatic double doors of the ICU swung open. I saw the small frame of my sister down the corridor just outside Dad's room. "Judy!" She twirled around to look at me, her thick brown hair brushing over her shoulders like a Breck girl as she rushed toward me. "What happened?" I whispered as we met halfway.

"I don't know," she said breathlessly while clutching her throat. "Maybe the paralysis has advanced. I don't know. They put him on a respirator."

"Where's Mom?"

"She's in there with him."

We hurried past doorways, catching glimpses of other patients lying silently in their rooms, their bodies contorted with illness and injury. I tried not to look, but morbid curiosity (and wishful thinking) got the best of me: *Dad's not as bad off as they are—he doesn't belong here and neither do we.*

When I got to the doorway of his room, I saw my mother—her back to me—leaning over Dad, one hand placed gently on his lower torso, the other tightly at her side, clenched into a fist. It sounded like I had entered a wind tunnel when I stepped into the room and heard the loud and rhythmical whooshing sound for the first time.

Then I saw my father's face.

Dad wasn't wearing his wire-frame glasses anymore. His eyes were cast blankly up to the ceiling, his dry mouth agape. A thick tube had been threaded down his throat as air was pumped from a bedside apparatus, mechanically inflating his lungs and then releasing. Dad seemed to gasp with each cycle of air, the big toothy smile wiped off his face, his thin hair clumped in beads of perspiration, the witty repartee silenced.

All I could do was stay at his side and watch the heart monitor, but the crooked lines on this screen seemed to be recording peaks and valleys of seismic activity. Memories began to flash and fade with each rise and fall of Dad's chest: Dad and I watching Jackie Gleason bid his final farewell to the Sammy Spear Orchestra or Dean Martin going off the air in '74. There were singing and stories, and a faint recollection of a car ride together—to a budding new life in a place called New York.

But the lines across the monitor kept changing patterns like erratic lightning. And as more air whooshed, Dad gasped for life, and I gasped right along with him.

I took his hand but was startled when he tightened the grip, not sure if it was the instinctive pull of a drowning man about to take me under with him, or the squeeze of the goddamn ham shaker reassuring me that everything was going to be all right—and that I'd better be getting my ass back in time for the lunch rush.

"He doesn't seem as distressed as he was before." Mom looked up at the heart monitor that was registering 105 beats per minute. "I think he's adjusting to the respirator." We watched the number drop to 95 a few minutes later. "Oh yes."

I fixated on the screen as if Dad were using his heartbeats to communicate, feeling my own pulse aligning with his. And as my own breathing fell in sync with each mechanical *whoosh* pumped into his chest, I started to get light-headed and had to get out of there.

"I guess I'd better be getting back to the luncheonette," I finally said, though Dad's eyes remained focused on the ceiling. "I have a feeling we're going to be busy today."

6.
SUNDAE TIMES

"Oh my God, this is out of control!" I clutched my Dutch Masters cigar box with the day's cash, jangling my keys at my little brother. He started to clear a path to the front door, which was now obstructed with bags of bread and stacks and stacks and stacks of newspapers.

"This is normal for Sunday," John said calmly. "Don't worry, I have a system."

"Well, this just puts the cherry on top of a perfect week!" I glared at him, wanting no part of his "system" even though he had helped Dad assemble the Sunday papers every weekend for the past year. I guess I was really upset about more important things—but freaking out at my baby brother seemed to be the only available outlet.

"This can't be worth it!" I whined as John dutifully cleared piles of comics and glossy magazines out of my path, restacking Real Estate, Sports, and at least five other inserts for the *New York Sunday Times* alone. "How much profit can we possibly be making from this?" I didn't really expect the fourteen-year-old to answer, nor had I expected to see Uncle Tony hobbling around the corner at five-fucking-freezing-thirty on my third day as the new boss at Clint's Corner.

"Hi, Uncle Tony!" John gushed, temporarily spared the profit analysis.

"Hey ya, kids!" Uncle Tony was an active member of the local Italian-American Association. But the only cause more important to him than one of their spaghetti-supper fund-raisers was the call to family duty. He waved at us and went right to work.

"Hi," I said, less demonstrative as Uncle Tony squatted slightly over his potbelly and tried to lift the largest bundle of newspapers off the sidewalk.

"John!" I admonished. "Don't let him lift those!"

"Heh . . . heh . . . heh . . . heh!" Uncle Tony laughed like he walked—in slow motion. "Don't you kids worry about me. Heh . . . heh . . . heh . . . heh!" Each self-contained chuckle landed on us like little pats on the back.

Once inside, I put the cigar box on the countertop next to the cash register. *What a waste of money.* I watched John and Uncle Tony transfer all the stacks of papers into the luncheonette as I walked over to switch on the lights. My own routine was already well established once the grill was lit: start the coffee, drink a cup, brown the bacon, sample the bacon, butter the Knipp's, devour a Knipp's, slice some cheese, eat some cheese—*What the hell are they doing!*

When I came out of the kitchen with a pan of home fries in my left hand, popping a sample into my mouth with the right, John's "system" for collating all the Sunday newspapers had taken over the luncheonette. The café tables had been paired off to create two work surfaces. All sixteen chairs had been pushed against the back paneled wall of the dining area, and a plank from the storage room had been placed across three of the turquoise stools. There were assembly lines everywhere with the classifieds, *Parade* magazines, and four-color comics ready to be stuffed into the main sections that were already thick with their Sunday ads. I looked at John.

"Thish ish out of control!" I grumbled through a mouthful of potato.

"Heh . . . heh . . . heh . . . heh!" Uncle Tony patted his belly like a department store Santa.

"All right. Let's get going on this." I put the home fries down and wiped my hands on my apron. "Okay, John—you do the *Press* and the *Daily News,* Uncle Tony—you do the *Register,* and I'll take care of the *New York Times.*"

"That's all right, Steven." John's voice cracked. "You can finish behind the counter. I have a system." John's voice was still changing well into his freshman year of high school. I noticed how tall he was getting, though he tended to hunch his shoulders, except when he tried to assert himself.

"John, three of us can get this done faster than two. Now stop arguing with me!" I walked over to the tables where the *Times* were piled. John peered out at me from behind his cereal-bowl haircut as Uncle Tony cleared his throat.

"You kids. Heh . . . heh."

"This is so out of control," I muttered under my breath as I reordered my sections. I didn't like that John had given the Week in Review more prominent placement than Arts & Leisure, but at least I felt like I was on my own turf. Collating the *New York Sunday Times* seemed to have a calming effect on me until I glanced over at John's misguided methodology with the *Daily News*.

"John! No!" The way I yelled at him, you'd have thought he had accidentally kicked out the plug to Dad's life support. "You're doing it backward. The comics are supposed to wrap around the outside!" He looked at me with eyes like Dondi in distress until Uncle Tony came to his rescue.

"That's all right, John. We'll fix them up," he assured, his eyes bulging like one of the caricatures in *The Far Side* when he looked at me.

"Forget it." I surrendered. "It's not important. I'll finish setting up behind the counter." I picked up my pan of home fries and carried them over to the grill as John and Uncle Tony went back to work.

"Morning, guys!" Coz the Cop breezed in. "Hi, Tony!"

"How ya doin', Coz?" Uncle Tony's leg was extra stiff from standing in one place for so long but he never missed an opportunity to shake a hand, making his way down toward the register like he was Ambassador to the Luncheonette.

"Can I get you anything, Coz?" I was running American cheese through the slicer.

"No, just here to pick up a *Press*. I'm on my way to seven-o'clock Mass. Here you go!" He dropped some change onto the counter then chatted with Uncle Tony for a minute. "Catch you all later!" He waved as Uncle Tony returned to his assembly line. I finished slicing the cheese, placed it in the Bay Marie, then went to collect the officer's change off the counter. That's when I realized that I had left the Dutch Masters cigar box with the day's cash sitting there. *Or did I?*

It was gone.

What did I do with it? I knew I hadn't transferred the cash to the register drawer yet, but I looked anyway. It was empty. *Maybe the cop stole it? No!* I got frantic. *Maybe I left it out in the car.*

"I'll be right back." I scurried out the back door as John and Uncle Tony looked up from their posts. I returned a minute later, flustered and confused. *Maybe I left it at home? No, I'm sure I had it with me when I opened the door this morning. Fuck!*

"Steven, what's wrong?" John spoke an octave up, as if he were about to be blamed for something.

"I can't find the cigar box with the cash. I thought I left it right *here.*" I patted the counter as if the box might be invisible. "John, did *you* move it?"

"I did." Uncle Tony stepped forward. "You left it out when you went into the kitchen to make the home fries, so I hid it for safekeeping." He pointed. "It's in the cabinet behind the register. You know, you really should be more careful."

If my eyes could have spoken to John, they would have said, *What the fuck are you looking at?* But none of us said anything for a few tense moments as I retrieved the box and we all went back to work.

"Uncle Tony." I finally broke the silence. "Why don't you sit down and eat something?"

"Oh, no, no." He wouldn't hear of it. "Don't worry about me."

"Uncle Tony, sit!"

"You kids. No really. Nothing for me."

"How do you like your eggs?"

"Scrambled."

I turned my back to him and spooned out a glop of Kaola Gold onto the grill.

"With bacon," he added.

I turned around. "Toast?"

"A Knipp's." He braced himself with two hands on the counter and climbed onto one of the turquoise stools. The perennial bags under his eyes drooped like two sad sacks as he turned to look at John, who was still working silently, his shoulders hunched over and rigid with tension.

I don't know why I was so hard on my baby brother. John was so loyal and reliable. Maybe I believed that no matter how much shit I threw at him, he wasn't going anywhere. And until I could figure out what I was feeling and who I was feeling it toward, then John would just have to do for my target practice. I didn't seem to know *anything* anymore. Though I knew John wanted to help. And I knew that he had cried on Christmas Eve when the ambulance rushed away with our father.

"John"—I swallowed—"can I get you anything to eat?"

"No, I want to finish up here first." He had just uncapped a black Magic Marker and waved the fumes away from his face then straightened up his shoulders. "I'll fix *myself* something later."

I prepared Uncle Tony's breakfast while John completed the last task in his system. There was a list of regular customers who had newspapers reserved for them. John made little stacks, wrote the customer's name on each with black Magic Marker, and placed them alphabetically across the chairs he had lined up against the wall.

This place is out of control, I thought as the three of us remained silent. That is—until my brother-in-law burst through the back door like he was making an entrance on a sitcom.

"Luuucy! I'm hooome!" Despite his swarthy good looks and his affected speech, Charles wasn't actually a crazy Cuban—he had probably just watched a little too much television in his day.

"Hiii!" Judy sang as she followed her husband through the back door of the luncheonette. "Hi, Uncle Tony. Hi, guys!"

"Hi, Jude." I kissed my sister. "You guys here for breakfast?"

"No, for God's sake, we're here to work! Charles knows how to cook on a grill. You take a break."

Charles came out of the kitchen wearing an apron—rolling his *R*s and corrupting his vowels like Ricky Ricardo. "Okay, Luuucy, you rrreally gut some splainin' to do!"

I started laughing for the first time in days. Taking a cue from the diner episode when Fred Mertz had yelled to Ethel, I called in an order to Charles: "Adam and Eve on a raft—wreck 'em!"

"Heh . . . heh . . . heh . . . heh!" Uncle Tony chortled. "You kids!"

"Okay, Steven, what do you want me to do?" Judy had washed her hands at the sink and was drying them on a towel.

"Well, church will be letting out in a few minutes, so you could slice up some porkroll for the rush." I pulled out the long tube of meat from under the Bay Marie and showed my sister what setting to use on the slicer.

"Is it supposed to smell like this?" She scrunched up her nose as she guided the New Jersey State meat across the blade.

"It's an acquired taste." I then pretended to vomit over the kitchen sink, sending Charles into a tirade of Spanish mumbo jumbo: *"Mi quiero la cosa kahootchy la mama!"*

It wasn't *that* funny, but I couldn't stop laughing.

And when John finally started giggling as if he had inhaled a few too many Magic Marker fumes, we were all off and running. Judy finished with the porkroll then slapped Charles across the back of his head when she passed him on the way to the soda fountain to do some cleaning. I watched her wipe down the pumps for the syrup and the stainless lids for the compartments of ice cream and toppings. That's when I got my idea.

There was a small blackboard over the soda fountain. I took it down, found a piece of chalk, and went to work. A minute later, I displayed the daily special:

EAT SHIT AND DIE!

Charles laughed so hard that he collapsed into a squat, Judy wiped tears from her eyes, and John turned red.

Oh, life was fun again!

But Uncle Tony just stirred his coffee and watched the front door like he was the lookout for customers. "Okay, kids. That's enough fun."

But I had another idea. There was a bumper sticker on Uncle Tony's car from a recent fund-raiser for his Italian-American Association. I took down the blackboard once again and rewrote the daily special:

KIDS DON'T HITCHHIKE!

"HEH . . . HEH . . . HEH . . . HEH!" Uncle Tony was much happier with this version as all of us "kids" howled along—just in time for the rush of starving communicants from seven-o'clock Mass at St. Jerome's. The church may have offered spiritual solace to its parishioners but it also provided the luncheonette with a steady stream of Sunday-morning customers, and hopefully a receptive audience for my antics. I was on a roll!

"Sounds happy in here this morning!" Googie the Gizmo opened his plaid blazer, hopped up onto his regular stool, and sniffed the air. "What's that cookin'?"

"My brother-in-law," I cracked.

"I was talking about the bacon!" He chuckled.

"I was talking about the ham!"

Everyone was laughing when the three Palladino sisters and their parents arrived straight from church. The five of them hopped up onto the spinning stools, their heights and sizes in no particular order, like a Catholic calliope, as Googie moved down a slot so as not to break up the set.

"I'll have a porkroll-egg-and-cheese."

"I'll have a porkroll-egg-and-cheese."

"I'll have a porkroll-egg-and-cheese."

"Charles, you got all that?" I sighed, still giddy from the morning routines as I set up the juices for the girls and Judy poured coffee for the adults. Uncle Tony worked the crowd and John worked the register as the Sunday papers flew off the chairs.

"Si, signore!" Charles confirmed the order, cracking up again when one of the Palladino sisters read the blackboard out loud. "Kids don't hitchhike?" She looked quizzically at her older sister as I burst out laughing. But the oldest Palladino girl had a different question.

"How's Mr. Sorrentino doing?"

Charles suddenly lost his accent. "I'll get the sandwiches," he said, looking to me to field that one. The young customers quieted for the update.

The smirk disappeared from my face when I answered little Catherine Palladino. "Not very well, sweetie. Thanks for asking."

"Will he be coming back?"

I was distracted for a second when I caught John out of the corner of my eye ringing up a check for one of the old regulars, wondering if he was doing it right. The fun and games were wearing off. I could feel myself wanting to run and correct him, maybe even fly back into a rage rather than deal with the question at hand. I wanted to believe that I knew everything.

"I don't know, sweetie." I set the juice glass down in front of her. "I just don't know."

7.
WAFER THIN

"Well, Happy New Year, stranger! What, are they holding you hostage there?"

"Not exactly. I'm kind of a willing participant."

"You sound so serious, lover boy—I mean liker boy!"

"Parris, something happened to my father. I'm not sure when I'll be getting back to New York."

He was silent as I recounted the events of Christmas Eve, ending just short of my little hand gesture. "He's paralyzed from his nipple line down," I said into the phone.

"Oh my God, lover. I'm so sorry."

"And things just seem to be getting worse. The day after Christmas, he couldn't breathe on his own, so they had to put him on a respirator. Have you ever seen anyone on a respirator? It's horrible!"

"Eek! How long will that be?"

"I don't know—don't wrap it in Saran—it'll get all slimy! Use the foil!"

"Darling, how can you think about sex at a time like this?"

"What? Oh, I wasn't talking to you. I'm at the luncheonette with my sister."

"She sounds like fun."

"You're really sick. I miss you."

"So come back to New York."

"I can't. I have to keep this business running."

"But surely you have plenty of help. How about your sister with the Saran Wrap?"

"Judy's a teacher. She has to go back to school right after the holidays."

"You know I'm violently opposed to education!"

"Really, Parris—okay, Stanley." I handed him his change. "Happy New Year!"

"Yep." He turned down the flaps of his hat and walked out the front door.

"How about Stanley? He sounds nice."

"Parris!"

"Then how about your brothers?"

"They're just kids. John's a freshman in high school. He's helping as much as he can. Although for some reason or another, every time he comes around, I turn into Attila the Luncheonette Manager. I don't know what's wrong with me."

"What about the other brother? Luigi or something?"

"Michael."

"Michael. Let's hire him!"

"Parris, he's got a job already."

"Well, so do you, pumpkin!"

"He has a regular paycheck with deductions. I'm an unemployed actor and occasional cater waiter."

"Exactly. That's why you must get in for that audition next week at the Ansonia. Remember? They want something with a swing. You were going to ask your father—oops. Well, little Luigi can still—"

"It's little Michael. And he's nineteen years old. But that's not the point. It's kind of expected of me—eldest son. You know. My father needs me right now."

"You said yourself that your father has supported this whole New York thing from the beginning. I bet he would *want* you to make this audition. Come on."

"All right, I'll try."

"Good. Now remember, you need something with a swing."

"I said *I'll try*."

"And how about tonight? It's New Year's Eve! We'll go to Times Square; we'll get drunk; we'll get mugged. We'll go back to my place; we'll get mugged—what do you say, love?"

"I can't."

Silence.

"Listen, it's a wonderful thing you're doing there, lover."

"You know, Parris, I really like you. Please wait for me. I'm sure I'll get back soon enough."

"You know I will. And darling, above all—keep the faith!"

Keep the what?

Growing up Catholic and gay in West Long Branch, I was already feeling alienated from the Church, though not in that love-the-sinner/hate-the-sin kind of way.

I was eleven years old the first time I had a crush on another guy. It was toward the end of fifth grade and my best friend had told me to come over to his house one night. His older sister had invited some of her fellow eighth graders to join her in the basement for that elementary rite of passage: the "boy–girl" party—and we were going to crash it.

Chatting away by the Cheetos was a dimpled frosh-to-be whose physique could have been chiseled right onto a piece of Greek pottery. I had first noticed him a few months earlier at a varsity basketball game after school, though I was infinitely more interested in the freckled shoulders and tank top than I was in the game. But seeing him up close in my friend's basement, I was practically hypnotized by his dark tuft of a cowlick bobbing around as he held court over by the chip table.

"Hey Steve-o!" He grinned and tousled my hair when I reached around him for the dip. I didn't know that Brent Jamison even knew my name.

I became intoxicated with the basketball player, reliving his small gesture of attention over and over in my head, imagining great affection on his part. Long after the party ended and the season passed, I looked for any excuse to ride my stingray bicycle over to Brent Jamison's neighborhood, hoping to catch a glimpse of him shooting hoops in the driveway.

Mondays were off-limits because I had to attend catechism classes at St. Jerome's to prepare for my confirmation the following year. But I was a boy on a mission, preferring to peddle around after Brent over peddling to church to become a Soldier of Christ. But one day, Sister Maria handed out something that I thought would be the answer to my prayers—literally. I read and reread the line at the top of the page: *Complete this novena and your prayers will be answered.* My efforts to win Brent Jamison's affection had only won me an occasional tousle and a "Hey Steve-o," so now it was time to bring out the big gun: a novena to Saint Jude, the patron of hopeless cases.

As per the instructions on the paper, I was to go to church every day for nine consecutive days. There was a prayer for each day with a fill-in-the-blank portion to state whatever it was you were petitioning for. It sounded simple enough: Just ask Saint Jude to make Brent Jamison fall in love with me, and—presto!

Every day for eight days, I stuffed the novena into my back pocket and hopped on my bicycle. I pedaled over to St. Jerome's and entered the large church, taking a seat in the rear pew. I read the day's prayer in a low but audible voice. When I got to the sentence with the insert-fantasy-here section, I would say, "Especially do we pray for *Brent Jamison to fall in love with me.*" On the way home, I would swing by Gallo's luncheonette, where I celebrated in advance with Yoo-Hoo and Drake's cakes.

But I never completed the novena. On the ninth day, I got home from school and grabbed my piece of paper, stopping first to read the contents of the final prayer: *May we not so much seek temporal good . . . may we incline ourselves toward the divine will, seeing God's good and gracious purpose in all our trials.*

Oh shit, a disclaimer!

I felt ashamed and despairing. I couldn't bear the thought that God might not answer my prayers, so I ripped the paper to shreds, and instead of rushing to the church, I headed straight to the luncheonette for some Devil Dogs.

Maybe it was time to give Saint Jude another shot.

Wednesday, December 31, the final day of 1980—one week of paralysis and counting. Judy and I locked the doors to Clint's Corner early that afternoon and left for the hospital.

"Who's Parris?" she asked when we got into the car.

"Just some guy I know in New York from auditions."

"Oh?"

"I don't know if I'm ready for this," I said, changing the subject.

"Neither am I."

It had been difficult enough seeing that tube going down our father's throat, but when the doctors realized that he'd be spending an undetermined amount of time attached to the respirator, they decided to perform a tracheotomy, an external perforation that allowed the tube to be inserted directly into his windpipe. All his nutrition and hydration was being fed to him intravenously while his throat was off-limits. It wasn't something we were looking forward to seeing.

We arrived at the ICU just as Mom and John were leaving for a cup of coffee.

"How's he doing?" Judy asked.

"He seems out of it." John's voice cracked.

"I don't know." Mom looked weary. "He can't talk. He's too weak to lift his arms to make any gestures, so there's really no communication. Father Larkin just went in to see him."

"Oh great." I wasn't exactly brimming with gratitude for the visit from our parish priest.

"Now stop that!" Mom said. "You can go see your father while the priest is there. You want anything from the cafeteria?"

"No," we answered simultaneously.

"See you in a bit." She and John disappeared into the stairwell.

The automatic doors of the ICU flung open for Judy and me. "Why do you suppose Father Larkin is here?" I was having a flashback to the time he slammed the confessional door on me when I had drawn a blank after "Bless me father for I have sinned . . ."

"He's just here to pray, I guess."

I guess I should have prayed, too. But in those days, the notion of God was becoming as incomprehensible to me as Father Larkin's booming brogue. "May dah piss of dah Lurd be always wit yah!" The parishioners at St. Jerome's had no choice but to look *up* to the priest—there had to have been stilts under those black robes! He would look down upon his congregation with love (and bloodshot eyes), his murky gray hair greased back from a face that was so flushed, it probably would have sent Linda Blair's head into another spin.

"He's a grrreat Gud!" his Irish accent rolled out from the pulpit one Sunday. "But He soomtimes works in mysteeerious ways!" Just the notion made me squirm in my pew.

But I really began to have it up to *here*—same hand gesture as paralysis story—with divine intervention, when Judy and I walked in on Father Larkin looming over our father who art in the ICU, pouring a cup of water down his throat. Dad was gurgling for life when we spotted the portable chalice on the nightstand and realized the priest had attempted to give him Communion.

From the sight and sound of things, we might just as well have stumbled upon an exorcism.

Here was Dad, the respirator tube entering his throat via a fresh tracheotomy, choking on the consecrated wafer. Clearly, the priest had panicked and was trying to remedy the situation with water, complicating matters more, as Dad then risked drowning—in addition to choking to death—on the body and blood of our Lord Jesus Christ.

Judy ran to Dad's side yelling at Father Larkin as I went running to the nurses' station, shouting like a good little heathen: "The goddamn priest just gave my father Communion!"

Within seconds, two of them were at the scene. One of them held Dad's head in place while the other inserted an instrument into his mouth and suctioned out the Holy Eucharist, which was then unceremoniously discarded into a trash receptacle next to the bed.

"We brought some doughnuts—" Mom and John had returned from the cafeteria by this point and stood back with Judy and me, watching in horror. But Father Larkin was nowhere to be found. You'd think he'd at least have had the manners to hang around for Last Rites, but apparently common Christian courtesy had gone the way of Extreme Unction.

As the nurses left the room, one of them stopped and patted the side of Mom's arm. "I hope that 1981 is a better year for you than 1980." If Dad could have spoken, this is the part where he might have perked up and said, "I'll give you a bad year: 1948—the musician's strike!" he'd proclaim. "Bing

Crosby couldn't record a thing for months and it pretty much killed the big bands! Now *that* was a bad year!"

But Dad's body was completely still, except for the rhythmical rise and fall of his chest. I wondered how the eternal optimist was really evaluating what was happening to him.

Mom and Judy brushed his forehead and touched his arms as John and I stood quietly off to the side. My eyes locked with Dad's but it didn't seem to be an appropriate time to talk. *Oh, by the way, Dad, can you recommend something with a swing?* I'm not even sure that he was seeing me. His eyes were dim and his expression blank. No vestige of that natural comic quality, just gravity.

My eyes drifted down to the plastic trash receptacle where the consecrated wafer had been tossed, along with a few cotton swabs, some latex gloves—and my faith.

8.
STAFF INFLECTIONS

After that infamous New Year's Eve when Dad almost came to Jesus, I was reminded why I had drifted toward Eastern philosophies to define my spirituality, though admittedly, I could just as well worship the heroine in a Jerry Herman musical. But with my ragged-eared copies of *Zen Buddhism* and *The Dancing Wu Li Masters* sitting back on my shelf in New York—right next to the score to *Mame*—I had to look around the luncheonette for solace.

I learned that scrambling eggs on a grill required a perfect balance of mixture, heat, and wrist action. First, the eggs and just the right plop of milk had to be whisked together in a bowl with just the right speed and turn of hand. Next, Kaola Gold was slathered onto the grill—not on the hot side, where the bacon or porkroll was browned, and not on the cooler side, where the home fries kept warm—but somewhere right in between. And once the egg mixture was poured onto the grill, it needed to be pulled and folded in a constant motion with the whisk to avoid browning and achieve a yellow and blissfully fluffy consistency.

It wasn't exactly nirvana, but with all the chaos that was swirling around my father those days, any scrambled semblance of balance made me feel better. I even found that at the counter, when some of the customers were funny and boisterous, others were serious and staid. And thankfully, there always seemed to be a nice one to offset one of the assholes.

Take Herck the Jerk, for example. Even though it had been years since the cops had to stop him from beating the shit out of his wife, there wasn't a law on the books to keep him from browbeating Norma, my part-timer.

"Gimme more coffee, sister!" Herck demanded. "Hey! Hey!" He scowled when she accidentally splashed some of it over the rim of his cup. Norma was usually quite fastidious with her service, but her hand shook when she waited on the old grouch.

"I'm so sorry, Mr. Herck, I, um—let me wipe that up." It was too late. Her rosy face had turned crimson for the third time that morning. It could have been attributed to her allergies, but when he blew a cloud of Lucky Strike her way, the red swelling around her neck was a sure sign that she had been exposed to extreme rudeness.

But just a few stools down, no one was more of a gentleman than Half Cup Harold, even when he raised his hand like a traffic cop to stop the coffee midpour. "Thank you, kind ma'am!" Harold might have retired from the bank years ago, but he still maintained the manners of a man dedicated to customer service, emptying a half portion from his little glass creamer into his coffee. "And Norma, dear—*when* you get a chance—I'd like a buttered roll—*please*."

"Yes, sir." Norma practically curtsied and backed away to the breadboard, whereas Dolores—if she were there—would have spiraled the Knipp's into place like a Frisbee before Half Cup Harold had even taken his stool.

But I liked the balance that Norma brought to the luncheonette, her retiring and modest yin a pleasant respite from her counterpart's wigged-out yang. Unlike Dolores, who had run her own business for years, Norma had simply waited for the kids to grow up before taking a part-time job. And when Dolores seemed hell-bent on recapturing her glory days as a luncheonette proprietress, Norma just wanted to make a few extra bucks, then get home to cook dinner. She didn't ask for much, though when she did ask for something, I could barely hear her.

"What?"

"Two orders of scrambled with bacon and white toast," she repeated a little louder. What Dolores would have brought to the grill with unchecked volume, Norma made up for in quiet calm.

And when it came to the sink, Norma was thorough, albeit a little slow—but she really knew how to wash a dish. Dolores could do the job a lot faster if you didn't mind encrusted yolk residue in your fork prongs or cereal in a soapy bowl that hadn't been rinsed properly. Again, it was all just a matter of balance.

And if Dolores had been there that morning, Googie and Stanley never would have had the chance to raise their empty cups.

But Dad's life was hanging in the balance, so I didn't mind that Norma had let the coffee run out. I was just trying to maintain some semblance of inner peace as I faced the Corey coffee machine, slid out the basket, dumped the old grounds into the trash, replaced the filter, opened a premeasured packet of Martinson's, and emptied the contents into the basket, which I slid back into place. I hit the button, and seconds later hot water automatically began to flow through the grounds. I placed an empty glass pot on the center burner just in time to catch the fresh coffee that poured forth from the spout. *Mmm, if good karma had an aroma . . .*

"Gimme some fire sticks, *fella!*"

"Right away—*fella.*"

I took a cleansing breath then tossed a book of matches at Herck the Jerk.

I was determined to filter him out of my universe, concentrating more on the show tune playing in my head and the smell of toast wafting through the air as the coffee brewed.

Once the pot had filled, Norma made her way around with refills before tending to the dishes piled high in the sink like she was worshiping at a sudsy altar. She smiled at me, perhaps in tacit acknowledgment that—especially on Dolores's day off—the clinking of flatware along the counter sounded more like the chirping of birds.

I imagined Dolores secured safely away at her house on Garden Street, wrapped in a worn chenille robe and wearing a hairnet, surrounded by Styrofoam heads as she groomed her collection of frosted wigs, her reserve of Banlon shells soaking nearby in preparation for the upcoming week of counter duty. I don't know if any of this was actually true, but I drew comfort just knowing—that at least for today—she was nowhere in the vicinity.

★ ★ ★

"All right, who the fuck's got the blue van parked out back?" Forks stopped midair and chewing temporarily ceased as everyone at the counter turned to see Dolores's head poking through the back door like an oversize sock puppet.

"Guilty as charged!" Googie the Gizmo raised his hand and shook his face like Jimmy Durante, his jowls rebounding like Jell-O.

"Come on, bay-bay, I'm right behind you. Let's move it so you're not blocked in. Now!" Her head disappeared from the doorway.

"Yes, sir!" Googie saluted, took another slurp of coffee, then ran out the back door with his keys.

Norma looked at me. "I thought she was off today?"

"So did I," I fumed.

I filled up a cup with seltzer at the fountain and poured it onto the grill, where I had just been cooking. The steam might just as well have been coming out of my ears when it rose up and evaporated quickly into the exhaust system. *What the fuck is she doing here today?* I cleaned the surface with a scraper and pushed excess breakfast gunk into the trap at the back of the grill.

"Good morning, Dolores." Harold tipped his cup toward her in a proper greeting.

"Good morning, Howard bay-bay." As usual she called him by the wrong name as she tossed her coat through the window to the kitchen as if there was no time to waste. "Good morning, bay-bay, good morning, bay-bay." She made her way along the counter, stopping briefly to acknowledge one patron in particular. "Jesus Christ, Herck, don't you ever smile? I think you'd better make a New Year's revolution. It won't kill ya!" He grumbled back something about shoving something or other up her something or other, but she seemed to take it as a compliment, tittering like a schoolgirl and performing some quick corrective positioning on her wig.

"Dolores, come take my money!" Googie the Gizmo waved a five at her.

"Comin', bay!" She rushed down to what seemed to be our two-thousand-pound piece of equipment aptly branded a National Cash Register. The old relic would get catapulted precariously toward the counter's edge every time Dolores slammed the weighty drawer shut. I had heard her complain to my father about it. "Jesus Christ, Clint, when the hell are you gonna submission a request to Angelo's Office Supplies and get us a commuterized register so I can get my coordination together!" With that, she had grabbed the large machine in a bear hug to pull it back into position as my father looked on. It was Dolores that Dad had really wanted to replace, but he hadn't figured out yet how to speak her language so he could tell her.

"There you go, doll, have a nice day!" Googie the Gizmo saluted her for the second time that morning as Dolores stashed the tip in her pocket before winding up her midriff like a belly dancer, and slamming the drawer shut with her stomach, sending the machine (and me) slightly over the edge.

"I'd like another half cup, please!" Harold patted his mouth with a napkin.

"I'll get it." Norma made her best effort but was too slow on the draw.

"I got it!" Dolores beat her to the Corey coffee machine. "Get'm a creamer, hon."

Norma's lips pulled into a pout and her neck started to inflame again as she was relegated to milk duty.

"I see you got the whole team here today." Half Cup Harold nodded to me. "Your dad's lucky to have all this help." I was about to tell him just *how* lucky when Dolores cut me off.

"You're tellin' me, Howard!" She poured Harold's coffee then put the pot back on the burner and turned to me. "I tell you, Steven, it's so wonderful what you're doing here for your father. You should have a hairlo."

"A what?"

"You know, a hairlo, like an angel has."

"Thanks." I was too weary to use the correct word in a sentence.

"But what you really need is a hairnet, bay. The board of health is gonna shut you right down when they see that mop of yours!"

"Dolores, why are you here?"

"To jerk off! Why the hell do you think I'm here—to work!" She yanked her wig firmly into place as Half Cup Harold started to choke, his coffee burbling down the wrong pipe. "Slow down there, Howard, hon."

"Dolores, may I see you in the kitchen for a minute?"

"*Boychick,* you can see me in the kitchen for an *hour!*" She slurped her tongue over her lips and waved bye-bye to her boys at the counter as she followed me back through the swinging doors.

"Dolores, you work from Tuesday to Friday. Today is *Monday!*"

"What do you think, I'm gonna sit home resting on my florals while your father's lyin' half-dead in the hospital? He's countin' on us, *boychick.* Your father needs us!"

"But Norma is here. I don't need you."

"Oh, you need me, hon. You don't know what the fuck you're doin' yet and Norma's a shitty counter girl—she don't move her ass!"

"But, Dolores—"

"I'm tellin' you, Steven, it's the first Monday of the New Year—we're gonna be very busy. A lotta customers will be asking how your father's doin' and they're all gonna want a little sandwich or somethin'.'"

"But, Dolores—"

"You know, when my Vern and I had our Pickle Place, he always told me, 'Dodo'—that's what he called me—'Dodo, our customers are countin' on us and we can never let them down.' "

"But, Dolores—"

Suddenly there was a clamor at the front door. Dolores looked out the service window. "Oh my Christ, here they come!"

"Here who comes?"

"The Syrians! They're back to work today. That's their bus to New York out front."

"But, Dolores—"

"Come on, *boychick,* you don't keep a Syrian Jew waiting!"

"Why, do they go bad?" I yelled after her as she flung open the saloon-style doors like we were in the middle of a shoot-out, and headed west toward the coffee station.

"I'm comin', boys! I got the coffees! Steven, you get the register! Norma, you do the dishes!"

It was too late. Dolores had taken charge. But it was also my first experience with the Syrian community in town that had brought some of their motherland's sensibility to West Long Branch—and I wasn't talking about the

Middle East. Most of them harkened originally from Brooklyn and the Upper East as they started to shout their orders.

"One regulah, to go!" The guy in the tailored suit turned to the guy in the fur coat over by the newspapers. "Elliot, you want a regulah?"

"Isaac, they're out of the *Times* already!" Elliot looked frantic.

"Make that two." Isaac turned back to Elliot. "I'm getting you a regulah!"

"Mistah!" Elliot shouted to me as he picked up an *Asbury Park Press* like he was handling someone else's dirty tissue. "You've got to order maw copies of the *New Yawk Times!*"

Dolores piped in. "I been tryin' to tell him but he don't listen!" She was lining up Styrofoam cups for the coffee orders as Herck the Jerk blew smoke and glowered at the gaggle of Jews.

"Gimme another coffee! I was here first!"

"And a poppy bagel with a shmeah! Elliot, you want a bagel with a shmeah?" Isaac didn't wait for a response. "Make that two—Elliot, I'm getting you a bagel with a shmeah!" He turned back to me. "So where's Clint?"

"He's in the hospital," I said as more men and women in tailored business attire came in waving bills and shouting orders.

"Three regulahs! Who's in the hospital? And whole wheat toast—and a juice!"

Dolores was running back and forth with the coffee orders. "Ohhh, you don't know what's been goin' on around here! Clint's in the hospital—he's got the syndrome real bad—here ya go, Roslyn, bay-bay, I saw you comin'."

"Hi, dahling. Milk, no sugar, right? Sweet'n Low on the side?" Another woman knocked on the front window to get her attention. "Make that two, dahling. Clint's in the hospital?"

"Oh, he's real bad, they put him on a perspirator and everything!" Dolores was tucking hair back under her wig as she rushed back to the Corey coffee machine, almost spinning Norma around at the sink.

"He's on a *respirator*—I'm his son Steven, by the way." I introduced myself to Isaac and Roslyn and told them what had happened to my father as I rang up the orders.

"Elliot, did you hear that? Clint's in the hospital! We have to do something for him—Dolores said he's got the syndrome—real bad!"

"That's terrible!" Elliot shouted back. "Isaac, get two more regulahs!" He gestured to the men who had just come in the door before coming over to me to introduce himself.

"Steven! Quit shakin' hands! These boys gotta catch the bus—dammit!" Dolores watched Norma serve the last of the coffee to Herck the Jerk, who sat smoking and glaring at the Syrians like they were a bunch of looters. "I'll make yuz fresh—it'll just take a minute!" she shouted while pulling out the basket and emptying the old grounds into the garbage. She quickly poured a packet of Martinson's into the filter, replaced the basket, and hit the button to start the flow of hot water.

Dolores had been right about the steady stream of customers that morning: old regulars from the back and Syrian Jews from the front. I kept up with the stream of orders at the grill and Norma kept up with the flow of dirty dishes. But when Dolores hit the button to start the Corey coffee machine, she had neglected to place an empty pot on the center burner, and now a steady stream of fresh coffee was flowing all over the station and out onto the floor.

"Those goddamn Syrians!" Herck the Jerk leaned forward over the counter when the rush had ended and complained to Dolores, who was down on all fours, sopping up the puddle of coffee with a wad of paper towels.

"Now come on, Herck!" Dolores wiped up the last of it, grabbed onto the counter, and hoisted herself up from the floor. "Don't talk about my Jews like that! They're good customers!"

"I don't mind the regular Jews but I can't stand those fancy New York ones."

"Honey, it don't make no difference if they're regular Jews, Syrian Jews, or even some of them cathartic Jews—they still gotta eat!"

"Ah, shit!" Herck slammed fifty cents down on the counter and stormed out the front door.

I went to scoop up the change. "He didn't even leave enough to pay for his coffee and roll!"

"That's all right, *boychick.* He said that in the old days Mr. Gallo always charged him fifty cents for a coffee and roll and now he ain't payin' any more than that. Your father said it's not worth the fight!"

"Well, my father's not here right now. I am!" Then I pulled out a concept from one of the self-help books sitting on my shelf back on West Seventy-seventh Street. "And I'll tell you what the problem is around here: Nobody has any boundaries!"

"Don't you give me any of that New York psycho shit! Your father needs us! We gotta keep this business running no matter what!" Dolores cupped her breasts in her hands and gave them a little boost. I was thrown off-kilter for a second as if they were illuminated and I was a deer caught in their beams. I barely noticed that Norma had said something.

"What?"

"I said I need three egg sandwiches for Lorraine's beauty salon, to go." Norma's face was crimson again.

By the time I had dropped the eggs onto the grill and popped the yolks, Dolores was on all fours again looking into the refrigerator under the Bay Marie.

"Steven, you better get your ass on the phone with Wenning's right now. Your turkey is low and this provolone is *nyeh dobsha.*"

I ignored her as I flipped the eggs.

"What's the matter, *boychick,* you don't understand Polish?" She slammed the refrigerator shut. "Ya got bad cheese here!" She stood up and watched me, her arms akimbo, as I placed the eggs onto buttered Knipp's rolls and wrapped each one in a sheet of foil.

"I'll take them next door." Norma bagged the sandwiches for the beauty salon, threw in some napkins, and disappeared out the front door like she was running for cover.

"Christ!" Dolores walked down to the phone to call the order in to our wholesaler.

I decided to make myself a sandwich while we were in the prelunch lull. I pulled a flake steak out of the freezer, creating a sharp sizzle as the paper-thin meat landed on the hot grill.

"Wenning's can't get here until tomorrow!" Dolores slammed down the phone. "I hope we don't run out of turkey in the middle of the lunch rush!"

"Dolores," I said while browning onions and peppers in a molten mound of Kaola Gold. "You can go home now. Norma and I will handle the rest of the afternoon." I flipped the flake steak.

"That's okay, *boychick,* you sit down and eat a little something. I'll finish setting up for lunch."

"No, Dolores, I want you to go!" I raised my voice since it was just the two of us now in the luncheonette.

"I'll just finish up them dishes in the—"

"No! Besides, you do a shitty job with the dishes. I want Norma to do them!"

"But she don't know how to move her ass! Let me help you—"

"I DON'T NEED YOUR FUCKING HELP!"

Dolores's eyes welled up and her lips began to quiver and curl like she was trying to form words, but no sound came out. She walked down to the end of the counter where she stored her Bic lighter, a plastic ashtray, and a pack of Pall Malls, sat down on the end stool, and lit up.

I slid my spatula under the steak and slipped it onto a half loaf of Nino's submarine bread, topped it with the onions and peppers and two slices of the provolone that Dolores had deemed *nyeh dobsha.* I carried my blue plate around to the front, grabbed a pack of Yodels off the rack, a can of Diet Pepsi out of the showcase, and sat down on the stool at the opposite end of the counter from Dolores.

Norma returned from Lorraine's but didn't dare speak. She looked relieved to have a sink full of dirty dishes, though she might not have liked being caught geographically in the middle: Dolores puffing away at one end of the counter and me eating with a vengeance at the other.

Carly Simon was blaring from the speakers about clouds in her coffee when my stomach started to gurgle. I had lost my appetite for the half-eaten sandwich and smacked it down onto the plate. "Goddammit!" I burped, wiped my mouth, and walked down to the other end of the counter.

"I'm sorry, Dolores. I'm having a really hard time with all of this." I took a deep breath, waiting for a response, but she refused to look at me. "You have to understand—oh, I don't even know what the hell I'm trying to say."

Dolores stared out into the space in front of her and said nothing. She drew deeply on her Pall Mall and looked like she was whistling when she exhaled, releasing a cloud of smoke before extinguishing the butt in the red plastic ashtray. She finally looked at me and nodded toward the sink. I followed her line of vision over to Norma.

"What?" I didn't know what she wanted me to see as the expression on her face changed and she puffed her chest out like she was about to make a profound proclamation. She finally spoke.

"I can fuck faster than Norma can wash dishes!" she clucked.

"Yeah? I'd like to see that."

"Let's go." She winked at me with her lascivious offer. But I knew right then and there that she was really taking me under her wing—like my own little twisted version of Auntie Mame.

I chuckled. Dolores and I had actually shared a moment—a crude one— but it was definitely a moment.

"So, *boychick,* you want me to slice up some ham for the lunch rush?"

"No! I want you to get the hell out of here before this wears off!" I felt a sense of peace and balance finally restored. "I'll see you tomorrow, Dolores. Thanks for helping out this morning."

"You sonovabitch."

Actually, I felt more like a cathartic Jew.

9.
IN GAGOOTS

Dad was a man of funny words.

If I sneezed, he might dispense one of his rapid-fire versions of "God-gotta-bless-your-lovin'-little-lovin'-heart!" Or if he wanted to amuse himself at the expense of an unsuspecting caller, he'd answer the telephone with a runaway "Hello-ello-ello-ello, sweetheart!" And if I fed him an inquisitive "yeah?" he'd shoot back with "huh?" Then I'd repeat my "yeah?" followed by another "huh?" until we were engaged in a standoff of "yeah?-huh?-yeah?-huh?-yeah?-huh? . . ." increasing in speed until one of us (usually me) cracked up or tripped over the word. Dad always had a roundabout way of communicating—preferring the wisecrack to the straight talk. But he still hadn't found a roundabout way around that tube that wound down his windpipe.

"How are you doing today, Dad?" Words escaped him when he tried to describe even the simplest of feelings, so considering the circumstances, I didn't expect a response.

"How is he today?" I asked my mother.

"Good. Good," Mom stuttered. "Walk me out. *Okay?*" Her eyes widened.

"Sure." I got the hint that something wasn't *okay*.

"Steven—is—going—to—sit—with—you—awhile." Mom spoke each word directly into Dad's face like it was a microphone before looking up at me. "I haven't run a vacuum through that house since before Christmas!"

Mom seemed to throw in the aside for effect or levity, but Dad just continued to stare at the ceiling like he had for two weeks. She talked into his face again. "I'll—be—back—later. Okay?" She kissed his forehead then watched for a response—but there was barely a sign of life.

"Come on, Mom, I'll walk you out."

"Bye, Clint. I love you!" Her singsong inflection seemed to fall on deaf ears, though it was normal for Dad to steer away from deep emotional expression. It's not that he wasn't best described as *sentimental,* but he couldn't even *sing* the word. If he could have responded to Mom in that moment, he probably would have gone for one of his old musical punch lines, like the time he had bastardized the lyric to an old Nat King Cole hit: "I Love You for *Seventy Mental* Reasons."

"There's something else," she whispered the second we were out of Dad's earshot, his hearing presumably one of his few remaining functions. "I need you to stay here and speak up for him."

"What are you talking about?"

"He's got the start of a bedsore at the base of his spine."

"What do you mean, is it like a rash or something?"

"No! The skin is actually breaking down from the pressure. There's hardly any blood circulation and he can't shift himself around in the bed. The doctor said he's *got* to be moved at least twice every hour!"

"How the hell do we do that? He's got all those tubes and the IV and stuff."

"The nurses will take care of it, but they're busy up here. You have to make sure they do it on schedule!"

"I'll stay here till you get back."

"Something about this bedsore really scares me," she continued. "This shouldn't have happened!" She looked over her shoulder to the nurses' station, not wanting to offend anyone.

"Mom, I'm sure they know what they're doing."

"Of course they do, but they get caught up in all the other complications." Her voice was rising. "Just make sure they move him!"

"Mom, okay. It will be okay." My heart was starting to pound. "What other complications?"

"He hasn't eliminated in several days."

Eliminated?

"I thought there would be problems with him soiling himself, but apparently it's just the opposite. We have to worry about him becoming impacted."

Impacted?

In that moment, I was feeling a weird sense of admiration for my mother, who had stepped up to the plate with gross aplomb. I guess all those years of interrogating her kids about the looseness of their bowel movements were finally paying off. But she wasn't finished with the funny words.

"He's also running a fever. It could be from the decubitus ulcer."

"The what?" I felt a chill and closed the lapels of my coat across my chest.

"Decubitus ulcer. That's the name for the bedsore. Or he might have a bladder infection because of the catheter."

I wanted to cross my legs tightly at even the sound of the word *catheter* but was actually nauseated thinking about that other term. If bedsores could talk, then *decubitus ulcer* sounded like the perfect onomatopoeia.

"Is that it?" I frowned. "You're not holding back a goiter or anything, are you?"

"Oh shit." She looked over my shoulder and rolled her eyes.

"What?" I asked as the automatic doors flung open behind me.

"My mother and father."

Poppy's gait was slower than usual as he entered the ICU with Nonny, whose sore feet compelled her short legs forward, her arms swinging like little paddles.

"Hi, Mama," my mother whined. She had discouraged them from coming to the hospital, knowing they'd be filled with questions before she'd gotten some answers of her own.

"Marie, dear. How are you doing? I've been calling. Did you get my messages?"

"Ma, I've been at the hospital day and night."

"I know, dear, you're busy." She turned to me. "Steven, dear. How are you?"

"I'm good, Nonny." I felt her smooth olive face against mine when we hugged, and smelled the sweet remnants of Aqua Net from her recent trip to the beauty parlor.

Poppy kissed my mother and tried to speak, but a lump in his throat cut off his speech. "Marrrie—"

It seemed like every time I saw him anymore, he was crying.

So much had happened since Great-uncle Freddy's viewing at the Damiano Funeral Home a month ago, but I'll never forget the sight of Poppy hovering over his brother's open casket, his hands gesturing up to God then down to the corpse, while rolling his *R*s and shrieking "Frrreddy! Frrreddy! Frrreddy!" Vida Damiano, the funeral director, was standing off to the side, apparently contemplating whether or not an intervention was in order. When she looked over to her brawny son, Buddy, who was standing by like a linebacker in a black suit, I whispered to Dad. "How embarrassing if they have to call over the bouncer!" Dad appreciated the humor in any situation, but under the circumstances, he contained his laughter in a beet red face and shoulder spasms. But it was Great-aunt Fanny who would finally restore order. She sat stone-faced in a big harrumph, glaring at her brother-in-law through one more chorus of "Frrreddy! Frrreddy! Frrreddy!" before she drew a deep breath, folded her arms, and spoke—loudly. "GIVE IT A REST, JOE!"

Joe Tarantolo sat down and shut up for one of the few times in his life.

"Now come on, Joe, that's enough!" Nonny handed him a handkerchief while looking around the ICU to make sure no one was watching. She wasn't being unsympathetic, but for the last few years, he'd been proclaiming every holiday, birthday, and special occasion to be his last, though his impending death had started to wear thin on her after two or three Christmases had gone by.

"Hi, Poppy." I kissed the old man as he wiped away his tears.

"How'sa Clint?" Poppy finally got words out.

"The same." Mom spared them the details.

"Marie, don't they know what's wrong with him yet?"

"No, Ma. I told you!"

"I know, dear."

"Mama, why don't you and Daddy sit with him a few minutes? Steven is staying but I have to run home." Mom nodded at me. "Remember, if they don't come in to move him in the next fifteen minutes or so, speak up! You have to be his voice—okay?"

"I'll look out for him—and *them*. Don't worry." I took my grandfather's arm. "Are you all right?"

He folded over his handkerchief and wiped his eyes again with the dry side.

"Thanks for coming by, Mama. Bye, Daddy." She hugged her parents.

"Marie, dear." Nonny stopped her just as she hit the button on the wall for the automatic doors. "Call me."

Mom's shoulders collapsed like she was carrying the weight of a small Italian province on them as the doors flung open and she left to go home and run the vacuum.

"Come over here, Joe. Say hello to Clint." Nonny stood at the bedside stroking Dad's hand as Poppy lagged behind in the doorway.

He entered the room with caution, like it was 1912 and he was that kid stepping off the boat from Sicily. But he was full of dreams then, of learning English and getting an education. What he got instead was a job at Jimmy Crapperotta's bakery in Toms River, New Jersey. Working for his brother-in-law taught him some invaluable skills, but his dream of becoming an educated man slowly slipped away with the wages he had to send back home. Now his cautiousness was due to mistrust and fear and old age.

I walked him around to the other side of the bed just as the tears started to roll again and Nonny bristled. "Now, Joe! Don't make a scene!"

"It's all right, Poppy," I said.

"I'ma good." He cleared his throat.

"Look at all those machines," Nonny observed as the respirator pumped more air into Dad and she squeezed his hand. "Oh, Clint, Clint."

But Poppy was more comfortable with another subject. "Howsa da luncheonette?"

"It's okay." I looked to Dad for a reaction, which barely amounted to an extra blip across the heart monitor. "We're busy."

"That'sa good."

Family business was Poppy's greatest source of pride.

By the 1930s, he had built up a small business empire of his own on South Broadway in Long Branch, including a grocery store, a rooming house, and—what would become his flagship enterprise—Tarantolo's Bakery. He may never have perfected his English or gotten an education as he had set out to do, but he had all the power and status he ever could have dreamed of on that one block, garnering him the ceremonious title of the "Mayor of South Broadway."

Poppy had made sure that his own three sons got the education that he had been denied, the irony being that there was no one to take over the businesses. In 1957, the year I was born, Poppy took my father under his prosperous wing, told him about the "secret" ingredient, and watched carefully as Dad began to bake the handmade crusty loaves, arguably the best Italian bread on the Jersey shore. (My father had been one of the few outside of the bloodline whom Poppy had told about the sugar.)

By 1961, Dad became the sole proprietor of Tarantolo's Bakery—sort of. Along with sole proprietorship came the role as sole keeper-of-the-struggle, as he tried to wrest control away from the Mayor of South Broadway. "Dictator" was the more apt title according to my mother. If her father had been cantankerous during his heyday, he was outright impossible when his glory days went on the wane. Poppy was unwilling to let go. Dad was growing intolerant of his father-in-law's pesky presence on the premises, not to mention his sense of entitlement to some of the cash right out of the register. Dad was more vested in keeping the peace, however, nurturing his first ulcer while leaving the arguments up to his wife and her father.

I wasn't aware of any of this when I was a kid. I just remember Dad singing as he slid the doughy formations into the oven, and Poppy, taking me next door and hoisting me up onto the bar at Commander's, plying me with Shirley Temples and slipping me a twenty here and there. I loved his gold tooth, his cherry-scented pipe tobacco, and the way he always took my side against my parents. "Letee stay!" he'd yell in his broken English at Mom for protesting against the lemon ice he'd bought me at Caputo's right before dinner.

But family tension aside, Dad respected Poppy, maybe even revered him after his own father died in 1962. He knew that with the bakery, he'd been afforded an opportunity he wouldn't have had otherwise—especially when there were more mouths to feed.

After Judy and me came Michael and John. There had been a couple of attempts to sell the business, but the day that the large brick oven at the heart of the operation collapsed, Tarantolo's Bakery closed its doors permanently. Poppy's glory days were over, and Dad moved on.

Poppy had nothing to control anymore. Not even his emotions seemed to cooperate as his tough exterior began to soften. After my final curtain call in *Fiddler on the Roof* senior year, Poppy was weeping and speechless. I wonder if he realized that I had tailored Tevye's character—who struggled with family, tradition, and power—after him.

"Steven, dear." Nonny looked up. "What are you doing for dinner?"

"I think I just want to go home."

"No! You come eat with us."

"*Letee* stay!" Poppy raised his hand to shut her up, though the respirator shushed all of us when it suddenly pumped a *whoosh* of air into Dad's chest—out of the normal cycle. The doctor had explained to us that the apparatus would give Dad air at regular intervals, though it would also respond to his own impulse for an extra breath if he needed it. I interpreted the off-cycle *whoosh* as a mechanical gasp, which frightened the hell out of me.

When the respirator fell back into regular rhythm, our conversation continued.

"You keepa da business open," Poppy lectured as he pulled out his wallet. "You needa help?"

"No, Poppy." I looked at Dad again. No response. "We're fine."

"That'sa good." He handed me a couple of twenties anyway. I think that as the old neighborhood had faded away, along with his health, he depended on his money more than ever to feel big and important. Poppy's body would stiffen and his face would seem to flush with rage if you ever tried to decline one of his handouts; so, in *his* best interests of course, I was always more than happy to take the cash.

"Thanks, Poppy." I stuffed the bills into my coat pocket.

"Steven, dear, you come eat with us tonight," Nonny interjected with her own form of currency. "I made some lemon chicken."

"I don't know." It wasn't that I didn't love Nonny's cooking, but I was feeling nauseated ever since Mom had told me about the bedsore. I pictured it festering away somewhere under the bedsheet, screaming its name in my mind's ear: *DECUBITUS ULCER!*

"No, you come," she baited. "I cooked up some *gagoots!*"

I wasn't normally fond of zucchini, but I couldn't resist the way she smothered it with olive oil, onions, and tomato. . . .

"All right." I gave in. "I'll come."

"And I have some nice fresh fruit—all cut up."

"All right already—I'll come eat with you!" I guess I needed a little smothering myself.

Not to be outdone, Poppy made another dip into his wallet. "You needa more?"

"No, Poppy, really."

"You take!" His arm was fully extended and completely inflexible as he pushed another twenty into my hand.

"Thanks, Poppy."

"You come-a *mange da gagoots!*" Poppy quickly stowed away his wallet when Nurse Karen entered the room with a smile as squishy as her shoes.

"Hello, Mr. Sorrentino! How are we doing there?" No response. She checked the urine that was collecting in a calibrated bag at the side of the bed. "Oh, *very* good," she said cheerily. "Now, may I ask you kind folks to step outside for a few? We're going to move Mr. Sorrentino and change the dressing."

"What do you mean, the *dressing*?" It sounded like Dad had a salad going on under there.

"On the *decubitus*," she peeped like a little pixie who'd just said *lollipop*.

"I want to stay."

"It's not very pleasant," she squeaked.

"I'm his son. I'm staying."

"Well—I suppose so."

"We're going now." Nonny patted Dad's hand. "So long, Clint dear."

Poppy's tears started to roll again.

"Come on, Joe, let's go!" Nonny shook her head. "Steven, dear, we'll see you in a little while?"

"I'll be there. I'm starving." I looked into Dad's face. He was still completely unresponsive, though that didn't stop my grandfather from trying. I was clinging to the lapels of my long black coat like a security blanket as I watched Poppy leaning over Dad, trying to say good-bye.

The hunger pangs were bad enough—but what I really couldn't bear was the thought of losing either one of these men.

Nurse Karen performed her task with relish, manipulating the pillows and sheets while strategically pushing and pulling Dad's body here and there. She showed me how to use the gravitational forces of my father's deadweight to maneuver him around the bed and into a new position.

She hit her hands together with a single clap—"Good!"—seemingly satisfied with the results and looking over the finished product as if she had just rearranged some furniture. "Are we okay there, Mr. Sorrentino?" No reply. She turned to me. "Okay, now I have to change the dressing on the bedsore. Are you sure you want to see this?"

"Yes." It had been a while since Dad and I had had a good bonding experience, and besides, the kid in me wanted to see what the hell a decubitus ulcer looked like.

I stood back as Nurse Karen went to work. She had positioned Dad as far up on his right side as was possible, giving her access to the area at the base of his spine. As she pulled back the hospital gown, the sight of my father's bare body embarrassed me. I wanted to spare him the indignity but was mesmerized like I had just come upon a car accident.

She had lined the necessary supplies up on the table next to the bed and now began to pull at the adhesive tape that secured the gauzy dressing just north of Dad's backside. The sound of the tape pulling off the skin sickened me, but my eyes were locked on the bandage that now started to loosen. As Nurse Karen pulled off the last piece of tape, she gently cupped her hand around the bandage so it would not fall onto the bed. She let the gauze drop into her hand and pulled it away, completely exposing the sore. I gulped when I saw the circle of redness about the size of a slice of baloney. But I stared right into the bull's-eye: a raw and fleshy hole at the core, as round as a quarter, with about a tablespoon's worth of flesh completely missing.

My morbid curiosity satiated (and stomach completely turned), I looked away as Karen patted and cleaned the sore before redressing it. All the while Dad was fortunately (or unfortunately) not feeling a thing—though I felt like I had just looked Death in the eye.

I stared at my father's face, trying to find him somewhere behind the blank expression.

Nothing.

"I'm here, Dad," was all I could think of to say once Nurse Karen had left the room.

No response.

I tried to remember what it was like to hear Dad talk his funny words or sing his funny lyrics, but I was distracted.

I checked my watch. Mom would be back soon and I'd go have dinner with Nonny and Poppy. But for now, I sat quietly at Dad's bedside, listening to the breathing and watching the heart monitor while that fucking decubitus ulcer devoured the memories like a piranha.

10.
SOME MISDIRECTED GRAPEFRUIT

Dad, you're walking again! It had been such a relief when he finally came off the respirator, but seeing him standing there in the back door of the luncheonette, smiling, well, I just couldn't believe it! I wanted to go to him, but there were so many orders to get done. The grill was full, the Bay Marie was almost empty, dishes were piling up in the sink. All the customers were there. What a wonderful kid you got there, Clint! I kept flipping the porkroll slices before they burned up. Dad, how did you do it? He still wouldn't answer me. Not that I would have been able to hear him over the music blaring out of the speakers. "In the Mood." Remember that one, Dad? Why won't he answer me? Oh my God! Parris? What are you doing in West Long Branch? Forget about me, lover, who's that? Oh, that's Pepsi Man, what a hunk, huh? Pepsi Man was naked. I tightened my apron. Suddenly all the floor tiles on the other side of the counter started to crack and fall into a giant pit. My apron was getting tighter and tighter and I couldn't move. Everything was being devoured. Tables. Chairs. All my sheet music and Broadway scores! Pepsi Man. Customers. Poppy. Parris! Why are you smiling like that? Run! Goddammit—run! What the fuck is wrong with you? Fuck you! My apron was tightening and the pit was growing wider and deeper. Fuck you! Everything was being devoured. Dad! Run! Run! Run! Fuck! Fuck! Fuck—

"Fuck!" The sound of my own voice woke me up. My heart was racing. The blanket was on the floor. I couldn't catch my breath.

I lay there, unable to fall back asleep, until it was time to roll out of bed and get ready for work. I wished I had never looked at that fucking decubitus ulcer.

"I putta too mucha shoogah!" Old Man Pascucci stood at the counter sucking on his corncob pipe and tapping his almost empty cup of coffee on the counter to get my attention.

"Just a *second,* Mr. Pascucci!" I wielded my spatula, wanting to pop him like an egg yolk on a porkroll-egg-and-cheese sandwich, but I resisted. Instead, I spoke in dulcet tones like a doctor in a mental hospital. "Dolores will be *right* with you, *okaaay?*"

The disheveled old man kept tapping anyway but I was determined to stay in control. After all, I was a nice guy.

Martin Leslie Pembrook sipped his tea, looked up from his *New York Times* crossword puzzle, and delivered his lines in clear staccato speech like a Barrymore. "Must you tap your cup like that on the counter? Can't you see the man is busy?"

But Old Man Pascucci was unfazed, extending his free hand out to the side in a half shrug, responding matter-of-factly, "I putta too mucha shoogah!"

"Well—Christ!" Martin Leslie Pembrook looked back down at his crossword puzzle, muttering, "What's a five-letter word for 'pain in my ass'?"

"Okay, *boychick*"—Dolores returned from table three—"I need an American cheese omelet with whole wheat, a toasted English, and an order of French toast on Italian bread." She pinched the elastic base of her wig between her fingers and wiggled it down an inch while lauding my innovative use of submarine-bread chunks for the French toast. "We're getting so goddamn continental here!"

"I putta too mucha shoogah!" Old Man Pascucci tapped again while his corncob pipe bobbed up and down out of the side of his mouth.

"Too much sugar, my ass! And if you tap that goddamn cup at me one more time, I'm gonna show you *another* way to smoke that pipe!" She poured coffee into his cup. "Here you go, bay-bay."

"Grrrazie!" The old man returned to his chair at table two, catching my eye as he proceeded to pour a stream of sugar into his cup.

"I don't know how you do it, son." Martin Leslie Pembrook put the used Lipton tea bag back into his cup and pushed it forward for more hot water.

"It's an art form, Martin," I answered over the shoulder. *Mr. Wonderful. Reporting for duty.*

The back door suddenly flew open, a gust of wind blowing in a tall wisp of a woman with an open coat and a brown paper bag.

"And speaking of pains in my ass—" Martin smiled at his wife.

"Good morning, boysss." Gertie hissed slightly as she greeted the group at large and tapped her index finger on Stanley's shoulder, prompting him to move down one seat like the previous guest on *The Tonight Show.*

"Thank you, SSStanley!" She whistled her words while settling her skinniness onto the stool next to her husband.

"Yep." Stanley was happy to comply, though Martin seemed less appreciative of the gesture as he watched Gertie open her brown paper bag and pull out a pack of Carlton cigarettes, a serrated knife, and half a pink grapefruit.

"Goddammit, Gertie!" He launched into her with all the mock exasperation of Lunt in a well-rehearsed scene with Fontanne. "How—pray tell—are they supposed to make a profit here if the customers bring in their own breakfast?"

"Excuse me—Marty—but whatever happened to *the customer is always right*—right, SSSteven? Go back to your crosswords, Marty."

"I'd like to give *you* five-across," he grumbled back like Ralph at Alice.

"Oh Jesus Christ, the lovebirds are here!" Dolores slid a bowl and spoon over to Gertie and poured the hot water for Martin. "Steven, where the hell are the sandwiches for my boys?" She winked at Big Bobby and Flip over at table one as they removed their JCP&L hard hats. "They ain't got all day!"

"Just a *second*—Dolores—dear." I stacked the eggs and porkroll slices onto buttered Knipp's rolls for the guys from Jersey Central Power & Light, wondering how they were able to climb utility poles with double orders in their stomachs. "Here you go, Dolores."

She scooted around to the other side of the counter to deliver the sandwiches. Big Bobby and Flip had placed their equipment belts on empty chairs, though their protruding guts still kept them at an uncomfortable distance from the table. "Here you go, boys. Eat up!" She scooped up their hard hats, holding them over her breasts like Brunhild, before tossing them onto the coatrack on her way back to the counter.

"SSSteven, sssweetheart," Gertie said as she sawed the inside of her grapefruit into little sections. "How's Clint?"

"Well, the good news is he's breathing—literally." I filled a glass of seltzer from the fountain and poured it over the grill to loosen the porkroll residue. "They're weaning him off the respirator as we speak."

"Oh, sssweetheart, that's maaarvelous." Even with wide-open vowels, Gertie managed to anchor the cigarette at the corner of her mouth as she sprinkled sugar over her pared-up grapefruit. "Ssso what's the bad news?"

"He's going to need major surgery now," I continued as Gertie scooped out the first section and froze with her spoon midair. Martin looked up from his crossword puzzle and Stanley scratched his head. It was like they were huddled around a campfire poised for all the grisly details of a ghost story. "You see"—I cracked two eggs into a stainless bowl with fresh milk and a touch of cinnamon—"he's got this bedsore that's been growing for weeks like a cancer." I blended the ingredients with quick wrist action, pausing to tap my wire whisk on the side of the bowl to release the gooey excess as Dolores chimed in.

"Steven, what the hell you doin'—tryin' to make us all puke?" I don't think she was referring to my French-toast mixture, though curiosity got the best of Martin Leslie Pembrook.

"For the love of God—just how serious is this—bedsore?" He had even commanded the attention of the cheap seats as Big Bobby and Flip looked up from their porkroll-egg-and-cheese.

Well, not since my repeat performances of "He's paralyzed up to *here*" had I felt so compelled to let Dad's medical update speak for me. I didn't know how to express whatever the fuck it was that I was feeling. But as long as I remained courteous and delivered service with a smile, I could just sit back and let the decubitus ulcer do the talking. That way, no one would ever suspect that I wasn't dealing with a full grill.

"It's *very* serious, Martin. It started out as a hole at the base of his spine the size of a golf ball." I dipped chunks of Italian bread into the egg mixture as I explained the daily scraping and submersion in Betadine pools that had failed to stymie the growth of the decubitus ulcer. "It's devouring everything," I added.

"Keep this up, *boychick,* and we can say good-bye to half our customers!" Dolores interjected, but couldn't resist: "So how big is this damn thing now?"

Gertie had a mouthful when I came up with the perfect description. "Well, now the hole in his flesh is the size of—well, actually—about the size of that grapefruit."

I watched the shock register on everyone's face as they looked into Gertie's bowl. I knew just how they felt. She gulped down the last section and winced.

"Good God!" Martin Leslie Pembrook spooned the teabag out of his cup and wound the little string around it to drain off the extra, as I stood there trying to steal even a few drops of the sympathy intended for my father. "That poor man! Good God!" he exclaimed again.

"*Rrranny bozke!*" Dolores crossed her arms over her chest with equal religious fervor. "Where's my goddamn order?"

"Coming right up!" I dropped the gooey chunks of French toast onto the grill.

"Well, you tell your father I looove 'm!" Gertie took one final drag. "And ssspeaking of bedsoresss," she hissed like the cigarette she pushed into the rind, "tell him you're adding grapefruit to the menu! Haaah!" She laughed in a single exhale as her tongue unfurled like a cuckoo clock on the hour.

"Goddammit, Gertie!" Martin gave her a little tap on the head with his pen.

That's when a woman I'd never seen before walked in the front door. Her face was nondescript but she had a shape like my glass timer for three-minute eggs.

The men were watching intently as she draped her coat over a stool, shook back her jet-black hair, and sat down. Unaware of her audience, she refastened the top button of her blouse that had popped out right along with Old Man Pascucci's eyes. I also noticed that Big Bobby and Flip had raised their cups of coffee like they were clinking steins of beer after a crude joke.

But Gertie wouldn't have any of it. She placed her hand over the top of Martin's head and turned it as if she were twisting the lid of a jar shut until he was facing forward again.

Stanley was more subtle. "Yep." He straightened out a crick in his neck, stealing a sideways glance at the curvaceous customer.

"Oh Christ," Dolores muttered to me. "Here she is—little Miss New in Town."

"She ain't so little." I wasn't referring to her height or weight, but what really interested me was the copy of the *Village Voice* she pulled from her bag and placed on the counter. Just the sight of the edgy New York weekly gave me a hunger pang. "I'll take care of her."

"Now be nice, she ain't used to us yet!"

"Don't worry, Dolores. I'm feeling a little homesick for New York today. I just want to steal a look at her *Voice* and maybe comb through the personal ads for a lark."

"I don't know about you this morning, *boychick*."

Big Bobby and Flip waved their empty cups in the air, presenting my nosy head waitress with an excuse to run over to table one, putting her in perfect earshot as I walked down to little Miss New in Town.

"Here you go boys." Dolores poured the coffees. "Now you'd better finish up quick so you can go back to workin' on your poles!" She slapped Flip so hard on the back that he burped.

"Hi there," I said to the woman sitting sideways on her stool, reading the *Village Voice* with her legs crossed. "I'm Steven."

"Oh, hello. Pammie." She put down her paper and rotated forward to extend her hand. "You're the New York son. Your father mentioned you. How is he doing?"

"Well." I looked around as if I needed props to do the story justice. I pointed down toward the bowl in front of Gertie. "You see that grapefruit down there?"

I didn't give her all the details, but by the time I finished the update, I was pretty sure she'd gotten the gist. I was also pretty sure that when she hurried out that front door—without her paper—she wasn't coming back.

Dolores walked over to the counter from table one. "Jesus, *boychick*." She looked out the window after little Pammie. "You really know how to charm 'em!"

I scooped up the *Village Voice* from the counter and flipped to the personals, contemplating how I might word my own: *GWM, 24, nice guy. Sings. Dances. Seeks special relationship with same. Warning: May need help containing my grapefruit.*

11.
SANDWICHED IN

After five weeks of poking and prodding and medicating and tube feeding and catheterizing and debreeding, Dad was finally taken off the respirator, freed from most of his tubes, and moved out of the intensive care unit and onto the fifth floor of Monmouth Medical Center, where he was propped up in bed and fed his first meal since Christmas: a ham-and-cheese sandwich on white bread with lettuce and mayo—hold the pickle.

His skin was as pale as the Hellmann's and his cheeks had practically disappeared below the crooked sideburns, but there was something momentous about the occasion: Dad could talk again. I had ached to hear his voice and couldn't imagine what his first words might be after surviving such an ordeal. I wouldn't be calling *Bartlett's* anytime soon, but I'll never forget Dad, wearing his wire frames again, smiling and speaking for the first time in five weeks— through a mouthful of sandwich.

"Hey, Shteve, howsh bishnish?"

Two weeks later, on my twenty-fourth birthday, I stumbled into the bathroom at five-thirty in the morning to shave and wash up like I did every morning before leaving for the luncheonette. So many people had told me that I looked just like my father, but—other than the fact that I wasn't looking so great right now either—I didn't see it.

Maybe I had become more critical with age, but I cringed at my own reflection, noting how my perm had almost grown out and my hair was beginning to flatten. This made me particularly intolerant of my Roman nose. I concluded that it was too big for my face and made me unattractive. For years I had wanted to get it "fixed," as if it were holding me back in my acting career or might even get in the way of my finding love. But neither of those things seemed within reach for now. I was trapped in New Jersey. If only life were as simple as getting a nose job.

A plastic surgeon was brought in after several methods of treatment had failed to heal or shrink Dad's decubitus ulcer. Its size had increased almost tenfold from the day I had watched Nurse Karen change the dressing two months earlier. And even though there was still no specific diagnosis for Dad's condition, this particular complication had become so critical that we'd almost forgotten that the man was paralyzed up to *here*.

The surgery was successful, though the recovery period was grueling, as it required Dad to lie facedown on his stomach for almost three weeks as the wound healed.

"*Brrruta.*" He was looking straight down at the floor but greeted me when my feet came into view. All I saw was the thin hair swept around the top of his head, his face smushed into a cushioned ring that extended off the front of the gurney. I bent over sideways and talked up into his face.

"Hi, Dad, how are you feeling today?"

When he lifted his head off the ring, the only color in his face was a big red circle around the perimeter. "Pretty good." His voice was hoarse. "How are things at the luncheonette?"

Well, other than the fact that I've completely unnerved a few customers with all the details of the nips and tucks and flaps and folds it took to reconstruct your backside—

"Good." I cocked my head all the way to my shoulder and knelt on the floor so he could see me without straining. "Everyone's been asking for you."

"Really?" he asked, as if the old regulars might have forgotten him.

"Of course *really*!" I snapped at him. "People are upset and they want you to get better!"

"That's nice." Dad dropped his head back down into the hole so he could bring his right hand up from under to scratch his nose. He popped back up for details. "Like who?"

Well, me, for starters.

"Stanley and Googie, and Martin and Gertie, all the Syrians, the two Anitas—oh, and Half Cup Harold always asks for you."

"Who?"

"You know—Harold, the retired banker who Dolores insists on calling *Howard*."

"Why do you call him Half Cup Howard?"

"Harold. Didn't you ever notice that he orders his coffee in half-cup increments?"

"Hey, every man's got to drink his coffee his own way."

"Woof. You don't get deeper than that!"

"Speaking of the great philosophers—how are you making out with Dolores?"

"Let's just say, now I know why you laid down the red line."

I could almost hear the fluid in his lungs when he attempted to laugh. "Uhhh," he groaned, then dropped his head back down for a rest.

My knees cracked when I stood back up and shook my legs out one at a time. Dad didn't say anything for several seconds, though I wondered what he was thinking as he stared at my feet.

"So, Steve," he said toward the floor, "how's New York, by the way? Have you been able to make any trips back?"

I walked over to the window. "What's that song you used to sing to Mom?"

He lifted his head up. " 'Embraceable You'?" he said into the air, since I was out of his line of vision.

"No. Mom told me that story about the one you sang her in a restaurant once?"

" 'If There Is Someone Lovelier Than You.' Hmm. Dietz and Schwartz." His voice was getting more hoarse, but the pitch rose. "Why? You thinking of using it for an audition?" He still couldn't see me.

"Maybe. I love the old ballads. Or anything with a swing." I watched him fiddling with his ear, the way he always did when he was concentrating or daydreaming. "Dad, you know how Pearl Bailey handles the microphone?"

"Oh yeah. She's really something," he said toward the wall.

"You gave me the idea once to sing 'Step to the Rear' into a hairbrush at an audition. I got a big laugh from it."

"Did you get the job?"

"No."

"You should be on television," he said, holding his earlobe between his thumb and forefinger and making gentle circular motions.

"Dad, do you think you'll ever be able to sing again?"

"Not today." He made another feeble effort to cough. "God, I could go for a cup of coffee and a cigarette."

"Oh, right!" I walked back over and squatted down. "I'll get you a pack of Camels. I think there's a vending machine in the ICU."

"I really want you to get back to New York," he said, looking into my eyes before dropping his head back down. "I feel bad. You in that luncheonette."

"It's okay." *You in that headlock.* "Dad, you've been on your stomach for two weeks. How can you stand it?"

He shrugged as best he could with his arms dangling off the sides of the gurney and his head in a hole. "It shouldn't be much longer."

"By the way, I bought some stainless pitchers from Kmart and got rid of those goddamn little creamers for the milk. And I started a new blackboard special—though Uncle Tony didn't approve."

"Yeah? What is it?" he looked up.

"Eat Shit and Die."

"Steve!" He tried to laugh, but the exasperation seemed to take all his air. He dipped his head back down into the ring like it was an oxygen mask.

"Okay, enough before I asphyxiate you." I knelt down on the floor again and cocked my head all the way to one side so I could look up into Dad's face. For an instant, I thought I saw the resemblance between the two of us that others had pointed out. Some of it was definitely in the nose, but I really saw it in the eyes. It upset me that for the first time in his almost three months of hell in that hospital, I thought I detected tears.

"You don't have to go," he said.

"I have to run to Pathmark," I explained, fighting back the lump in my throat. "Aunt Angie and Aunt Mary are coming in to help with the meatballs later this week."

"Okay."

"I'll be back again tomorrow."

I stood up and kissed him on the back of his head. I didn't know what to say or do. I looked back from the doorway on my way out and watched for a few seconds as Dad remained facedown in the ring, motionless, like he'd gotten his head caught in a trap.

12.
...NO, BUT HE'S GETTING CLOSE!

"Hello, Parris?"

"No. It's Jack. Who's this?"

"It's Steven." *Who's this?*

"Just a minute, I'll get him."

I was sitting at the end of the counter near the National Cash Register, rubbing the day's grill smoke out of my eyes. I waved to John, who'd come in after school as usual to stone the grill and sweep up. I was trying to be nicer to him these days instead of treating him like he did everything wrong. The fact was, he did everything right, so it worked best to keep a little distance from each other, since neither one of us knew exactly what would set me off. I don't know if he realized it, but we *both* preferred the original owner to the more volatile stand-in. He waved back at me, smiled tentatively, and went to work.

"You do a great job, John!" Dolores said for my benefit while wadding up paper towels and spraying Fantastik all over the place.

"Jesus, Dolores, that stuff is strong!" I squinted.

"That's cause this shit ain't any good by itself. I had to add ammonia!" She was wiping down everything but the Knipp's rolls when Parris finally came to the phone.

"Hello, liker boy! Long-time-no-hear-from!"

"So who's Jack?" I was spinning around on one of the turquoise stools, then reversing direction, wrapping and unwrapping myself in the long curly phone cord.

"He's a good friend, lover. We got cast in this wonderful experimental piece at the Playhouse down in the Village. It all takes place on Mount Olympus!"

"Oh great, so he's a Greek god?"

"Wait till you see us in our togas!"

"Yeah, wait till you see me in my greasy red apron."

"Oh, Steven, Steven, Steven. How's your father doing?"

"Ugh. I don't know how he does it. He's been recovering from major surgery for almost three weeks now, and believe it or not, he's had to spend the entire time lying on his stomach! And I haven't heard him complain about it once." I brought Parris up-to-date while watching Dolores wipe under the hood of the Bay Marie, wondering how much cleaning fluid she had sprayed onto the cold cuts in the process.

"And how are *you* doing, lover?"

I was about to fill him in on the finer details of my short-order existence when John walked over to me from the fountain, clutching the grill stone in one hand and holding up an empty glass in the other.

"Steven," he whispered, "we're out of seltzer." I detected that adolescent crack of change in his voice, reminding me that I was older and bigger.

"Oh, for Christ's sake! Wait just a second, Parris." I unraveled myself from the phone cord, hooked the receiver on the side of the counter, and stormed over to the half-empty showcase. "Here!" I slammed a can of Sprite on the counter in front of him. "Use this instead."

"That wasn't what I meant—"

"John, please! I'm on the phone!"

"Okay." He spoke as if he had his finger on the trigger and I'd just dared him to shoot me. "Whatever you say." He pulled back the flip top until the can opened with a *pop!*

"Goddammit," I said into the phone as John went back to the grill. I watched him hold the can high in the air, tipping it forward so that the Sprite came cascading down onto the hot grill surface with a dramatic and smoky hiss. Dolores slammed down the hood of the Bay Marie and ran to stop the spectacle, but she was too late.

"Oh, no, no, no, doll! You can't put that shit on the grill! It's got sugar in it. You'll make it all sticky!"

"*He* told me to do it," John announced triumphantly while pushing away his bangs, which had become soggy from the steam.

"Hold on a second, Parris—there's no seltzer, Dolores!"

"Well, then we better check our gas, *boychick*. Come on!" Dolores put down her spray bottle and headed toward the back door while pulling the Banlon away from her neck so she could fan some cool air down into her cleavage.

"Sounds like you're running out of gas, lover."

"Parris, hold on again." I put the receiver down on the counter and ran to catch up with Dolores. "What do you mean *check our gas?*"

"The tank, *boychick*. Where the hell do you think we get the gas for the seltzer?" Just inside the back door, she pointed out the silver tanks that were slightly smaller than kegs, hooked up to lines feeding into the soda fountain. "Look at your dials, hon. You're outta gas. And your syrup's low on this other one. You better call Pepsi Man." She yanked at her stretch pants and giggled at the sheer mention of the burly brute in the tight blue uniform—though she wasn't the only one excited at the prospect of bringing in our big drink of soda.

"I'll get right on 'im," I said without thinking.

"Not before I do." Dolores slurped, then checked my face for a reaction—but I quickly slipped back into my hometown nonchalance reserved for all matters of sexuality.

"I mean I'll call him to come service our tanks." I heard myself digging in deeper. "Oh, go disinfect the slicer!"

I passed John on my way back to the phone as he scoured the grill surface like he was taking revenge on somebody's face.

"Everything all right, lover?"

"Let's just say, Parris, that the Pepsi man cometh."

"Do you know what you need, dearest?"

"What?"

"Sex."

"Shut up!" I looked up as if John and Dolores could hear him, stretching the phone cord all the way to the front window for more privacy. "I can't get into New York anytime soon if that's what you're suggesting."

"Daaarling. Surely they have sex in New Jersey."

"Listen, the only thrill I get these days is drooling over this Pepsi guy when he's loading in the Yoo-Hoo."

"Well, that's a start!"

"I swear that I am the only gay man in this town." I sighed. "I guess I could drive over to Asbury Park. There's this bar called the Odyssey, but it's so sleazy."

"But if people just knew that you were gay, the others would start coming—pardon my pun—out of the woodwork. Advertise a little."

"I'm not ready for that. Not here, anyway. Not while I'm stuck in this family thing. I mean, I *want* to help. But if Googie the Gizmo or Uncle Tony or my grandmother tells me one more time how wonderful I am—I'll puke!"

"Dearest, I wish—"

"Just a second." I covered the receiver with my hand but my voice would have carried through steel-enforced concrete. "JOHN! Don't empty the goddamn grease trap into the garbage! I already changed the bag! For Christ's sake!"

"Lover, who *are* you talking to?"

"That's my baby brother. Who'd you think I was talking to?"

"It sounds more like you're talking to a hatchet killer."

"Yeah, well, so I'm a little impatient these days."

"Oh, is that what you call it?"

"I know, I'm being an asshole, but he's the only thing around here that's smaller than I am." I was looking out the front window at the two Anitas smoking in front of the dry cleaners when Dolores came up from behind and startled me.

"*Rrranny bozke!*" She took the Lord's name in Polish vain as I twirled around and came face-to-face with her fogged lenses and a loaded spray bottle.

"You're bein' awfully hard on your brother, *boychick*."

"I'm on the phone."

"Yeah? Well, I got one word of advice for you—don't spite your ass to spite your face!"

I ducked and covered as she shot an ammoniated mist of Fantastik over my head before walking away.

"And who's that?" Parris begged on the other end of the phone.

"That was Dolores." I watched her go back to the Bay Marie and brandish her spray bottle at me one more time like it had long-range capabilities.

"We like her."

"Parris, I just want my father to be okay and for all of this to be over."

"I know, liker boy. But it's really wonderful how you—oh, just a second." I heard garbled words on the other end of the line. "Listen, lover, I gotta run. You take care now and I'll see you soon?"

"Yeah, yeah. By the way, Parris—"

"What's that, love?"

"Who the hell is Jack?"

"Good-*bye,* love. And for God's sake, do yourself and the little hatchet killer a favor—make that call to Pepsi Man!"

13.
RIGHT IN THE MEATBALLS

"What the hell is this, *boychick*?" Dolores pointed a rock-hard loaf of Nino's submarine bread at me like it was a rifle. "You left five of these out in the kitchen last night—what's wrong with you!"

"They're for the meatballs!" I flipped the porkroll to brown the undersides as two slices of Wonder bread popped out of the toaster.

"Stale bread?" Dolores tried to nudge the end of the loaf under my apron and lift it like a skirt, but I retracted with a series of wiggles, never once losing control of my spatula. I scooped up the eggs.

"Yes, stale bread! I have to soak them. My aunts will be here in a little while to help me with a new batch." I slipped the porkroll slices, a mound of home fries, and the toast onto the plate next to the eggs. "Here you go, Norma." Dolores lifted the stale loaf like it was a tollgate so Norma could pass through to deliver the order to Half Cup Harold.

"Give me that!" I swiped the loaf out of Dolores's hands. She followed me out from behind the counter, through the swinging doors, and into the kitchen.

"I'm tellin' ya, hon, when my Vern and I—God rest his goddamn soul—had the Pickle Place, we used plain old-fashioned bread crumbs." She watched me pull out a three-inch-deep lasagna pan and fill it with water. I tried to explain that once the bread was soaked and drained, it would add a nice light texture to the meatball mixture. But the information seemed to be lost on her as she suddenly became wistful. "Oh, my Vern and I"—she snapped her bra straps—"we made a good sandwich."

"Don't make me picture it," I said under my breath.

I had always suspected there was sex going on in West Long Branch, though I never actually experienced it firsthand. I grew up playing the chaste little kid who delivered newspapers and ate all his macaroni, secretly pining away after the school jocks. It wasn't until I moved into Manhattan that I began to blossom, sprung free from the old hometown role and the secret crushes that had gone with it.

But there I was, back home again, neutralized under the greasy red apron that was wrapped tightly around my midsection. The only real action those days was in my head, though I did seem to share one unspoken fantasy with my head waitress.

"I thought you said Pepsi Man was comin' in today?" Dolores had pulled a gold tube out of her apron pocket and was refreshing her pink lipstick.

"He's supposed to," I said while submerging the first loaf of bread, holding it down until it no longer popped back up to the surface. Dolores recapped her tube and smacked her lips like she was preparing for a big date. I wanted to go on one, too, but just the thought of Pepsi Man shoving his big invoice in my face reminded me that my opportunities seemed to fall into one of two categories: what I didn't want, or what I couldn't have.

"Oh boy, that counter's fillin' up again." Dolores waved from the service window at Carmen, who smiled back through his zits. "That kid looks like he ain't had a vegetable since Johnson was president. Come on, *boychick.*"

I was dunking the second loaf into the water. "I'll be out as soon as I finish here—you've got Norma helping you for now."

"Yeah, but she don't move her ass and the boys from Jersey Central will be here soon and we still have to do the takeouts for the beauty parlor and—"

"All right already! I'll finish with the bread later," I conceded while holding the hard loaf underwater like I was drowning it. I dried my hands and followed Dolores behind the counter while she shouted the order.

"Ham and eggs for Carmen! Toasted bagel—extra butter!" Dolores flew past Norma with the coffeepot, barely hearing her coworker's comment. "What?"

"I told you already—we're out of bagels," Norma squeaked.

"Shit! Carmen doll—we're out of bagels, so I'm gonna toast you a nice Knipp's roll, extra butter!" She didn't wait for his response before yelling down toward the Bay Marie. "Norma—toast me a nice Knipp's roll, extra butter!"

I cracked two eggs into a bowl and dropped four slices of ham onto the grill, first shaking the thin slices into little bunches. "Just like your father," Dolores commented, "but you can take your dear sweet time—we can all get *fucked* by the time Norma butters the goddamn roll!"

Half Cup Harold tried to retrieve the spoon he'd bounced onto the counter, knocking his fork onto the floor in the process. He pretended not to hear what Dolores had just said, but I could no longer ignore the whole damn issue of sex—especially once it walked right in the front door and took a seat at the counter.

"Hey Steve-o!"

Brent Jamison hadn't tousled my hair since freshman year at Shore Regional High School when I just happened to run into the senior stud outside the locker room after a varsity basketball game—but the nickname had stuck. And it still got my attention when the pin-striped attorney saddled up to the counter lugging his attaché case like it was a gym bag.

"Brent!" I really didn't mind the crush of his handshake, though farther down I was experiencing a more painful reminder of what I missed most about New York. Well, maybe not pain—though there was a notable weakness in my legs.

"Great to see you again, Steve-o!" When he leaned over to place his attaché onto the footrest under the counter, his designer jacket buckled under the stress of containing a set of shoulders like barbells. The look might not have been what Evan Picone had intended, but it worked well for the former upperclassman—and me.

"Brent," I stuttered again, not knowing what to do with my hands. It didn't help when Brent raised both of *his*, open-fingered, to comb back his hair and showcase the expanse of his chest, before mounting the stool like it was a Harley.

Norma saved me from my loss for words.

"Can I get you a cup of coffee, Mr. Jamison?" She had just done some dishes and was wiping her hands dry.

"I got it!" Dolores pushed her aside and slammed an egg cream down in front of Brent. "I know what ya like, bay-bay!" She yanked her wig down in a defiant gesture of victory as a blush of crimson washed over Norma's face.

"Thanks, Dolores. You remembered! And thank *you,* Norma!" Brent tried to console the retreating part-timer, but the back of her neck had already begun to redden and swell.

"Christ." Dolores pushed on her hips as if they had popped out of the sockets. "I'm goin' in the back for a smoke."

She disappeared into the kitchen as I watched Brent's lips wrap around *new job blah-blah this* and *new baby blah-blah that*, his update buying me some valuable staring time. It wasn't until he blew through his straw and hit me in the face with the wrapper that I realized he had asked me something. "I *said*— how is your father doing, Steve-o?"

"Oh, better, thanks." I would have delivered Dad's medical report with my usual panache, but *bedsore blah-blah this* and *grapefruit blah-blah that* weren't nearly as entrancing to me as Brent's untamed cowlick. "So when did you move back from Connecticut?"

"Pennsylvania," he corrected me. "And—like I *just* finished saying— Candy and I moved back when I finished law school last year and I went to work in my father's firm." He seemed to be searching my eyes for signs of intelligent life. "You're not paying attention there, Steve-o. You got something on your mind?" Brent winked at me as Dolores burst through the swinging doors from the kitchen, swinging a loaf of hard bread.

"Yeah." She handed it to me like it was an old torch. "Meatballs!"

"Aunt Mary, do you think this will be enough?" I was tipping the pan to drain the excess water into the sink, careful not to spill out any of the bread.

Aunt Mary looked over her shoulder. "Plenty!" She was standing at the marble slab in front of the service window, unwrapping packages of ground chuck from Pathmark and crumbling the meat into a five-gallon green vat. "Just make sure you drain it really good now."

"Sorry we're late." Aunt Angie's voice was like gravel as she handed her sister a bag through the service window. "Here's the parsley. Hi, Steven!" She undid the large fabric buttons of her lamb's wool, hung it on the rack just outside the kitchen, then entered through the louvered half-doors. "Is that Tony's old black coat hangin' there? You're still wearing that thing?"

"Yeah, believe it or not." My worn cashmere suddenly looked like an old man's coat hanging there next to Brent Jamison's swank trench. "So where's Uncle Tony?"

"The lot's full. He's parking next door at McDonald's." She coughed while pulling out a lighter and a pack of Salems before slotting her pocketbook between two gallon cans of Hunt's tomatoes. "Okay, let's get going here." She placed the cigarettes on the windowsill, patting them as if she were instructing a small dog to stay.

I flattened the bread with my hands one last time to drain off the rest of the water. "I think this is ready. How many eggs do you need?"

"How much meat you got there, Mary?" Aunt Angie asked.

"Almost fifteen pounds." Aunt Mary was crumbling the last package into the vat. "About twenty eggs, you think?" The two sisters nodded at each other.

"I got 'em." By the time I pulled two cartons of eggs out of the refrigerator and placed them on the marble slab, Uncle Tony had come in the back door and was leaning on the shelf outside of the service window.

"Hi, Mary. Hi, Steven," he said while catching his breath. "Angie, you sure that's enough parsley?"

"You want to help, Tony?" Aunt Angie growled while pulling out some stems. "Go sit down!" she continued while her sister laughed.

"Steven"—Uncle Tony ignored her and looked over to the coat rack—"you still wearin' that old coat I gave you? God bless you. Heh . . . heh . . . heh . . . heh. What a good kid. Heh . . . heh . . . heh . . . heh."

"Tony!" Angie chopped. "Sit!"

Dolores tried to lure Uncle Tony over to the counter with a cup of coffee but wasn't successful until she waved a slice of spiced ham at him like a hankie. "I'll make ya a nice sandwich!"

"Is that *sopressata*?" His eyes lit up at the sight of the thin Italian cold cut.

"We can pretend, doll!"

I watched him from the service window as he placed both hands on the counter and lifted himself onto one of the stools, keeping his good leg planted on the floor for balance. A few stools down, Brent Jamison did a semispin and winked at me, setting my own footing a little off-kilter. But I looked away. "I'll get the cheese."

"And garlic salt," Aunt Mary requested.

"And black pepper," Aunt Angie added.

Aunt Mary had already begun to blend the bread and meat through her fists as I poured two jars of Locatelli cheese into the vat and sprinkled in the spices. Once Aunt Angie had dropped in the chopped parsley, she plunged her hands into the vat alongside Aunt Mary's. I began to crack each of the eggs, pouring them over my aunts' bare flesh as they scrunched and squashed the mixture through their fingers.

"Ooh, I got an itch." Aunt Mary pulled her right shoulder up to her nose to avoid getting runny yokes and raw meat on her face.

I'm glad the board of health wasn't here to cite my aunts for not wearing any gloves. I suppose they should also have been wearing nets on their heads. But as the overhead fluorescent lighting illuminated Aunt Angie's lacquered bouffant and Aunt Mary's hurricane-proof permanent, I was reassured that all that processed hair wasn't going anywhere.

"Steven, we'll need a pot for the sauce and a couple of skillets filled with olive oil. Okay, dear?" Aunt Angie wiped her brow with the back of her hand, careful not to get any raw egg in her silver hair.

"I tell you—you'll never get meatballs like these in New York!" Aunt Mary punctuated her point with suction sounds as the mixture oozed through her fingers, two fistfuls at a time.

"That's for sure!" Aunt Angie concurred before directing her chronic smoker's cough away from the lunch special.

★   ★   ★

"Umm. Something smells good back here, Steve-o!" Brent rested his forearms on the sill of the service window and sniffed. The aroma of meatballs browning in hot olive oil blended with the smell of tomatoes simmering on the back burner with fresh garlic and onion. I sniffed, too, more intent on zeroing in on Brent's cologne.

"Oh yeah. I love that smell." I played along. Just across the ocean gray concrete floor, the two old sisters were standing on the multicolored woven mat from Kmart like it was a little island. "How are you doing there, ladies?" They were hunched over the large skillets, turning each meatball over and over with a fork to brown them evenly and keep their shape. They didn't hear me over the crackling.

"So, Steve-o." Brent extended his arm through the service window and tapped me on the shoulder to get my attention. "You didn't tell me what you've been up to the past four years. Did you finish college?"

"Well, no. Um." I avoided eye contact, preferring to watch Aunt Mary lay Scott towels on the counter to drain the finished meatballs that Aunt Angie was pulling out of the oil.

"Oh yeah, Steve-o. I forgot. You were in all the high school musicals. Are you doing any theater?"

"Well, not right now!" We were interrupted by the sound of my tanks clanking together near the back door. *Oh great, Pepsi Man has come!*

Brent smiled at me. "Well, of course, Steve-o. I didn't mean right *now!*" He winked at me as Pepsi Man appeared in the window and took a sniff for himself.

"Man, dat smell good—here's da bill," he grunted as he leaned into the sill and presented me with the invoice. "Where's de uddah guy?"

"He's been in the hospital for three months," I said coldly.

"And Steve-o is taking good care of things," Brent added with another wink as Uncle Tony nudged his way into the window between the fragrant attorney and the soft-drink stud.

"He's a good kid! Heh . . . heh . . . heh . . . heh." He raised his chin into the air as the other men nodded my way. Uncle Tony's eyes welled up as he proudly proclaimed the F-word: "Family!"

I felt like I was on display, but Aunt Angie seemed oblivious to the three men peering through the window. She rolled fresh balls in her palms and placed them into the smoky olive oil while Aunt Mary pulled some of the dry ones off the paper towels and began to plop them into the pot of bubbling tomato sauce. At least I was sequestered away in the kitchen, in the safety of the women.

"Hold it!" Dolores came crashing through the swinging doors, raising a fork like she was in a Hitchcock shower scene. Angie and Mary stepped away from the multicolored woven mat from Kmart just in time for her to stab one of the meatballs then devour it in one fell swoop like a python. "Oh *boychick!*" She swooped her chin out and up to complete the swallow before stabbing another, looking me straight in the eye to declare her utter satisfaction.

"Luscious!" she cooed before gobbling down the other one.

14.
TWO LEGS— OVER EASY

The next phase of Dad's recuperation began at the end of March when he was flipped over like a breakfast special. The decubitus ulcer had finally healed, but the effect of lying prone for so long, in combination with the paralysis, had severely affected his blood pressure and circulation. Learning to sit up again became the next hurdle. Any attempt to elevate his upper body made him extremely nauseated and faint. Physical therapists had to raise him on an incline in small increments—about five degrees higher each day—so he could slowly adjust to new altitudes.

I was still convinced that my father would walk again someday, based solely on the fact that there was still no official diagnosis or prognosis for his condition. But that hope (and denial) was fading fast, like the color in Dad's face each time they added a few degrees to the workout.

Other than my newly acquired grill skills, there wasn't much more I could offer my father outside of a snide comment or two from the foot of his bed during my daily visit. On Monday, March 30, 1981, we had to break two unrelated news stories from the night before: The house had been robbed, and Aunt Mary had had a heart attack.

"There go the diamonds *and* the meatballs," I snipped.

"Steve!" Dad reprimanded me as best he could from a twenty-degree incline. But that dry cough didn't fool me—I knew there was a laugh hidden in there somewhere. That's when Uncle Tony hobbled in carrying a Kodak Instamatic and the other news of the day.

"Can you believe they shot that goddamn Reagan this morning?" He aimed the camera at Dad. "Say *sopressata*!"

The flash went off before we could react. "Heh . . . heh . . . heh . . . heh." He took one more for good measure. "Don't worry, Steven, I'll give you a copy to hang up in the luncheonette."

Dad and I looked at each other as Uncle Tony advanced the film on his way out the door—no doubt planning to swing by Aunt Mary's room in the coronary-care unit.

It took weeks before Dad was able to sit up again and even longer before he could dangle his legs off the side of the bed.

"Okay, Mr. Sorrentino." One of the therapists would hold him up while the other took his ankles. They turned him sideways until his legs extended off the bed, parallel to the floor. "Now take a deep breath and exhale slowly as we let your legs down." Dad did his best not to throw up, but within seconds the blood drained from his head and flowed down to his lower extremities without the benefit of a vigorous circulation to recycle it. They quickly returned him to a horizontal plane, massaging his legs and head until he regained his equilibrium. "Good work!" they'd encourage him.

The physical therapists weren't the only ones paying Dad a lot of attention. His new doe-eyed roommate smiled at him—constantly. Phillip had suffered severe head trauma in a truck accident and had recently emerged from a coma—more than a little dazed in his newfound consciousness. Without warning, the young man would wake up from his nap, walk over to Dad, and climb into bed with him. He'd lie on his side, leaning on his elbow so he could prop up his head while batting his big blue eyes and smiling sweetly at my father. Dad—always one to go with the flow—would calmly exchange pleasantries with his bed buddy while hitting the call button.

Phillip loved to watch Dad's therapy sessions. He would step into slippers and sit on the edge of his own bed like he was at a taping of *Wonderama*, his eyes wide as saucers and his hands folded in his lap, as Dad managed to hold his new position for thirty whole seconds one day. "Good work!" Phillip mimicked the therapists.

The seconds eventually turned to minutes as Dad became more tolerant of having his head up and his legs down. I don't know where the hell they thought he was going, but this exercise came to have great significance in Dad's recuperation.

I'll never forget the sight.

It was April of 1981—almost four months into Dad's hospital stay. I had closed the luncheonette and arrived at Monmouth Medical Center at about four o'clock in the afternoon. As I approached Dad's room I could hear my mother and sister's voices, their tone more spirited than usual, especially given the recent news that Dad was battling yet another strain of pneumonia and a bladder infection.

The first thing I noticed when I got to the doorway was Phillip sitting on Dad's bed—grinning like a kid at Christmas—though Dad was not in it at the time. Phillip looked like he was about to burst his little pajama buttons as Mom and Judy turned to catch the look on my face.

Dad looked, too. He smiled at me like a kid who'd just discovered training wheels.

It was the first time I ever saw my father sitting in a wheelchair.

"Wow, Dad." My stomach fluttered. "Let's see."

"Ah, jeez." He wheeled himself forward a few feet and did a little turn as Phillip looked back and forth from me to Dad, waiting to catch my reaction.

The maneuver was small, but its significance wasn't lost on me: Dad was moving of his own accord. It was just a little turn, but it was like he'd just hung a Louie onto the road out of there. For the first time in months I felt hope that this whole nightmare might finally be coming to an end. It wasn't exactly time to run and buy my train ticket, but maybe a little celebration was finally in order.

15.
CITY OF LITES

The sausage-and-provolone omelet with extra potatoes and a toasted Knipp's roll had barely made a dent in my hankerings, and wolfing down the second package of Ring Dings drove home the fact that no amount of luncheonette food—salty or sweet—could really hit the spot, especially when what I was really craving was a little—well, let's call it affection.

Why hasn't he returned my calls?

I was just getting to the creamy center, watching the wall-mounted extension near the back door when Angelo startled me.

"Big Steve!" He reached over the counter with his unlit cigar and tapped imaginary ashes on my head. "Where's my coffee?"

"Angelo!" I almost dropped my Ring Ding. "I didn't see you come in."

Herck the Jerk looked up from his chain-smoking and sneered like he had just seen a Syrian Jew.

"I've been standing here for ten minutes," Angelo teased. "You know, I'm going to have to report this to your father!" His muttonchop sideburns rounded into bushy parentheses when he smiled.

"Good, maybe he'll fire me," I said, reaching for the coffeepot.

"Gimme some!" Herck the Jerk shot the words out of his gray shriveled face while pushing his cup forward.

Dolores stood by, tapping her foot, her knuckles resting on her hips in an attempt to appear menacing, but the effect was more that of a giant loving cup. "I think you've stuffed enough *cheska* into your face for one morning—now where the hell are my orders?"

"Whah ordersh?" I savored my last chunk of Ring Ding and noticed that Big Bobby had pushed a couple of tables together.

"I asked you for six porkroll-egg-and-cheese sandwiches for the Jersey Central boys!"

"No, you didn't!"

"Right there!" She pointed to a kitchen check lying on the shelf next to the grill.

"Dolores. How many times have I told you? I need the orders *shouted* to me, not written down. You're familiar with shouting, right?"

"Bad day, *boychick*?"

"What do you mean?"

"You've been starin' at that goddamn phone all morning like it's gonna explode!"

"So what's it to ya?" My voice rose.

"Who the hell are you waiting for anyway?" she yelled back.

"No one!"

"Good. Now I can shout: SIX PORKROLL-EGG-AND-CHEESE!"

"Thank you—COMING RIGHT UP!"

"Put one on for me, too, big Steve!" Angelo puffed.

"And one for me, too," Dolores added. "My break's comin' up and I'm havin' a hyperglycerin attack."

"*Hypoglycemic.*"

"You get those, too?"

Herck the Jerk snarled through his yellow teeth but said nothing.

I pulled a fresh porkroll out of the Bay Marie, peeled back the burlap covering, and placed it on the electric slicer. *This ought to shut everybody up,* I thought as I pushed the meat across the spinning blade twenty-four times to cover the eight sandwiches, stopping only once when I thought I heard the phone ring. My heart was pounding when I quickly switched off the machine before realizing that the sound I had heard was Dolores practicing on the new computerized cash register that Angelo had delivered a few days before.

"This thing don't make no sense!" she complained as Angelo walked over to explain the new key configuration for the third time.

I scored the porkroll slices, tossed them onto the grill, and began frying the eggs, when Dolores's girlfriend Vivian made an entrance that was louder than her Hermès scarf.

"DASHA!"

"VWAJ!"

"You behaving yourself, girl?"

"Like a goddamn nun!" Dolores covered her privates with both hands. *"Vesushoinih!"*

"AAAHHH!" Vivian screeched with laughter, doubling over with a flexibility that defied even her own self-proclaimed age range. She was still panting when she straightened up, her bleached coiffure falling into place with a single shake. "Steven, do you believe her!" she asked at full volume. "Do you know what she just said?"

"Drier than yesterday's corn muffins. I know, Vivian." I had already learned enough choice vocabulary from these two gals to get myself arrested in Krakow.

"How's your father doing?" Vivian settled onto one of the stools, patting down the collar of her silk blouse and checking her reflection in the napkin dispenser.

"At least he's out of bed," I said.

"Oh?" She looked up.

"In a wheelchair," I clarified.

"Well, you tell my boyfriend I was asking for him." She yanked out a napkin and dabbed her eyes. "A wheelchair, huh? You tell him I was asking, okay?"

"Don't worry, Vivian, I'll tell him."

"Let's go, *boychick*—PORKROLL-EGG-AND-CHEESE!" Dolores shouted as Flip led a small stampede of work boots through the front door and joined Big Bobby at his table.

My face was reddening from the heat of the grill. "You know, Dolores," I whispered while popping the yolks for the sandwiches, "someday I'm going to hear that order just one too many times and I'm going to murder someone!"

"What order?"

"PORKROLL-EGG-AND-CHEESE!" I shouted into her ear.

"Hon"—she pulled back as if she were the intended victim—"I don't know who the hell it is, but you'd better go make that phone call—ya-know-wadda-mean!"

"Hello?"

"Parris, it's me."

"Liker boy! How *are* you?"

"Where have you been?"

"Oh, I am so sorry about that, lover. A *lot* has been going on around here. I must catch you up."

"Well, that's what I wanted to talk to you about. I decided to—"

"Steven!" Dolores interrupted. "Ring up Vwaj, will ya?"

"Just a second, Parris. Dolores is having trouble with our new cash register." I put the receiver down.

"Hey Vwaj? Nice *poyzladki*, huh?" Dolores continued to mix English and Polish with Vivian, but from the way I was being looked up and down, I could tell they were talking about my ass.

"Dasha!" Vivian chided her.

"Oh, if only I were twenty years younger—ya-know-wadda-mean!"

"Dasha, you mean if only you were *forty* years younger! AAAHHH!" Vivian laughed at her own joke and banged on the counter three times. "Here, Steven, take my money!"

"Who was that?" Parris asked after she left.

"That was Vivian. She's Dolores's best friend."

"Loud, but she knows how to make a point. I like her."

"Listen, Parris. I need a break."

"And you deserve one, love."

"That's why I was thinking—we're closed on Easter. Maybe the night before I'll come into New York, see your show, and maybe—"

"Oh, that's what I wanted to tell you, love. I've quit the show!"

"Quit the show?"

Angelo walked up to the register. "Big Steve!" He grumbled something while inspecting the cigar display that had dwindled down to a couple of loose Muriels and a package of Tiparillos.

"Just a second, Parris." I put down the receiver then pulled a cigar out of the rack and handed it to him. "Here you go, Angelo. It's on me."

"Oh no, I couldn't. Really." Despite his protest, he swiped the cigar from my hand and stored it in his shirt pocket. "But as long as you're giving the store away—I'll take one for the road!" He grabbed another for good measure.

"Thanks for giving us a break on the cash register, Angelo."

"Your dad owes me big for this one. I'm gonna have to pay him a little visit at the hospital." Angelo grinned while pulling out his overstuffed wallet to pay for his coffee. "He'd better watch who's pushing that wheelchair!"

He dropped a buck on the counter, tapped his unlit cigar over my head one more time, and walked out the door.

I picked up the receiver to continue my conversation with Parris.

"Mafia?" he asked.

"Nooo! That's my father's best friend."

"Sounds sweet. A little dangerous—but sweet."

"Gimme a pack of Luckys!" Herck stepped up next and demanded.

I couched the phone between my shoulder and ear so I could hand him the cigarettes. "Sorry, we're out of matches."

"For Christ's fucking sake!" He slammed down his change on the counter and stormed off.

"And whose best friend was *that*?" Parris quipped.

"Nobody's. So what happened? Why did you quit the show?"

"Are you sitting down, love? I got cast in a twenty-four-city bus-and-truck of *Hello, Dolly!*"

"Oh my God! That's my favorite musical. I did it in high school. Shit, Parris, now you officially—"

"Hold on a second, love." Parris cut me off. I heard a muffled voice in the background.

Now you officially have everything I want.

"You know, Parris," I said when he returned to the phone, "*Hello, Dolly!* is my father's favorite musical, too. I have *got* to tell you a story about him and that show."

"I can't right now, love. I have *got* to run."

"Well, maybe if I come in before Easter?"

"I'm sorry, love. I can't. I'm leaving that Monday. So much to do."

"Oh."

"But listen, I'm going to be on the road for almost a year. We're going everywhere. Isn't that fab?"

"Fab."

"Jack's flying out to see me in St. Louis—or maybe Frisco. You'll fly out, too."

"I can't."

"But, lover, you've got to get out of there."

Silence.

"You're the best, love. I want to hear that *Hello, Dolly!* story about your dad. I'll call you later. Okay?"

"Okay."

"Bye, liker boy. I'll call you later," he repeated.

"Good-bye." My shoulders dropped like I had just run onto the platform to find the train pulling out of the station without me. I hung up the phone—pretty sure that I wouldn't be hearing from Parris again.

"ONE PORKROLL-EGG-AND-CHEESE—TO GO!" Dolores shouted from the other end of the counter.

"COMING RIGHT UP!" I shouted back with one hand over my heart and the other frantically reaching for the Ring Dings to quell my craving.

"More *cheska*? What's the matter with you, *boychick*?"

"Oh nothing," I answered while tearing open the cellophane wrapper. "Just a little hyperglycerin attack."

16.
WON'T YOU COME HOME, PEARL BAILEY?

There is a scene from the Broadway musical *Hello, Dolly!* when its eponymous star returns to one of the grandest restaurants in New York for the first time since the death of her husband. The staff of waiters and cooks, in anticipation of her entrance, buzzes and gallops around the stage in preparation. And just as all the excitement reaches fever pitch, a particularly zealous member of the male chorus comes running onto the stage and tugs at the tails of the head-waiter and exclaims, "She's here!" as the orchestra holds its musical breath, the string section trembling on a high note that begs for release, and all eyes turn up-center to a curtained doorway at the top of a grand staircase as they wait for her to appear.

When I was ten years old, my parents went into New York to see the first all-black company of the hit Broadway musical with Pearl Bailey at the helm. Mom let me keep the illustrated souvenir program they bought in the lobby, but it was Dad who unwittingly gave me the biggest memento of the show. I'll never forget how he described that climactic restaurant scene.

"And then—a really deep slide on the trombone pulled the orchestra into this big, brassy entrance music." He described the drag on the tempo and the fluttering of banjos as the curtains at the top of the stairs parted and Pearl Bailey appeared in a crimson-sequined gown with a matching feathered headpiece that made her look like a giant red peacock.

There was something about how Dad described *that* trombone and the way Pearl Bailey came down *that* staircase in *that* red dress to the sound of *those* banjos. His recollection was so vivid that I felt like I was right there in the theater alongside him—just like when we shared the sofa for our TV variety shows. But while Dad described the scene, his eyes welled up with tears. He didn't express his emotions very well, but I knew how much he loved a great musical experience. And in those moments, when he shared one of them that vividly, I knew how much he loved *me,* too.

I never got a chance to tell Parris that story—or that I was falling in love with him.

But it didn't matter. I'd rather have flipped on the old *Dean Martin Show* to hear Dad's running commentary or maybe listen to one of his stories—like the night Pearlie Mae came down *that* staircase—just one more time.

Mom had stories, too, though I wouldn't have unleashed her at a cocktail party in those days with all her unsavory yarns of bedsores and bowel movements. Despite them, I did appreciate how strong an advocate she had become for Dad in the hospital. Most recently, she had come back from her meeting with the head of rehab. Dad needed to learn to transfer himself along a board between the bed and the wheelchair, but there was one slight problem, she explained to me. "Can you believe they don't have him in the right bed? It's too high!" She shook her head and cursed. "Dammit!"

But there was something more ominous about the appointment with Dad's neurologist. "We're meeting with Dr. Herman today." She didn't elaborate but something told me to close up the luncheonette a little earlier that afternoon so I could get over to the hospital for one of Mom's updates.

"Well? How did it go?" At first, I couldn't get her to look me straight in the eye.

"He says that your father has a rare neurological disease."

"Well? What is it?" I folded my arms while she took the notes out of her pocketbook and began to sound out the unfamiliar words in slow deliberate syllables.

"A–cute—trans-verse—my-el-i-tis. Acute transverse myelitis," she repeated. "Dr. Herman said there's a one-in-a-million chance of getting it." She looked out into the air, seeming to ponder the irony of finally winning some lottery.

"But what does it mean?"

"*Acute* refers to the speed with which it happened." She had to look at her notes again, struggling to explain it the way Dr. Herman had in their meeting, pacing the words slowly, as if adjusting to the sound of the new information. "*Transverse* refers to the place on the spinal column—like the vertebra that affects the nerves from the nipple line down—and *myelitis* is like poliomyelitis."

"So it's like polio? And what the hell causes polio?" I badgered my mother for more details from the piece of paper she was holding with all the answers.

"He thinks that it was probably viral?" she said, scanning her handwritten notes that spilled into the margins, and talking in question marks. "The way I understood it, a virus went to attack his spinal column?"

Come on, Mother, you're not making perfect sense here!

"Yes, I'm sure I heard that right. And he had some—wait." She looked to the paper for some more of her new words. "Yeah. He had an *autoimmune* response that kicked in and inflamed the—let me see—the *myelin sheath*?"

"And this was caused by a virus?"

"I don't know," she answered like she was talking out loud to herself. "He also said there's a chance it may have been a blood clot, but they would have to open him up to know that for sure. At least I *think* that's what he said."

"What do you mean you *think*?"

For the first time in our conversation she turned and looked me straight in the eye. "Maybe *you* should make an appointment to talk to the doctor and *you* can get all the answers."

I unfolded my arms and put my hands in my pockets. "I'm sorry, Mom."

It was like I was looking at her for the first time in months.

I had forgotten how pretty she was, though I didn't dare tell her. She cringed when either of two things was aimed her way: cameras or compliments. But Mom knew how to fight. Her freckled skin was a little paler than usual, and small bags had appeared under her eyes recently like battle scars, but otherwise she was vibrant and healthy. *Oh my God*, I thought, *it's my mother.*

Since Christmas Eve, she and I had been functioning more like business partners: coordinating schedules, doing the books, and processing all the medical information that came our way. I hadn't had time to contemplate my own loss—no less hers. She had stories about Dad that went way back before mine. And maybe that is what kept her going.

Marie and Frank had not been the obvious match. She was the eldest of five of the enterprising "Mayor of South Broadway," while he was the youngest of eight in a family whose not-always-gainfully-employed father crammed his brood into the small concrete house on Winter Street, which sat literally on the other side of the tracks.

But they both got their nicknames in similar ways.

When it became clear to the three older brothers that little Frank could throw a football more telephone-pole lengths than anyone else on the block, they began to compare him to a Heisman Trophy winner named Clinton Frank. The kid may have had some of the same power and durability as the Ivy Leaguer, but given his background, Yale wasn't likely in his future. Nonetheless, little Frank Sorrentino came to be known as "Clint."

And when Marie got together with her rather large brood of siblings and cousins to play softball, her uncle Eddie assigned each of them the name of a famous baseball player. Marie was more academic than athletic, but her association with Pete Reiser of the Brooklyn Dodgers seemed to stick.

When "Pete" became a junior at Long Branch High, she found herself sitting next to one of the Gizmos (as the gang in the leather jackets called themselves) in the back row of Miss Chamberlain's English class. During the school year, Clint perfected a little routine to get Pete's attention. When they took their seats and waited for class to begin, Clint would lean over to Pete, take a *very* deep breath, then sing—no, *race* through all the lyrics of an old song

before the bell rang and Miss Chamberlain stepped up to the blackboard to
begin her lesson:

Have you seen my sweetheart fair?
Hol-la-le! Hol-la-lo!
None with her can yet compare.
Hol-la-le-la-lo!
Did you see her as she went by?
Hol-la-le! Hol-la-lo!
I am waiting for her reply.
Hol-la-le-la-lo!

Breathe!

Only Pete could hear the pianissimo words that rolled off Clint's tongue
in his easy baritone as she giggled, especially when the bell seemed to ring
perfectly on cue just as he sang the last word.

It wasn't until after graduation that Clint realized his sweetheart fair was
actually waiting in a bakery in Long Branch. A more tentative dating relationship that had included movies at the Baronet or strolls through the penny
arcade on the Long Branch boardwalk, now heated up with some spicy linguine fra diavolo at the West End Manor restaurant.

One night in 1950, Clint gave the piano player an extra big tip to play
Howard Dietz and Arthur Schwartz's "If There Is Someone Lovelier Than
You," which he sang sotto voce to Pete right at the table, though he didn't
rush this particular rendition to make a bell. On the drive home that night,
Pete noticed that Clint had begun to behave awkwardly. Initially, she chalked
it up to stress over his impending assignment overseas with the U.S. Army's
34th Battalion, but she was speechless when he fumbled around for something
in the glove compartment, then presented her with a diamond ring.

When Clint returned from Korea in 1952, it seemed only appropriate to
celebrate the special occasion at the West End Manor. As the reunited couple
walked arm in arm into the establishment where they had not been for almost
two years, they looked at each other in astonishment when the piano player
winked at them and began to play "If There Is Someone Lovelier Than You."

Frank "Clint" Sorrentino had practically sung his way into Marie "Pete" Tarantolo's heart—and right up to the altar on December 14, 1952.

I looked at my mother's tired eyes and think I understood what it was like to have been swept away by Dad's music. Maybe that's one of the reasons we were both hanging in there. But she seemed so composed and resolute, while I was ashamed to admit how angry I was inside. The truth was—I wanted to grab that piece of paper out of her hand and skip to the part about *acute luncheonette* and the prognosis for *me*. Instead I took a breath.

"I'm sorry," I repeated. "So what's going to happen?"

"Well, he said there are three possible scenarios. In the first one, there is complete recovery. The second one—partial recovery. In either of these cases, he would hope to see some sign of the nerves regenerating in the first couple of months, though that hasn't happened with your father."

"And the third scenario?"

Mom looked back down at the paper as if she needed to be cued. "In a third of the cases, there is no recovery at all."

"Do you mean to tell me that Dad will never walk again? Is that what he said?"

She nodded.

"And how did Dad take all this?"

"Well, he gets the worst news of his life—" She looked away from me, unable to complete the sentence. It was the first time since Christmas Eve that I saw her start to break down. "After the doctor left, we just held each other and cried."

"Oh, Mom." And that was the first time since Christmas Eve that I hugged her.

"I'm going in to see him," I said after a minute.

"Good." She wiped her eyes. "He'd like that."

Phillip came over and hugged me when I walked into the room. "How are you doing, Dad?" I asked as my father's roommate rested his head on my shoulder.

"I wheeled myself halfway down the hall and back today," he answered. "Pretty good, huh?"

"Wow," I said while walking Phillip back to his bed.

"Good work!" Phillip chimed while nodding his head and kicking off his slippers.

"How are things going at the luncheonette?" Dad asked. He was blowing into a clear tube containing a Ping-Pong ball, a little contraption they had given him in rehab.

"Same old. Vivian misses you." I watched him struggle to provide enough air to keep the ball afloat as long as possible. "Oh, and Angelo complained that we're running out of his cigars. He told me this morning that we're discriminating against him because he's a Jersey City Italian."

The ball fell to the bottom of the tube as Dad started to laugh, though it quickly disintegrated into wheezing.

"Do me a favor and ring for the nurse." His voice was as hollow as his face. "I need to get back into the bed now."

The nurse showed me how to lock the wheelchair and remove one of the armrests. This is the part where we would have placed a level board between Dad and the bed so he could make the transfer on his own—if the bed had been the right height.

Dammit! I could hear my mother's voice in my head.

Instead, we each took an armpit and lifted him from the chair, seating him on the bed with his legs dangling freely over the side. He reached overhead with one of his hands and grabbed onto a trapeze suspended from the ceiling, using his free hand to pull his legs up onto the mattress one at a time. He then placed both hands on the trapeze and hoisted himself over to the center of the bed before releasing the trapeze and dropping back breathlessly onto the pillows.

"Don't say I never took you to the circus," he panted.

Well, actually, it was a gay old time in New York that I really had in mind, but now that seemed so trivial.

"So, Steve, we have to talk about the luncheonette."

"Don't worry about that, Dad. Not now."

"We'll work something out. I want you to get back to New York."

"I don't need to get back right now. It's not like I have a job waiting for me—or anything else."

Phillip was sitting at the edge of his bed, hinging on my every word. He looked so innocent and alert, like a little puppy. His life had changed dramatically, but he'd been given a second chance, free from any memory of getting thrown through the windshield of that pickup truck. He smiled at me.

"By the way, Dad, I was talking to a friend of mine the other day. He got cast in a big tour of *Hello, Dolly!*" I watched Dad's eyes light up.

"Oh, I love that show," he said, yawning.

"Remember when you saw Pearl Bailey in New York?"

"Yeah, she was really something."

"I swear, that night when you came home and told me all about it, I was stagestruck!" Dad's eyes began to glisten with moisture like he was going to tell me the story all over again. "Remember when I finally got to see her do the role in the revival a few years ago? Remember? I got to go on opening night. She made her entrance down those stairs in the restaurant scene just like you had described it. But at the end of the number—did I tell you this? At the end of the number the audience gave her such a standing ovation that they couldn't get the show going again. So Pearl Bailey gestures to the pit, bends over to gather up the bottom of her big red dress, turns around, and walks back up the stairs, and does the entire number all over again—right from her entrance! It was the most amazing encore I had ever seen!"

Phillip looked like he was about to burst into applause. My father had fallen asleep.

Dad's mouth was open like he was trying to collect enough air for a good snore, but it never materialized. I kissed him on the forehead and waved good-bye to Phillip. The wheelchair was parked in the far corner, the late-afternoon sun shining through the window and onto the spokes, casting a shadow across the floor like a spiderweb. I looked at Dad one more time, wishing we could march back up the stairs and take it again from the top of the number.

Guest Check

TABLE	SERVER	240128	GUESTS

PART II

TAX

17.
HOME SICK

One fine sunny day in the middle of the merry month of May of 1981, my mother—taking a *very* deep breath—declared that with all due respect to the neurologists, the urologists, the nurses, the infectious-diseases specialists, the plastic surgeons, the priests, the social workers, and the physical therapists— thank you *very* much—she was getting Dad out of the hospital before they killed him.

But could *we* take care of him?

I'm not sure that even my father had the confidence to come home, concurring with the doctors' fears that he was still too weak and needed more hospital time to rehabilitate. But Mom prevailed, the experts had to admit that "now was as good a time as any," and during the third week of May, plans went into effect to bring Dad home after five long months.

The plan was simple enough: Mom would take the day off from her job at the Frank Antonides School and go straight to the hospital for some last-minute consultations with the doctors and nurses. She would then gather up the get-well cards, collect her paraplegic husband, and place a call to the West Long Branch First-Aid Squad. Dad couldn't be transported by car, so the same ambulance that had rushed him away on Christmas Eve would now deliver him back home.

"What a big day! Huh?" Norma was coming around the bend with some plates and silverware she had just bussed from the tables as I stared out the window of Clint's Corner. "You must be so excited!"

Honestly? I didn't know what the hell I was feeling. I was waiting for the ambulance to emerge from the firehouse across the street while eating a Knipp's roll—lightly toasted, extra butter—with a Drake's crumb cake in my free hand for backup. "Yeah, excited."

Norma smiled at me until Dolores nudged her along. "Hey, hon, you gotta move your ass—we got customers!"

Norma scurried back to the sink as Dolores put her hand on my shoulder and stared out the window with me. "Big day, huh, *boychick*?"

"What if we can't take care of him?"

"I'm tellin' ya, you people are doin' the right thing. I gotta hand it to your mother. She knows what's right—we always do. It's called mother's tuition."

"Dolores, it's not like he's coming home from college!" My stomach was knotting as I continued to fixate on the door of the firehouse.

Unlike Norma, who had picked up on the more obvious excitement of the day, Dolores had clearly tuned into the more complex emotional fabric of my anxious state as her voice began to crack with carefully chosen words of comfort:

"I bet yuz are all scared shitless."

Tombstone rested his elbows on the counter. Fortunately, the stubble on his face stuck to his callused hands like Velcro, keeping his head from crashing down onto the Formica. He flinched when Dolores shouted his order down to me at the grill.

"I need a dozen fried eggs on one plate—no potatoes, no toast—for Tombstone!"

"Uuuh!" The gravedigger groaned at me from behind eyes that were more bloodshot than usual. "Make sure they're sunny-side, runny, and extra greasy!"

"Jesus Christ," Dolores muttered to me. "If I had a match I could instigate his breath."

"*Ignite*," I corrected.

"Yeah, big night." She poured the coffee.

Tombstone groaned again.

I had argued with him over the price of his breakfast the last time he came in shit-faced from the night before. Just because he wanted to down a dozen eggs in one clip, it was still the equivalent of six breakfast specials, and I wanted to charge him accordingly. He demanded credit, however, for not eating the toast and potatoes. We finally settled on five dollars, which he still thought was excessive but I had him over a barrel: After all, we both knew that twelve runny fried eggs cooked in a heaping slather of Kaola Gold was the only surefire cure for his hangover.

"Dasha!" Vivian swept through the back door at full volume as Tombstone came unhinged at the heightened pitch of her morning greeting. *"Dzienyeh dobry!"*

"Uuuuh!" His head dropped deeper into his hands.

"Dzienyeh dobry, Vwaj!" Dolores greeted her girlfriend. "You got the lemons, doll?"

"Two dozen!" Vivian handed Dolores a bag from Nannini's food market over on Wall Street as she hopped up onto one of the turquoise stools with all the enthusiasm of a game-show contestant.

"Dobsha!" Dolores approved while inspecting the merchandise.

"Lemons?" I looked at Dolores.

"For the lemonade, *boychick*." She was emptying the bag into a bowl near the fountain. "Listen, I been in this business for thirty-eight years and I'm tellin' you, it's a big seller!"

"Steven, she's *so* full of shit!" Vivian cackled.

"My eggs!" Tombstone growled from under his palms.

Uuuuuh, I thought as I spooned mounds of Kaola Gold onto the grill and began to crack a dozen eggs, plopping them one at a time into the grease.

"All right, Norma," Dolores announced, "let's get started on the simple syrup."

"Simple syrup?" I asked.

"For the lemonade!"

"And dare I ask how you make this simple syrup?" Bubbles of grease were starting to spit out from under the eggs.

"Christ! It's a good thing you got me here!" Dolores flattened out her apron and rattled off the recipe like she was squaring off with Julia Child. "You just pour your five pounds of sugar into your big pot where ya got your water boilin' and you stir the shit out of it until it all disappears and gets nice and thicklike and then you get it all boiling again and then ya cool it off and put it in your fountain there to pump into your fresh lemonade!"

"No wonder they call it simple syrup." I slid my spatula under one of the eggs, my stomach taking another turn. "It sounds so icky sweet."

"Ask Vivian. She loves that shit." Dolores turned to her girlfriend for backup. "Tell Steven how I even used to put simple syrup in my dikeries." Vivian started to laugh but I just *had* to ask.

"Do you mean *daiquiris* or did you actually feed it to lesbians?"

"Tell 'm, Vwaj, how I made the best!"

"Steven, I don't know what the hell she's talking about!"

"Oh, fuck yuz all!"

Vivian slammed her hands down on the counter and dismounted, doubled over with laughter. She had to walk in a circle to neutralize her spasms as Dolores did a random sweep of the counter, hurling spoons and juice glasses into the sink.

Norma pulled her hands out of the suds just in time. "I'll go boil the water."

The fried eggs stared back at me from the plate like a dozen yellow eyes. I retched just looking at them, but really almost lost my Knipp's when Tombstone began to devour the runny dish with all the slurping frenzy of a lion hovering over a disemboweled gazelle. I turned my head in disgust and walked back down to the window.

That's when the white door across the intersection began to rise, its hinged sections disappearing one by one into the ceiling of the firehouse, revealing the ambulance that had been backed in to accommodate quick exits. As it slowly emerged, the warm May sun flashed off its shiny surface like lightning bolts. The vehicle hesitated as the door slammed down behind it. It snuck into the Monmouth Road traffic and headed toward the hospital. That was my cue to head home.

I wanted to vomit.

★   ★   ★

The front lawn that had lain dormant during a particularly cold and brutal winter was now a brilliant carpet of green. The azaleas under the picture window were resplendent in full white and fuchsia blooms.

As I waited for the ambulance to arrive, I paced back and forth along the sidewalk, periodically looking up at Uncle Tony, who had maneuvered himself—gout and all—up a ladder and onto the roof for some badly needed repairs and a ringside seat.

Poppy and Nonny arrived in their Chrysler New Yorker, which backfired as they pulled up in front of the house. I watched the car clip a piece of the lawn and recalled my mother's recent contention that her eighty-three-year-old father "really shouldn't be driving anymore."

The once-cantankerous old Sicilian had mellowed with age and bad health, though he was still the family patriarch—the big *Goomba*. As Nonny waved to Uncle Tony up on the roof, I helped my grandfather across the lawn and into the house, painfully aware that I was running out of men to lean on.

The artificial Scotch pine had long been disassembled and stored away in the attic with the lights and ornaments. The heavy winter drapes in the living and dining rooms were replaced with the spring sheers, part of Mom's semiannual rotation. The living-room furniture had also been rearranged to its spring/summer position, most notably the couch shifted to the opposite side of the room and the upright piano pulled from the corner to the center of the main wall.

But there was one new piece of furniture that didn't quite gel with the marble-topped end tables and velveteen upholstery.

We had brought the wheelchair home the night before, setting it up in front of the fireplace like a throne. Its pillow, however, was not a royal bolster, overstuffed for comfort, but rather a Roho Air Flotation Cushion to prevent tissue breakdown that might lead to decubitus ulcers. Dad's worn recliner in the corner by the bookcase was suddenly obsolete.

John stayed home from school that day and was meandering around the house. Our exuberant black Lab mutt ran from room to room, sensing a change in routine and jumping on everyone in sight. "Reggie!" I yelled when he almost knocked Poppy onto the couch. *How is this going to work out?* I thought as I chained him out back to get him out of the way.

"They're here!" John yelled more with caution than excitement as I joined him at the picture window. We watched Mom park her Buick Special Deluxe behind Poppy's Chrysler while the white Ford ambulance backed into the driveway. John and I looked at each other, our eyes welling up, though I resisted the impulse to burst into tears.

My heart thumped as I watched Sonny and Rich jump out of the passenger side and scurry around to the back to open the doors. Joyce, who had also been part of the original team on Christmas Eve, stepped out from the cab looking cool and in charge as my mother crossed the lawn and stood behind her, holding a pocketbook and a shopping bag stuffed with Dad's things. Joyce made a broad gesture with her right hand and gave some instruction that was inaudible from my vantage point. They slowly pulled the gurney out from the back of the ambulance.

At first, all I could see were white sheets, wrapped snugly around a human form. Once the entire gurney was over the driveway, its metal legs unfolded like an ironing board to give it table height. The squad members on either side obstructed my view of Dad's face. Mom ran slightly ahead to get the door as the gurney was turned to make the trip along the sidewalk to the front porch. That was when I saw my father's broad if tentative smile. He looked so pale in the warm May sun, yet his face was animated with small talk. He even managed a candidate's wave to his brother-in-law on the roof.

Up till that point, it had been like watching a silent movie. Once the front door opened and the action moved inside, the picture became a talkie and the action three-dimensional as I joined the first scene of Dad's new life at home.

I still fought the impulse to cry. Poppy made up for both of us. I don't understand why I resisted the connection to Dad. It was like I wasn't ready to let him back in the house. I was grateful for the distraction of the paramedics, whose presence provided a buffer between Dad and me, though he did keep looking my way. "Hey Steve, is the coffee on?" Dad's signature line was hoarse and rusty, but it was his best shot at acknowledging a heartfelt moment.

Mom dropped her bags in the kitchen and returned to the living room as Joyce pulled back Dad's sheet. He was wearing a gray sweatsuit and a pair of slippers over his swollen feet. Sonny and Rich lifted him off the gurney and into his wheelchair, settling his body onto the Roho Air Flotation Cushion.

Mom stepped in, wrapping a tether around his upper body and tying him into position so he wouldn't topple over from his own deadweight. I guess that's what you do when your husband is paralyzed up to *here*. He looked up at me again and smiled.

No Dad. Not yet.

The first-aid squad members sang a chorus of good wishes to my father as they walked the gurney back out the door.

"Now you call if you need anything, okay, dear?" Joyce lingered behind as Dad took her hand in his, holding on like a security blanket. They were momentarily speechless.

"You call me, Marie." She kissed Mom on the cheek, waved to John and me, and walked out the door.

For a moment, the only sound in that room was Poppy blowing his nose and Reggie howling from the backyard. Mom was the first to speak. "John, let him in. We'll have to teach that damn dog not to jump on your father—if that's possible."

Back in the house, the gangly mutt bounded through the kitchen despite his lack of traction on the tiled floor, and within seconds he rounded the corner into the living room. His posture changed instantaneously when he caught sight of my father sitting in the wheelchair at the far end of the room. Lowering his head, he reverently crept toward Dad, his hindquarters wiggling, his long tail sweeping back and forth.

The three of us lurched slightly forward, poised to lunge in the event that Reggie might overpower the defenseless master of the house. What he did instead was poke his nose once or twice into Dad's armpit, eventually placing his head on the armrest of the wheelchair, mesmerized and peaceful as Dad pet him.

Okay, get me out of here.

"Okay, I have to get back to work," I said.

Dad's ears perked up. "Tell everyone I'll be in soon!"

"Clint! Oh no," Mom chided.

"Oh Pete, not today for God's sake! I meant *soon*. I just want to get back to my luncheonette! Jeez!"

I leaned over and kissed Dad on the forehead, resting my arm around his neck as he reached around to hold on to me.

My stomach started to turn.

Something hit home with me in that moment, quietly at first, like the beginning of a malignancy.

Okay, I admit it: I liked it better when Dad was in the hospital.

As long as he was on the fifth floor of Monmouth Medical Center, I could still fantasize that some antidote would come along, that everything was only temporary, and that soon I'd be moving back to New York City, my life back to normal. But I might as well have been pumping my head with simple syrup. I had to face reality: What was once tentative was now home to stay—and so was I.

I was totally confused. *How can this be?* See Dad. See Dad smile. See Dad starting a new life. So why did I feel like someone was dying?

I pulled back and stood up straight, looking down at my father in his wheelchair. I was amazed to see that Reggie had shifted positions and was now down on all fours, licking his master's legs to jump-start the healing.

"Welcome home, Dad!" I said with a big goddamn smile on my face.

He looked up at me like he wanted to say something, but we both looked away and let the moment pass.

18.
WEIGHTING TABLES

"Almost ready!" Mom trumpeted the return of the family meal, checking her pan of baked ziti or chicken Divan or whichever of her old signature dishes was bubbling in the oven that night. "About five more minutes, I think."

She shut the oven door, went to the sink to scrub her hands, and returned to check on something new brewing on an extra-pristine stovetop. An aluminum pot—large enough for a Christmas Eve lobster sauce—gaped open, its contents rattling like something was trying to get out, steam rising up into the exhaust vent. There was no tomato sauce bubbling up in the pot or seafood simmering—or anything else savory and edible, for that matter—but rather some of the trappings of Dad's new life dancing about in the boiling water. She turned the dial to "off" and picked up a pair of long metal tongs that rested in a white dish next to the burner.

Dad watched from his wheelchair as Judy and I set the table.

"I'm going to get myself ready," he said.

"No, Clint, you can cath later," Mom said while dipping the tongs into the pot and carefully removing small Plexiglas containers, rubber stops, and tubing—all the sterilized supplies Dad would need to catheterize himself.

"Well, then I want to get dressed for dinner."

"All right, I'll come help you in a minute."

"No, I want to do it *myself.*" Dad started to push his wheels forward as Mom pursed her lips in protest. "I may as well start now." He wheeled out of the kitchen, getting momentarily mired in the pile carpeting of the hallway before plowing his way down to the bedroom. Having practiced certain maneuvers while in rehab, he was determined to begin the ritual of getting dressed—on his own.

"Pete!" he called a minute later. "Where's the hook?" Mom ran down the hallway to find the device Dad needed to retrieve clothes out of the closet. Once she'd found it, he sent her back to the kitchen.

I can only imagine what he was doing in the bedroom that night as we all waited for him at the table.

Opening the closet was a challenge. Dad had to figure out how to position the wheelchair so he could both reach the door handle and keep out of the path of the swinging doors. Once inside, he looked up at the wooden dowel that he had installed twenty-four years ago at the standard sixty-six inches off the floor, now well beyond his reach. Grounding himself by hooking one arm around the handlebar of his chair, he held the long hook with the other and extended it up into the closet to grab a pair of pants and a shirt. I have no idea how many attempts it took or whether or not the clothing fell to the floor that first time, but I do know that he never called for help.

My siblings and I had already sat down at the table and started picking at bread. Mom checked the casserole in the oven one more time and we all checked the clock.

Once the clothing was draped over his lap, Dad pulled back from the path of the swinging doors and used the hook to shut the closet. He then backed his chair along the right side of the bed, laying the clothes out so that they would be accessible to him when he was ready for them.

Doing a quick visual check and satisfied that everything he needed was in place, he secured the brakes and began the arduous task of transferring himself out of the wheelchair and onto the bed. Lifting his legs out of the bracings, he then reached over and pulled up on the pins so he could remove the leg rests, leaning them on the right side of the chair, his legs now dangling freely. Next, the left armrest had to be lifted out of its sockets to create an unobstructed path between Dad and the bed. He was ready for the transfer.

"Pete!" He called for my mother again, this time to untie the tether that held him into the chair from behind.

"Okay, Clint, I'm coming!" Mom ran to Dad's assistance. Judy gave the salad another toss and asked me how things were going at the luncheonette. She had stopped coming in on Sunday mornings once the smell of the porkroll started triggering her morning sickness.

"I hope Dad makes it to the table before the baby comes!" I cracked while tearing off another chunk of bread.

Once Dad was untied, he sent Mom back to the kitchen, where she lowered the oven temperature to "warm." The casserole was done, but she wouldn't be serving it for a little while longer.

The plastic sliding board was thirty inches long, a foot wide, and slightly convex lengthwise. He positioned one end of it just under his left buttock and the other on the mattress, spanning like a bridge between him and the bed, which, unlike the one in the hospital—thank you, Mom—was the correct height!

Until Dad could perfect this little technique, it was a treacherous journey from chair to bed. He used all the strength he could muster in his arms and hands to push down at his sides, lifting his torso slightly to travel across the board in a series of lifts and shifts. When he reached his destination, he let his upper body fall back onto the pillows then reached up for the trapeze that had been installed over the bed, pulling himself into a seated position. Still holding on with one hand, he reached with the free one and pulled at the tops of his pants, lifting his legs up onto the bed and placing them in an extended position out in front of him.

Dad's breathing was labored at this point, so he rested a minute.

Removing his sweatpants was accomplished in a similar series of lifts and shifts, grabbing the trapeze alternately between his left and right hands to lift the body slightly as the free hand pushed down the pants a few inches at a time. Once they were down around his ankles, he bent at the waist, dropping his upper torso over his thighs. He could then easily reach his feet in a stretch that had been impossible until paralysis had eliminated any sensation of strain he would normally have felt in the legs, back, and abdomen in such a position.

It had taken my father almost forty-five minutes to change his clothes that night, but he was now ready to get back into his wheelchair and come to the dinner table. Reaching once again for the trapeze, he hoisted himself up to a seated position, freed one hand, lifted each of his legs by the pant material, and dropped them one at a time over the side of the bed. He repositioned the sliding board—this time under his right buttock—and began the maneuvers that would carry him off the bed and back into the chair, cautiously leaning forward so as not to fall backward and knock the lamp off the nightstand.

When Dad arrived at his destination, a journey of less than three feet, he placed the sliding board back onto the mattress, then hooked his arm back around one of the handlebars to brace himself. He could then safely reach down to the floor without falling out of the chair. This allowed him to retrieve the left armrest and two leg rests that he had placed there earlier, and drop them back into their slots on the wheelchair. He then reached over and again lifted each of his limp legs by the pant material and dropped them back into their respective braces.

"Pete!" he yelled once again to my mother so she could come tie him into the wheelchair. By this time, we had run out of bread and salad and baby talk—waiting patiently in the kitchen for his arrival.

"You need help getting to the table?" she asked.

"No."

Mom came back into the kitchen and took her seat, looking toward the hallway with the slight impatience of someone waiting for a bus.

Nobody spoke.

We heard Dad's leg rests clank against the wall when he made the tight turn out of the bedroom into the hallway. The wheelchair creaked as he plowed his way through the thick gold pile. A few years earlier, the plush carpeting had been one of my parents' rare attempts at opulence, but now it was just another obstacle.

We sat silently at our places as the rubber tires pulled free from the rug and Dad made the left turn onto the tiled kitchen floor, finally on solid ground. Mom shut her eyes and flinched when Dad's leg rest nicked the refrigerator door as he swung around to the table, not yet attuned to the new spatial relationships.

Since the table was nestled into a corner, Dad could no longer sit at the head. It now made more sense for him to sit on the side that was accessible from the center of the room, where I usually sat. I moved to the head of the table.

We watched him roll the chair forward and take his new place. Resting his elbows on either side of his plate, he dropped the full weight of his head into his hands and sighed from exhaustion.

"Great job, Dad." Judy wiped her eyes as I nodded in agreement.

"Let's eat!" Mom chirped. She popped up from her chair and finally pulled the overcooked casserole from the oven.

Dad lifted his head out of his hands, sat up straight, and inspected the table.

"Who ate all the bread?" he groused with a big smile on his face.

I was the obvious suspect but I couldn't answer. There was a lump in my throat the size of a dinner roll.

19.
BETWEEN A TOILET
AND A HARD PLACE

"Itchy," I explained when Googie the Gizmo stopped in the back door to stare at me balancing on one foot in front of the grill, frantically digging the heel of my left sneaker into the flesh of my right ankle.

"Let me know when you hit something," Dolores needled while rushing a coffee and roll down to Googie's regular spot before he had a chance to get there himself.

"Will an artery do?" I asked, switching feet to work on the other one.

Herck the Jerk unleashed a cloud of trapped smoke when he lowered his copy of the *Asbury Park Press* to get a look at the floor show, but the jig was up when we all heard the squeal of air brakes out front.

"Oh Christ, here they come!" Dolores sounded the alarm as the morning bus unloaded and the Syrian Jews rushed through the front door of the luncheonette.

"Shit!" Herck sucked so hard on his Lucky Strike that his lips practically disappeared from view before raising the paper back up in front of his face.

"Two regulahs, to go!" Isaac shouted from the register, then turned to the man standing by the newspapers. "Raymond, you want a regulah?" All I could see were tailored pants, an open newspaper, and a felt-brimmed bowler nodding in the affirmative. Isaac yelled back down to Dolores and me, "Make that three!" He turned back to Raymond. "I'm getting you a regulah!"

"And a poppy bagel with a schmeah!" Elliot stuck one foot in the door and waved to me. "Quick!"

The more they demanded, the more Herck groaned from behind his classifieds. It seemed that the very things he detested about the local Syrians were the same things I loved: their abruptness and energy and New *Yawk* pronunciations. I pictured them descending upon the rug and garment and diamond and whatever other districts in the city where I used to live and work, not unlike my own frenetic little community lining up like cattle outside the Minskoff Studios right in the heart of Manhattan's theater district. God, I missed it!

I hadn't known what to expect the first time I attended an open call for a musical, listed in *Back Stage* under the deceptively ambiguous category of *singers who dance*. Granted, there was more nerve waiting on that line than there was talent, but each group of twelve they brought in packed more kick than a mile of Rockettes. I was a pretty good dancer, though I needed repetition to pick up a routine. I tried to follow the bitchy Bolshevik with the upwardly sloped nose and pinched butt cheeks when he started in with "zis and zis and one two sree and turn and kick and jump and yah!" But when he flitted back to his cigarette after only one demo, then turned and commanded, "Now *you* do!"—I knew I was fucked.

The actual audition was a disaster, but the postmortem at the Times Square Howard Johnson's with a dozen dejected queens made it worth the price of admission. I must have made a fool of myself, gesturing madly with my arms and smiling as if at gunpoint, anything to draw attention away from the missteps and tripping going on below. But once I got together with my group of cast-off "singers who dance" and rehashed the whole debacle—complete with reenactments of our own frenzied performances and imitations of Zbig zee Dance Kapitaine—something clicked: I was happy.

Not only did I feel part of a community for the first time since leaving home—but it was an unapologetically gay one, at that. It didn't matter that I almost fell flat on my face. I could still burst out laughing just picturing what I saw in the studio mirrors that day and remembering how it felt afterward to be falling in love with my New York life.

"Quit dancin', *boychick*. These people gotta get to work!" Dolores was lining up Styrofoam cups as the Syrians shouted more coffee orders from the front of the luncheonette and the itching on my ankles intensified.

Roslyn walked farther down the counter so she could talk to me at the grill. "Good morning, dahling. You know—cawfee, milk, Sweet'n Low on the side—how's Dad?"

"Pretty good, Roslyn. He wants to come back really bad. Maybe soon."

"Fantastic! God bless. You remember to tell Dad I was asking for him."

Herck the Jerk especially hated the one with the Chanel suit and the dry toast. He extinguished his cigarette, the fourth in a row, and slammed down fifty cents on the counter.

"I'll tell him, Roslyn." We watched Herck disappear out the back door.

"Mahvelous. And some toast, to go. You know—dry. The way Clint does it." She winked at me.

"Goovno!" Dolores cursed after spilling one of their "regulahs" all over the stainless-steel workstation. She wiped up the mess, then pulled out her spray bottle.

"What's that smell?" Roslyn scrunched up her nose.

"Straight ammonia!" Dolores responded proudly while giving the surface an extra spritz.

"At breakfast?" Roslyn pinched her nostrils and frowned at me.

"Dolores, get the register. I'll finish here."

My eyes watered as I wiped the surface dry, filled the rest of the coffee orders, and marked each cup with a grease pencil, the itching still nagging at my ankles.

"And two blacks—no sugar," Elliot interjected while jumping ahead of Roslyn. "Did you say Clint's coming back?"

"He's gonna try—maybe in a couple of weeks. It'll be the first time he's been here since Christmas Eve."

"Fantastic! I'm gonna write another check!" He yelled to his companions down the other end, "Did you hear that guys? Clint's coming back!"

The chattering klatch of designer suits slowed and quieted for two seconds with affirmative *ahs* and nods. Raymond lowered his paper and smiled at me. He had mobilized the local community of Syrian Jews while Dad was in the hospital, then personally presented him with a check, one of the first major contributions to the Clint Sorrentino Fund, which some of Dad's friends had recently established to help cover his staggering expenses.

I stopped what I was doing and walked down to shake his hand.

"Thank you so much, Raymond."

He cupped both his hands around mine, gave it a single shake, then just as abruptly as they had arrived, the Syrians rushed back out the door and boarded the New *Yawk* express. I wished I could have hitched a ride, but I just stood there on one foot, frantically scratching myself with the other, and watched the bus pull away from the curb.

The intense itching on my ankles had begun about the same time as the construction on the house. Uncle Tony acted as "contractor" for the project and was there for the deliveries of cinder blocks, lumber, windows, and piles (and piles) of sand. Reggie was happy as a mongrel lark picking up two-by-fours like they were sticks and running up and down the new little hills in our yard. I, on the other hand, was the one that picked up the sand fleas. At first I thought the small red marks were mosquito bites. Then the itching became so intense that I scratched my ankles raw and actually caught the little buggers jumping around on my flesh. Why no one else—not even the dog—got infested was beyond me.

The important thing was that the Clint Sorrentino Fund was making it possible to convert the large screened-in porch in the back of the house into a wheelchair-friendly den—complete with an easy-to-navigate Congoleum floor, Dad's desk, and a wide-open parking spot in front of the television. Adjacent to the room, a huge bathroom would be constructed with some unique amenities. Dad would be able to roll the wheelchair under a specially designed sink, reach the spigots, and see himself in a tilted mirror. There would also be a drive-in shower and a higher-than-standard-toilet-and-trapeze setup, saving Dad the indignity of having to use a portable commode in his bedroom like a child in potty training.

But apparently Dad was impatient that the addition was not being completed fast enough.

"Steven, you'd better talk to your brother quick. He says it's an emergency!" Dolores held the phone out to me, though her lips kept moving after she finished talking, a twitch that sometimes replaced wig adjusting when she got nervous.

"What is it, John? . . . What? . . . What!" I couldn't believe what I was hearing. "Oh shit!"

"What? What, *boychick*?" Dolores begged after I hung up the phone.

"My father fell on the tile floor in the bathroom! I gotta run home."

"Oh Jesus!"

"Dolores, keep an eye out?"

"Oh my Christ, just get going!"

"Okay, okay. I'm going!"

"But before you go—"

"What?"

"Stop at Nannini's on the way back and pick up some extra lettuce. I got a feelin' we're gonna have a scourge of salads today!"

Although I wondered how Dolores was able to predict a "scourge of salads," the bigger question was, what the hell was my father doing in the bathroom? The new one wasn't built yet and the old one was practically inaccessible to him. John had said that Dad wanted to "experiment" with getting onto the toilet so that he wouldn't have to use his portable commode anymore. But the wheelchair could barely fit between the tub and the sink, making a transfer from the chair to the toilet almost impossible. "How could you let him even try it!" I had yelled at John on the phone.

I arrived home simultaneously with my mother, who had gotten the same call at her secretary's desk at the school. She looked flushed as we both ran into the house with visions of broken pelvises and a trip back to the ICU. We could hear what sounded like moaning and crying coming from the bathroom as we ran down the hall and came upon a sight that neither of us was prepared for.

There was John, sitting doubled over on the edge of the tub, his shoulders bobbing up and down in spasms, and Dad, on the floor, half-naked, tears rolling down his cheeks, pinned between the toilet and the radiator.

The two of them were laughing hysterically.

"Clint, what the *hell* were you thinking?" Mom scolded my father. The only response she got was a spray of laughter back in her face.

"Shit!" I squeezed my way past the wheelchair and slipped around the other side of the toilet, almost tripping on Dad's plastic sliding board that had fallen onto the floor during the failed maneuver. I managed to lift him up by the armpits, getting his legs all twisted up in the process as I dragged him backward and plopped him back into the wheelchair like an oversize rag doll. And the more I glared at John, the harder he laughed back at me.

I wanted to kill my brother, but I had to admire my father's tenacity. After all, we both had lofty goals: I wanted to get back to New York City, and he wanted to get back onto a toilet.

"Did you stop at Nannini's for the extra lettuce like I asked ya to?"

"No, I didn't stop at Nannini's for the extra lettuce like ya asked me to!"

"You'll see, ya little sonovabitch . . ." Dolores continued to mumble something under her breath. A counter full of old regulars clamored for food and I jumped back into service, ladling out the chili with one hand, flipping flake steaks with the other, while pulling my heel up along the opposite ankle for a good scratching. Apparently a few more freeloaders had jumped aboard when I had run home to scoop Dad up off the bathroom floor.

"Howdy, Mr. Steve," Stanley greeted me while hunching forward and pounding the bottom of a ketchup bottle. "That's some fancy footwork ya got there."

"Believe me, Stanley, my dancing days are over."

But apparently my libido was still alive and kicking. I could feel my face getting as red as my ankles when Brent Jamison slotted himself through an opening at the counter, loosened his tie like he was gearing up for some hot lunch, and got a gander.

"Hey Steve-o!" He chuckled as he looked me up and down like he had just caught his prom date in a robe and curlers. "Did I catch you at a bad time?"

"Oh, don't mind me." I fanned myself as if the heat from the grill had caused the flush. "How are you, Brent?"

"Great!" He flashed his dimples while combing back his Dick Tracy hair with one slow stroke of his right hand. "How about three bowls of your famous chili for me and my buddies over there?"

"You got it, man!" *Man?* I hated when I slipped into Jock English, but it was a good cover when I was picturing him naked.

"I know you're busy, Steve-o, but I want to show you something real quick." He leaned over the counter and flashed his open wallet at me. I oohed and ahhed on cue, though I was paying more attention to his cologne than to the pictures of his baby.

"Oh, he's adorable," I fawned.

"She."

"She."

"So I hear your father will be coming back to Clint's Corner soon?" Brent slipped his wallet into his breast pocket, allowing me a quick peek at his fine tailoring. "You must be so happy!"

"Yeah. I'm really, really happy." I started ladling out the chili, providing my usual service with a big goddamn smile.

"Good for you!"

What Brent saw on the surface was some imaginary headline from the *Asbury Park Press*: LOCAL BOY SAVES AILING FATHER'S BUSINESS; HAILED AS FAM-ILY HERO. If *Back Stage* had covered the same story, however, it would most likely be titled: SINGER WHO DANCES FORCED BACK INTO CLOSET TO RUN FAMILY BUSINESS; SECRETLY BLAMES AILING FATHER.

"Do me a favor, Brent."

"Whatever you want, Steve-o. Anything."

"This place is a fucking madhouse today." I placed the three bowls of chili on the counter in front of him. "Could you bring these over to your table?"

"Sure thing, Steve-o." Brent dutifully delivered the chili to his paralegals as I watched from an old familiar closet that was now wedged uncomfortably between the cold Formica counter and a hot grill. There was nothing worse than an unrequited crush, and the knowledge that in the end, all he really wanted from me was lunch.

The itching was getting unbearable. So was Dolores's insistence that every patron order a particular side dish with his or her lunch.

"I need two well-done burgers and a cheese omelet with sliced tomato! And I'll get the three—yes, *three*—salads!" Dolores stuck her tongue out at me, as her prophecy of the Great Salad Scourge of '81 was being fulfilled.

She moved down to the Bay Marie to get the lettuce while I stood at the grill ladling and flipping and scratching like I was doing some strange short-order ballet.

"Oh, we gotta do somethin' about those fleas—this is making me fuckin' crazy!" Dolores stopped midsalad. "I'm gonna take care of you, *boychick*!"

Brent had just stepped up to the counter for a refill on his Pepsi.

My new sense of normalcy was now covering a broader range of behaviors, so I didn't question the fact that Dolores had dropped to her knees on the floor behind me. I was flipping the burger as I felt her rolling up my pants and pulling the socks down as far as they could go. That was when she applied the wet cloth to my raw ankles and I felt a sensation that was indescribable.

"AAAAAHHHHH!" I screamed in pain, bringing all activity in the luncheonette to a halt. "What the hell did you just put on my skin?!"

Dolores jumped up and away like a kid who had just lit a firecracker.

"Straight ammonia!" she shot back defiantly as if making a political statement.

"Are you fucking nuts?!"

"Does it still itch?"

"Well—" I must admit she had me there.

"What I tell you, *boychick*? I said I was gonna take care of you."

Brent was watching from the counter with his empty Pepsi glass, laughing like a hetero hyena and shaking his head. "Ohhh, Steveooo."

I may have listed *horny* and *frustrated* on my growing list of complaints for the day, but at least I could now scratch off *itchy*.

20.
MY FATHER, MY HOUSE

"I really want to get back to the luncheonette," Dad said one night at dinner.

"That's great, Dad," I affirmed, "but first we have to get you out of this house."

Work had already begun to replace the aging roof, but down on the ground—with the support of the Clint Sorrentino Fund—Uncle Tony was overseeing the project that would make 40 Girard Avenue wheelchair accessible.

I closed the luncheonette early one Saturday afternoon—about two o'clock—much to the chagrin of Tino and Larry, two of the kids who were still feeding quarters into the pinball machine, and a couple of blue-haired ladies from Lorraine's beauty salon who pouted when I gave them their grilled-cheese sandwiches—to go! But the house where I'd grown up was about to go through a major transition and I needed to be there.

A flurry of family activity spilled off the front porch, out onto the lawn, and up the ladder to the roof. Dad watched from behind the screen door, his right elbow anchored on the armrest as he tugged and pinched his earlobe, taking in the activity with his sister Rosie, who stood behind the one family member who was now shorter than she was.

Dad's brothers Ralph and Joe had run a long extension cord from an outdoor outlet hidden behind the bushes in the front garden to power their buzz saw and electric drills. They had laid out a series of two-by-fours and some sheets of plywood across the front lawn. They trimmed and shortened them into various lengths and shapes, slowly attaching the pieces with bolts and nails to create sections. Uncle Mickey, the oldest of the brothers Sorrentino, didn't participate anymore in the heavy stuff, though he did offer a pointed suggestion here and there, waving to Dad, who smirked back his approval.

And you couldn't miss the white-haired foreman at the center of all this activity with his bright red polo shirt stretching across his gut like a corset, and a Linden Lumber apron supporting him like a pocketed truss stuffed with nails, and a laugh that was as rhythmical as the hammering.

"Heh . . . heh . . . heh . . . heh." Uncle Tony looked up at the crew laying out a new section of shingles on the roof.

"Tony!" my brother-in-law Charles yelled. "The head on this one is loose!"

Uncle Tony braced his stiff knee when he leaned over to pick up another hammer and tossed it up onto the roof. Charles ducked and held his footing but slipped effortlessly into exasperated-Cuban-bandleader. "What are you, crrrazy or somethin'!"

Mom crossed the lawn when Poppy and Nonny pulled up in their Chrysler New Yorker. She greeted her parents but shook her head when she noted the wide space her eighty-three-year-old father had left between the car and the curb.

Nonny waddled up the small hill from the street as Poppy lagged behind on Mom's arm.

"How you doing there, Mr. Tarantolo?" Uncle Tony called to his fellow senior, acknowledging the hierarchy.

"I'ma good," Poppy puffed as I met him halfway across with a lawn chair.

I kissed him on his shiny forehead as he settled down to watch all the hammering and sawing, slipping me a twenty like I was a cabana boy.

But all activity stopped when the bulldozer from Becker's Tree Service arrived. The brothers laid down their tools and picked up their iced teas as the sisters stood in a bunch on the front lawn, holding their pocketbooks. Aunt Mary looked somewhat gaunt, still recovering from her March heart attack. She and Aunt Angie had their sweaters slung over their forearms, though Aunt Rosie was wearing hers. "I'm freezing!" she complained on that warm May afternoon. I watched from the ground; the rest of the crew moved down to the edge and sat, dangling their legs over the front gutters. John had wheeled Dad onto the front porch and was standing next to him in adolescent repose, both hands in his pockets, his shoulders pulled up stiffly, as Mom followed them out of the house and threw a blanket over Dad's legs.

The engine began to roar and everyone watched silently and idly as the cold yellow machinery began to rip up the azaleas and Chinese evergreens, and the other shrubbery that nestled just beneath the picture window. This little patch of landscaping had for years provided an elegant and inviting entrance to the brick house, but was now being cleared for the construction of a concrete ramp.

I watched Dad watching all the activity. His hands were folded in his lap. His teeth were showing, but they were more in a clench than a smile. He had designed the house all by himself twenty-four years ago, one of his crowning achievements, then built it with the help of Mickey, Joe, Ralph, and their brother-in-law Tony, who rounded out the fraternity of masons and carpenters who approached this particular project with craftsmanship and care.

But now the structure seemed so flawed as Dad sat in his wheelchair, trapped up there on the front stoop. His masterpiece seemed to have turned into a prison—or maybe just an obstacle course.

When I was nine years old, I spent a lot of time playing in the basement. One rainy day, perhaps out of boredom, I ventured into the dark storage room at the bottom of the stairs. Dad had finished off the rest of the cellar with paneling and floor tiles but had left this one room in its original form with concrete-block walls, exposed ceiling beams, and the furnace smack in the middle of the room. Wedged back into the corner was an intriguing relic: an old Hoover hutch that my grandparents had ordered from Sears & Roebuck, now packed with Dad's tools and some Maxwell House coffee cans filled with nuts and bolts.

I blindly circled my right arm above me in the dark until I located the pull string to turn on the light, a plain bulb screwed into a ceiling socket. Once the room was illuminated, adequately at most, I eyed the Hoover hutch and realized that I had never looked into its bottom cabinet. On an impulse, I knelt down on the concrete floor, swung open the white creaky doors, and entered my father's world.

My first discovery was a tall stack of heavy black albums—or so I thought—until I noticed the 78 printed on each one. The only time I had ever used that setting on my record player was when I wanted to make the Beatles sound like Alvin and the Chipmunks. But these were the real thing. *RCA* and *Decca* and *Columbia* were printed large on the labels. I sifted through the stack: Bing Crosby's "White Christmas" and "I'll Be Seeing You," Ella Fitzgerald sings "I'm Beginning to See the Light" with the Ink Spots, "Till the End of Time"—both the Dick Haymes and the Perry Como versions—Sinatra's "Ol' Man River." I recognized most of the names, but was really excited by the familiar titles, each echoing a song that I'd heard Dad sing while baking the bread or driving the car. I had stumbled upon Dad's repertoire, safely hidden away near the furnace, yet beating like a heart there in the core of the house.

I noticed something else at the back of the cabinet.

I reached behind the stack of 78s and pulled out a long clump of scrolled papers. I resisted sneezing from the dust as I unrolled them across the floor, my right hand holding down the open end so they wouldn't curl up. As the first few inches were revealed to me, I noted the inky blue color of the paper and the words scrawled on the bottom right-hand corner: *Drawn by Frank Sorrentino.*

I had discovered the blueprints to the house.

I was already familiar with every three-dimensional nook and cranny: the double closets, the arch between the living and dining rooms, the columns in the basement, the placement of the windows, my bedroom. And there it all was on paper. Every unique detail of the house had been part of Dad's drawing before any of it ever existed.

Something about that discovery excited me—and triggered a yearning that I didn't understand. But the blueprints turned out to be the beginning of one of Dad's best stories: the house.

Dad used to take my brother Michael and me on "tours" of his creation, pointing out the Tennessee flagstone he'd used to build the fireplace, adding how he'd constructed it entirely by flashlight over a series of nights. Then we'd walk outside and look at the red and gray bricks he'd special-ordered from an out-of-state quarry, their content low in salt and alkaline. "These will never fade or get that damn chalky look!" he'd point out to Michael and me as we imagined him laying one brick at a time, for hours and days on end, until finally the house appeared.

The yearning I felt intensified when Dad showed us the simple tools of his old trade. The metal trowel with the battered wooden handle had gradually molded itself to his hand with each day's work. He used it to apply wet cement that would hold the bricks together like the thick icing of one of my mother's layer cakes. Periodically, he laid down the trowel and checked his accuracy with a level, which was nothing more than a two-foot-long piece of metal with floating water bubbles encased in glass at its center. The position of the bubbles in respect to two little black calibrations was my father's only assurance that the finished house would not be lopsided.

That's it! I thought. I wanted to create a house, too—just like Dad!

He explained how he'd complete a section of wall, wait about an hour, then spray it down with water. "That keeps the concrete from cracking," he continued, defying us to find a single flaw in his work.

Yeah, yeah, yeah. Michael was much more interested in the technical details, though my mind had begun to race in another direction. I headed for the basement again, spread my drawing paper out over the old kitchen table, picked up my pencil, laid down the ruler, and began to design my own three-bedroom ranch—just like Dad.

My first drawings were crude and childlike in their stick-lined simplicity, but they grew more sophisticated and detailed with practice. "Hmm," Dad said as he looked over my first attempt at a split-level, but never offered any advice. "That's really good."

But the yearning got stronger as I began to design a new house every week, moving onto colonials and bi-levels and Tudor mansions.

And the stories continued.

Dad talked about the day the bricks were delivered in the winter of 1957, when he and his brothers eagerly lined up to unload the truck. Rather than carry the bricks, they tossed them to save time and energy. Forming a brigade, they threw the bricks two at a time through the air from brother to brother. As Ralph threw the two red blocks to Joe, the wind would cause them to separate midair. But just as Joe caught them, they would knock back together before he dropped them lightly onto the growing stack in front of him. Each *clop* of the bricks marked their progress. I could almost hear the rhythmical beat of the story like it was one of Dad's boogie-woogie-eight-to-the-bars.

Then he'd talk about the roof, the "hip" roof he had designed with its multiple surfaces, unlike the standard A-frame that the neighbors had. "Look up and down the street," Dad had said proudly. "It's the only one like it!"

One day I watched Dad shin his way up along the shingles until he reached the cupola at the apex of his hip roof. Up till then, the cupola's purpose was to provide ventilation to the attic, but that day it became the resting place for an iron rooster to swirl around and indicate the direction of the wind. I watched him standing at the highest point of the house, mounting our new weather vane and looking like he had just conquered the world. Watching Dad stand precariously atop the roof took my breath away, my legs weakened in empathetic response to his risk of falling.

But that was it: the yearning. It was for my father. The man who had channeled our relationship through the television set, and communicated through songs and stories, also connected with me through the house. Dad *was* the house.

But now Dad's creation challenged him at every turn: traveling from the bedroom into the hallway required moving the clothes hamper and doing a tricky K-maneuver, the closet rods were too high, there was no shower large enough to accommodate the special waterproof wheelchair, and—as he found out the hard way—the toilets were inaccessible.

Oh—and if you were in a wheelchair—there was no way in or out of the house.

The men from Becker's Tree Service finished clearing the wreckage of the front garden and reloaded the bulldozer onto a flatbed truck. Another crew would pour the cement for the permanent ramp a few days later, but in the meantime, my uncles had crafted a temporary one out of wood that attached to the porch and veered straight out into the middle of the front yard.

Rather than drive pilings into the ground, Uncles Tony, Ralph, and Joe had fashioned various combinations of bricks and cinder blocks to support the crude wooden structure. A couple of taps with the hammer here, and an extra brick wedged in for support there, completed the temporary ramp.

"All right, Clint." Uncle Tony hooked his thumbs onto his Linden Lumber apron and stood back. "Let's try it out!"

It was like Dad was on a launchpad. I held my breath as he released the brake on his wheelchair, rolled down the creaking boards, and shot out onto the lawn. The family applauded from the ground and along the edge of the roof.

Poppy wiped his tears with a handkerchief as Rosie, Angie, and Mary clamored around their brother like he had just returned from an Apollo mission. Uncle Tony scatted the sisters away so he could push the wheelchair across the thick grass and onto the sidewalk, positioning Dad for a full view of his masterpiece as everyone went back to work.

By that time, I had climbed back up the ladder to join the work crew laying new shingles. I looked down to the ground at my father sitting there, smiling in the warm sun. He looked happy just to have made it outdoors.

But the way his chair was positioned, he had to look up sideways and over his shoulder. It was a strain for him to see me. My legs went weak when I caught Dad's eye as he now watched *me* stand precariously on his hip roof.

In the next few weeks, Dad gained more strength. His nerve was returning, the concrete ramp was completed, and he now had easy access to the driveway. The Clint Sorrentino Fund was going to buy him a specially equipped van to get around, but in the meantime, we practiced getting him in and out of the car.

The initial excitement surrounding that first trip down the ramp had worn off and Dad was now ready for a more ambitious journey. And I would be there again to join him.

First stop: the luncheonette.

21.

POP, POP, FIZZ, FIZZ

"Steven!" Dolores shouted, her hand over the receiver. "It's Angelo, he wants to know what time you expect your father?"

"Noon!" I told her for the fifth time as she spoke back into the phone.

"You'd better get here early if you want a good seat . . . Yes, bay-bay, we got your cigars . . . Okay, bay-bay . . . Get here by noon, for Christ's sake!" She hung up the phone just as Old Man Pascucci approached the counter and tapped on it with his empty Pepsi glass.

"You putta too mucha ice!" he accused Dolores as she grabbed the glass out of his hand. He turned his attention to me. "How'sa you papa?"

"You better watch out, Pascucci," Dolores warned. "He's comin' back today and that'll be the end of all these free fuckin' refills!"

It was her own fault for getting the word out that Clint was coming back to the luncheonette. All the old regulars began pouring into the place and filling up the seats like first-nighters.

"Can't wait to see your father!" Half Cup Harold raised his third refill of the morning toward me in a salute. Then Googie the Gizmo came in wearing a new Yankees cap and an extra splash of Old Spice, took his regular stool, and ordered a large cola.

"*Goovno!*" Dolores cursed from the fountain. "Of all days to run out of gas! *And* the showcase is low on cans! Shit!"

"Don't worry, Dolores, I already called Pepsi Man for a fresh tank."

"*Dobsha boychick!*" She lit up at the mere mention of our man with the biceps that were bigger than liters, instinctively pulling the lipstick out of her apron pocket and freshening her application. "These people are all excited that your father's comin' back and they're gonna be thirsty!"

"I know, Dolores." *I'm feeling a bit dehydrated myself.*

"Dasha!" Vivian entered through the back, posing in the doorway so that Dolores could get a load of her new ensemble. "How do I look?"

"Like a common *dzeevka!*"

"Aaaaah!" Vivian wailed with laughter, gingerly wiping a tear from her eye without smearing the mascara. "Oh, Steven, that Dolores! I'll take a Diet Pepsi," she ordered while scanning the room. "Where the hell's Clint? I thought he was coming back today."

"Yeah!" Googie and some of the old regulars murmured like an unsettled audience waiting for the curtain to go up on Act Two.

"Yes, yes, he'll be here around noon!" I assured the impatient bunch.

Big Bobby and Flip were sweating under their JCP&L hard hats when they came in for their late-morning porkroll-egg-and-cheese sandwiches and soft drinks—but they had to wait a little longer than usual for some service. Dolores and I were too busy ogling Pepsi Man, who had just restocked the gas tanks and was now squatting down to load six-packs of Yoo-Hoo into the showcase. We even ignored Gertie, who had ambled in with her brown paper bag, as we strained from different vantage points for the best glimpse of what-ever else Pepsi Man might be packing.

But at least Martin Leslie Pembrook acknowledged his wife. "Well, that's my cue to exeunt!" he boomed while refolding his *New York Times.*

"What do I have to do to get some ssservice around here?" Gertie took the adjacent stool. "Dolores, give me a cup of coffee and let me borrow your lighter. Hello, Steven, dear." She looked at her husband in deliberate after-thought. "Oh. Hello—Marty." He raised his pinkie and downed his last ounce of tea in response.

"How ya doing there, Gertie?" I tried not to be too obvious, but my eyes kept drifting over to Pepsi Man, noting how he filled his tight blue uniform with all the subtlety of a Cro-Magnon.

"Peachy, dear. Now get me two ssslices of rye toast. No butter." Gertie's words slurred slightly as she opened her brown bag and pulled out a pack of Carltons and a jar of Skippy. "And bring me a complimentary knife so I can ssspread my peanut butter."

"Goddammit, Gertie!" Martin rose from his stool. "Why—pray tell—can't you just order something that's on the menu?" He tapped her lightly with the *Times* before tucking it under his arm. "I'll see you at home, my dear. And Steven, my best regards to your father. I'll catch him tomorrow when there's less brouhaha." He winked at me before making a slightly grand exit out the front door.

"Whiskey down, comin' up!" Dolores blindly slipped the rye bread into the toaster, not once taking her eyes off the hindquarters currently on display at the Pepsi showcase. She pulled the elastic waistband of her stretch pants and let it go with a snap.

I wasn't quite so obvious, though I did bound down to the front end of the counter, practically pushing her out of the way, when Pepsi Man knuckled up to the cash register with his invoice. For some reason or another, I was jockeying a little harder than usual for his attention.

Gertie was oblivious to our little game as she spun around on her stool and crossed the sticks she called legs. "Where's that father of yours?"

"He'll be here any minute!" I yelled from the register, prompting another round of buzz from the old regulars.

"Is de uddah guy comin' back?" Pepsi Man grunted.

"Yes." *You catch on quick, Magilla.*

Just then I realized that Dolores and I (though we never discussed it) had established a little routine with Pepsi Man. Whenever he approached me at the cash register with the bill, she would grab her spray bottle and run out to clean the tables. Basically, I would take the front, and she would bring up the rear, with the burly Pepsi Man in the middle, unwittingly taking part in our bizarre little threesome.

"Dat's nice. I'll see him on Tooooosday when I bring de uddah stuff." He grunted a reference to the Mountain Dew as I counted bills into his plate-size hand.

"Porkroll-egg-and-cheese for Bobby and Flip!" Dolores shouted as she ushered them over to table two, her thick lenses trained like a set of binoculars on Pepsi Man's *poyzladki* as he headed out the door. "And a ham-and-cheese sub on two plates for my kids at the pinball machine!"

I watched Pepsi Man climb up into his truck like he was scaling a tree. He pulled away from the curb, leaving an open space for Mom to park the car when she got there with Dad.

That's when I noticed that almost every seat at the counter was filled, and only table one was left unoccupied. I went to the Bay Marie to make the subs, shaking thin slices of ham and bunching them into little mounds to bulk up the sandwich.

"Just like his father!" Dolores pointed out to Vivian over the rising decibel level of the lunch crowd.

It was almost noon.

Googie the Gizmo shook his jowls back and forth and stuck his fingers in his ears as Tino and Larry fed more quarters into the pinball machine and Old Man Pascucci tapped his glass on the counter for another refill. Gertie spread more Skippy and laughed at her own jokes, her *S*s as sloppy as the tray full of Carlton butts that were piling up in front of her.

"Steven!" Flip yelled when he saw my mother gesturing for me outside the front window.

"He's here!" Big Bobby yelled above the racket.

I was dangling another slice of ham over the sub. "Dolores! Finish these sandwiches, my father's here. I have to help get him in."

"Oh Christ!" Dolores nervously began to adjust all her accessories—wig, glasses, bra, then finished the job off with a series of pats up and down her body as if she were flattening out lumps and air bubbles. There were tears in her eyes as I pleaded with her.

"Dolores, please, the ham sandwiches!"

★ ★ ★

Getting Dad out of the Pontiac was no easy feat. I helped Mom lift the collapsed wheelchair out of the trunk and set it up next to the open car door. As I placed the weighty Roho Air Flotation Cushion back into place, I noticed that Lorraine had come out of her beauty salon next door and was watching from the sidewalk, both hands over her heart.

Next, we balanced the plastic board like a bridge between the car seat and the wheelchair. The angle of the car door made the transfer awkward and difficult. But Dad's determination to return to Clint's Corner, even if just for a cup of coffee, superseded any obstacles. He placed his hands flat at his sides and began the series of lifts and shifts, inching his deadweight across the board and into the wheelchair.

Mom stood by patiently holding the attachments. Big Bobby and Flip watched from a few feet away, holding their hard hats under their arms as if in reverence. When Dad completed the transfer, Mom dropped the left armrest back into its sockets with a click. I slid the two leg rests into the swivel hinges, then lifted his limp legs and repositioned them into the braces. I finally backed Dad away from the car and swung him around as he noticed the silent audience for the first time.

"Dad, look." I pointed across the street where Al was waving from his Amoco station. Dad waved back as I pushed him forward. He got a kiss from Lorraine's shampoo girl and a handshake from Flip.

"Welcome back, Councilman."

Big Bobby pulled back the front door, its hinges making a rumbling sound like the deep slide of a trombone just prior to a grand entrance. We could hear customers inside buzzing, and silverware clanking and fluttering like the strumming of banjos.

I pushed down on the footrest behind the chair and leaned Dad back as if I were delivering a new appliance. Taking a deep breath, I pulled him up that one stubborn step and into the luncheonette. The tempo of sounds dragged to a halt. Everyone silently watched the door as I turned Dad around to face the old regulars.

Googie the Gizmo and Half Cup Harold looked on from their places at the counter. Tino and Larry let the last pinball roll into the gutter and stepped forward with cautious schoolboy curiosity. Gertie had put out her cigarette and gotten off her stool, standing next to Vivian, who had quickly checked her reflection in a napkin dispenser before joining the impromptu receiving line.

None of these people had seen my father for almost six months, from back in his walking days. They seemed relieved that the ingratiating smile was still in place, but were momentarily silent, like a hesitant chorus waiting to sing "Hello, Dolly!" when Dad sounded his return to the luncheonette.

"What the *hell* do I have to do to get a fresh cup of coffee around here?" And just like at home a few weeks before, when he had rolled down the temporary wooden ramp and onto the lawn for the first time, he was greeted with a round of applause.

Dolores was the first to throw her arms around Dad. "The goddamn ham shaker is back! How ya doin', bay-bay?"

Their new height differential put him in peril of suffocation, her Banlon shell muffling his voice when he evoked their old feud. "Dolores, you staying behind the red line?"

"Oh, you're a goddamn doll!" She burst into tears, released his head from her bosom, and ran in the back to blow her nose.

"How's my boyfriend? Look at you!" Vivian blew a kiss. "I tell ya, Clint, Steven's taken good care of us, but that Dolores—*nyeh dobsha!*" She cut her own laughter short with a gulp and fiddled with her faux pearls.

"That'sa nice," Old Man Pascucci observed, his corncob pipe bobbing up and down.

Dad looked better than he had in months. His face had begun to fill out again as had his shoulders from using the trapeze and maneuvering his weight around on his own. Even without the use of his legs, he looked like a man strutting on his own turf.

"Look at this." Dad's voice was choked with emotion, his eyes bright and glistening behind the gold wire frames. "The whole gang is here!" He rolled himself forward like Roosevelt inspecting the troops.

"Welcome back, dear!" Gertie bent at the waist, kicking one leg back like a flapper as she kissed Dad on the cheek. "I hate to open old wounds, but you know your ssson is a ssstubborn sssonovabitch like you are." She sprayed him with every *s*.

"Like father, like son," Dad played along.

"So can we sssettle this once and for all? Now that you know that life is too short, it won't kill you to keep a couple of grapefruit and a jar of SSSkippy on hand for me. Whatever happened to 'the customer is always right'? Hahhh!" Gertie's laugh released in a mist as Dad subtly tried to wipe a spray of spit off his face, but she caught him. "Welcome back. I love ya, honey." She wiped his cheek with her hand. "Sorry, did I get any on ya?"

"Howdy, Councilman! Where the hell you been?" Stanley tripped through the front door just as the horn across the street at the firehouse sounded its three noon blares.

Clint was back and the lunch rush had officially begun.

There was a restaurant on Manhattan's East Side that held weekly open calls for their Monday-night talent showcase. When it was my turn to audition, the guy in the black turtleneck at the piano asked me for my sheet music.

"Uh, if you don't mind," I said, "I'd like to accompany myself."

"But that's why we have David here." The manager bristled, looking up from her clipboard.

"I know, but I've spliced two songs together and changed the tempos and I'm not sure if—"

"That's all right, Kaye." David got up from his bench and joined her at the table. "Let him try."

"All right," she looked at her watch. "Go ahead. Let's see what you got."

"Thanks." I handed her my photo and résumé then sat down on the bench. I had cut and pasted the sheet music to "Bidin' My Time" and "Wrap Your Troubles in Dreams" together, combining the two old standards into a little medley. I cleared my throat, put my hands on the ivories, and began to belt out the two songs with a runaway tempo and a little bit of a Jolson edge to my voice.

"That's not how you do those songs," Kaye the manager complained when I finished. "They're supposed to be ballads, not up-tempos. But thank you."

"And thank *you,* ma'am."

Bitch.

"And thank you," I nodded to David as I gathered up my sheet music and made my way through the main dining room. I may have changed things around a bit, but at least I had done it my way.

"Wait!" David stopped me at the front door. "Can you be here at seven for rehearsal? We go up at nine." He grinned.

The butterflies immediately kicked in, but I walked out of that restaurant that day and strutted up Third Avenue.

"Quit daydreamin'! I need four bowls o' Manhattan with extra rubber bands for your father. Move your ass!" Dolores zipped past me to get the setups for table one. I ladled out the chunky red clam chowder then lined the bowls on the counter for her to pick up.

Dad was positioned like a talk-show host at table one with Mom at his side, glowing in the shared spotlight. Angelo had walked over from his store around the corner looking like a proud papa about to give away all his cigars. Even Uncle Tony had hobbled in just in time to fill the last seat at table one and celebrate his brother-in-law's return. The three men quipped at one another like it was a Rat Pack reunion, constantly interrupted by Vivian and Gertie and a virtual who's who of West Long Branch lunchery. Even the two Anitas from the dry cleaners left their presses for a rare joint appearance.

Everyone seemed so goddamn happy. And no one's goddamn smile was bigger than my own.

"Your dad said to set everyone up on the counter with a free Pepsi— thank God we got our gas today!" Dolores yelled over her shoulder while ferrying the chowder out to the table.

Angelo walked up to the counter, his cigar in one hand, Dad's empty cup in the other. "The boss would like another cup, please—from the *fresh* pot! Boy, service is slow here today!" He beamed, happy to have his best friend back, a new rigor to his needling.

I grabbed the full pot off the center burner and turned just in time to catch an explosion of laughter from table one, with Dad at the core delivering the punch line. He looked like Dean Martin surrounded by his Golddiggers, back in his regular NBC time slot.

I poured his coffee, placed the pot on the burner, and turned around to find Angelo sitting back comfortably in the huddle.

"Thanks, Angelo!" My father acknowledged his friend's kindness as I tried to catch his eye.

I began filling up the glasses with Pepsi and delivering them up and down the counter to the extra-thirsty bunch.

"Drink up!" I encouraged like one of the bartenders over at the Larchwood, though all my patrons spun around on their stools and thanked my father.

But just as I felt the ache of being left out, Dad looked up, eyeing the signs strewn across the fountain ledge like sheet music on a piano, announcing the French toast, salads, and some of the other changes I had made to the menu in his absence. He fiddled with his earlobe as he studied my personal touches.

"Looks good, Steven." He smiled at me. "Thanks for everything."

I stood up straighter and sucked up that little dose of attention like the noisy last drops of a fountain soda through a straw.

"It's good to have you back, Dad," I said.

22.
AS LONG AS THEY SPELL YOUR NAME WRONG

"Ugh!" I helped Dad adjust the patterned tie he had chosen for the special occasion.

"You just don't appreciate a classic!" he rebuffed.

"Well, let's just hope your public does!" I shot back. "Though no one will even notice the tie once they get a load of that classic beige suit!"

"I'll change."

"No! We'd like to get you there before 1982!"

Dad laughed at me but the fact was, he had become quite adept at using his hook and trapeze and transfer board, and had gotten into his summer suit in under a half an hour.

"Are you nervous, Dad?"

"Naaah."

Well, I was. It wasn't unlike the stage fright I'd experienced before the talent showcase that time in New York. It was more like going out on stage without really being sure what role I was playing.

"Come on, Clint." Mom came into the room all dressed up and perfumed. "Let's get you tethered in."

"No," Dad said firmly. "Not anymore. If I need to steady myself, I'll just hook my arm around the handlebar."

"Well, okay then." She hesitated. "Let's get you into the car!"

I watched Dad roll himself out the front door and down the new concrete ramp to the driveway like he'd just been cut loose. He was getting stronger and looking more confident as he lifted and shifted himself into the passenger side of the Pontiac.

Mom and John climbed into the backseat. "Let's go!" Dad said as I slipped behind the wheel and backed the car out of the driveway, butterflies in my stomach like I was taking a new act on the road.

On Sunday, July 5, 1981, committee members of the Clint Sorrentino Fund held a cocktail party at Squires Pub, a popular West Long Branch restaurant located just a mile up Monmouth Road from the luncheonette. The fifteen-dollar ticket price didn't just include a donation to the fund, whiskey sours, and goat-cheese pastries. It was also an opportunity for a nervous public to break the ice with the borough council member and luncheonette proprietor. Most of them had not seen him since before he became a paraplegic.

Apparently there was little trepidation, however, as the final tally for the event yielded a whopping seven hundred presold tickets. In proportion to the size of the town, it would be like a million Manhattanites showing up for a single event.

As we approached the driveway of Squires Pub, I noticed the simple message that had become the mantra for the Clint Sorrentino Fund, posted in large block letters out front on their events board: WE CARE CLINT.

With its ample banquet space, the atmospheric restaurant was also the venue for many a local wedding, class reunion, and campaign headquarters on election night. When my father was first elected to the borough council in 1976, we had gathered with the town's Democrats in one of the large ballrooms. The Republican candidates and their crowd were also there but had been strategically booked into another of the large rooms at the opposite side of the building.

Tonight's event, however, had been touted as a "nonpartisan" affair and would meld family, friends, and the town's political factions all into one.

The lot was already filled to capacity, but we pulled into an extra-wide space near the entrance and took advantage of one of Dad's new perks: handicapped parking. Basil Plasteris, the owner of Squires Pub, was there to greet my father.

"Welcome, Councilman!" He watched us pull the wheelchair out of the trunk and reassemble it next to the car. Some of the patrons entering the restaurant passed quickly and disappeared inside, while others stopped and silently gawked at the peculiar routine with the transfer board.

"Here, let me help," Basil offered once I had pulled Dad around to the small set of stairs at the entrance.

"No, thank you. I got it." *Uh, that would be my role, bud.* Basil stepped away as I leaned Dad far back in the chair and pulled him backward, one step at a time, up to the restaurant entrance.

Once we were inside, the hostess and waitresses momentarily stopped work to greet their familiar patron. Some of the diners ceased conversation to either wave or just stare curiously as I pushed my father through the main dining room on the way to the banquet hall.

I thought about how momentous an occasion it had been six weeks earlier when Dad had rolled down the wooden ramp and onto the front lawn, the family clapping with excitement. And when he tested the public waters this past week at the luncheonette, the customers had burst into applause as well.

But as my father began to grow stronger, his ovations got bigger.

When I rolled Dad through the entrance to the noisy hall, a few people at the front of the crowd noticed him, put their drinks down on their tables, and began to clap. They were just some of the hundreds of people in attendance that night who were seeing him in the wheelchair for the first time. As I pushed him farther into the room, the excitement spread like a wave, and within seconds, everyone was standing and cheering.

Dad wept.

★   ★   ★

TABLE	GUESTS	SERVER
	160	

LUNCHEONETTE

Angelo was standing next to Dad when Dominic Nannini finally made his way to the front of the line. Mr. Nannini ran the small food market on Wall Street, but that night he attended in his official capacity as president of the West Long Branch Lions Club. When he presented Dad with a check for five hundred dollars, Jason Grossman of the *Asbury Park Press* snapped a photograph of the three men for the next day's edition.

"Hold one second." Grossman scribbled onto his pad, checking some facts as well as the spellings on *Nannini* and *Sorrentino* and *Valenzano*.

"And this is my son Steven," Dad introduced me to the reporter. "He's taken over my luncheonette."

"That's spelled with two *t*'s." My snide comment seemed to be lost on the reporter, so I clarified. "In *luncheonette*—get it?"

"You're looking good, Clint." Paparazzi pushed me aside when the mayor of West Long Branch, Henry Shaheen, leaned over to shake Dad's hand, the flash of the bulbs reflecting off his shiny scalp.

"That's because I'm feeling good, Mayor." Dad looked up—way up—at the man who was hovering over him like Daddy Warbucks over an orphan. "You can't get through something like this without the support of friends." The reporter from the *Asbury Park Press* furiously scribbled the sound bite for his article.

Mayor Shaheen was the latest in a succession of West Long Branch Republicans who'd held that office and most of the council seats for over half a century. But when my father was elected to the council five years before, he was one of the few Democrats to break the stronghold that the Grand Old Party had held over the local government. The political rivalry intensified as the dynamic of the old institution changed, but Dad seemed to have won the respect and admiration of his adversaries.

"We miss you at the meetings, Clint. It's just not the same without you!" If there was tension between Dad and the Republican council president Robert Shirvanian, it was barely detectable.

"I'll be back soon, Bob. I just need to build a little more strength."

"How *are* you feeling, Councilman?" The reporter from the *Daily Register* picked up the cue.

"I'm flabbergasted!" Dad took in the room. "Look at all this—ordinarily I'm in bed by now!"

Everyone chuckled except the reporter, who continued to dig. "Do you think that some might perceive this to be a political event?"

Shirvanian readjusted the knot of his necktie and bristled. And I think if Angelo's cigar had been lit, he would have extinguished it on the cub's forehead, though he chose to intervene more civilly. "Republican, Democrat, whatever." He tossed off the question. "They're all here for one reason: because they love this guy. That's what it's all about!"

The reporter looked up from his pad and noted the three men all in one frame. He turned to his photographer. "Get that one."

Dad and Shirvanian smirked at each other like rival quarterbacks before a coin toss as the photographer from the *Daily Register* snapped another image of the evening—which, like most of them, included some big guy with a cigar grinning at my father's side.

"What the hell are you doing, Angelo?" Dad strained to look up to his best friend, who had towered over him even in the days when they could stand side by side. "Get me a martini!"

"Hell no, I'm staying right here with you so I can be in all the pictures!" Angelo rested one hand on my father's head while primping his own full brush of salt-and-pepper hair with the other.

"I don't want you standing next to me!" Dad swatted Angelo's hand away from his own fragile comb-over. "You make me look bald!"

"I'll get you a martini, Dad!" I stepped back into the frame.

"Make that two, big Steve!" Angelo teased while scanning the crowd for another photo op.

"Oh no, no, no, no!" A sharp-eared waiter had happened by. "Two martinis—coming up!" He rushed away.

Well, I guess I'll just disappear into the background.

I managed a big goddamn smile while negotiating my way around Democrats and Republicans, cops and firemen, aunts and uncles, the Syrian contingent, that guy that always requested extra porkroll on his sandwich, Martin and Gertie, my pregnant sister, and a few Gizmos—as I made my way over to the bar to have a little too much to drink.

The first whiskey sour had pushed its way down in spasms, but I was adjusting nicely to the third when I heard a familiar greeting: "Hey Steve-o!"

I looked up at Brent Jamison and wondered what right he had to look better than a Kennedy. "Nice suit," I slurred.

"Oh, hey, I want you to meet my wife. Steve-o, this is Candy."

"How do you do?" I extended my hand.

Dear, sweet, lovely Candy.

"How do *you* do?" Candy whined through a pronounced underbite, extending her hand just enough for me to shake her fingertips before she withdrew, whipping her hair back like a cheerleader and clamping onto Brent's left arm.

I think Dad and I saw this happen to Humphrey Bogart once.

"Honey, the sitter can't stay too late. I want to get home to the baby."

"Oh right," I said. "How's he doing?"

"She," they corrected me simultaneously.

"Oh, right. She."

"We can stay a little longer." Brent nodded to me. "The night is young—right, Steve-o?"

"Hoooneeey!" When Candy dug into his arm a little deeper, I wanted to hand Brent a saltshaker from a nearby table—a little trick Dad and I had learned from *The African Queen* for removing leeches.

"Okay, okay." Brent relented in singsong, "Mommy and Daddy have to get home." He pulled out his keys and kissed his Candy on the side of her flip. His anxious wife was almost home safe, that is, until Dolores approached with a frock that was louder than a six-piece wedding band.

"Boy, this is some fuckin' shinding, ya-know-wadda-mean?" She filled out the angular garment in ways Butterick could never have imagined.

"Hey, baby!" Brent carefully extracted his wife from his arm so he could give Dolores a little peck and a hug. "Dolores, this is Candy!"

Go on, Dolores. Kill the bitch.

"Oh, honey, you're a lucky girl. That husband of yours is quite a piece of *cheska!*" She normally used that word in reference to a Drake's crumb cake, but I could glean from the context that—in this case—it would be loosely translated as *stud muffin.*

"Down, Dolores! Or she might not let him come in for the chili anymore!" I slurred my words and let out a slow cocktail-party laugh. "Uh huh, huh, huh."

"Nice to meet you," Candy nipped as she reattached to Brent. "We were just leaving."

"Okay, okay. I have to be in court early tomorrow anyway. I'll see you during the week, Dolores. Take care, Steve-o!" Brent looked over his shoulder and winked as Candy hauled him out of the banquet room.

"So, *boychick*?" Dolores watched me watching Brent. "Lookin' for some legal advice?"

I blushed. "No, I was lookin' at *those*." I shifted the focus to her floral-print cocktail dress with darts that could etch glass. "Nice daisies!" Flattered, Dolores touched herself like she was honkin' a pair of horns. I laughed at the distraction but my thoughts drifted back to New York, where a wink from a handsome guy had a much broader range for misinterpretation.

Coverage of the fund-raiser hit the newsstands in the July 6, 1981 editions of the *Asbury Park Press* and *Daily Register* with the respective headlines: FRIENDS MAKE A DIFFERENCE and SORRENTINO "FLABBERGASTED" AS 600 FRIENDS PAY TRIBUTE.

Not all the stories were told, but for the most part, coverage of the big event was accurate, though the *Press* would report one item that was particularly disturbing to me: "His son Stephen has taken over the running of the family business . . . a luncheonette . . ." I don't know what made me flinch more—the fact that they misspelled my name or that seeing my new role printed in black and white somehow made it official and irreversible.

Either way, news flash: Dad was back in business—and I wasn't going anywhere soon.

23.
ONE SPECIAL DELUXE— COMIN' UP!

I wasn't exactly under house arrest, but true freedom seemed to be at a premium those days. Funny how I could even squeeze a semblance of independence out of the license plate of my new car: KYK-128, which I preferred to read as "KICK!-128."

I had never owned a car before, which is why I referred to it as "new" even though it was actually my mother's old 1969 burgundy Buick Special Deluxe, a knockoff of the sportier Skylark. My mother had meticulously kept the white interior clean and the body was practically mint, barring a few scratches. It was a simple gesture when she officially turned the car over to me that morning, but it represented my first sense of freedom since the whole ordeal with my father had begun eight months before.

With money from the Clint Sorrentino Fund, Dad had been able to purchase a used cream-colored Chevy van, specially equipped for a disabled driver. That purchase had precipitated the switching around of our family vehicles. Once Dad had the van, Mom officially got the Pontiac, and I was given the Buick—each of us upgraded and a little more independent.

⋆   ⋆   ⋆

"You're free!" Dolores proclaimed on the morning the Buick became mine. "Now get the hell out of here so you can be back in time for your sister's anniversary party!" She watched as I unloaded twenty cartons of eggs from a large cardboard box marked *Pennfield Farms*.

"I know, I know, but I want to bring the box with me." I checked each dozen for cracks before stacking them in the kitchen refrigerator. "Are you sure you'll be all right without me?"

"Your brother's here. Your father will be here in a little while yakkin' it up. We'll be fine, *boychick*." She spied out the service window like a prison matron watching her charges through one-way glass. "And I'll keep Norma's ass movin'!"

"You be nice to her."

"Go!"

Seeing the skyline from my new car was exhilarating as I approached the entrance to the Hudson River tube that would take me into Manhattan.

It was much like the day more than four years earlier when Dad had helped move me into my Upper West Side apartment. I remember losing radio reception when we entered the Lincoln Tunnel. But just as we came out the other end, something with a boogie-woogie beat suddenly blared out from WNEW-AM, simultaneous with the Manhattan sun hitting us like a spotlight. Dad immediately picked up the song—midlyric—as I grinned with anticipation, believing I had entered my forever.

But the light at the end of the tunnel was different this time around, without Dad to navigate his way around the songs and the streets. I missed that part of it. The journey wasn't quite the same without him.

I took Tenth all the way uptown then snaked my way in and out of the side streets of the West Seventies until I found an empty space. I got out of the car and read and reread the parking signs until I was absolutely sure the spot was safe and legal, pulled the large Pennfield Farms box out of the backseat, and locked the door. As I walked away, I looked back and read and reread my little declaration of independence: KICK!–128.

★ ★ ★

I would return to my apartment in a few weeks to move out the big stuff, but for now, I placed the empty Pennfield Farms box on the floor, opened the desk drawer, and began to pack up a few of my prize possessions.

I started with the sheet music. Sondheim's "Anyone Can Whistle" had been my big audition ballad and sat at the top of the heap that included scores to *Cabaret, West Side Story,* and *Man of La Mancha.* I thumbed through an old "fake" book and came upon "Everybody Loves Somebody." It may have been Dean Martin's signature, but it was my father's performance of it while shaving or baking bread that I most identified with the song. I stacked it all neatly into one of the corners then slipped in my theatrical résumés and eight-by-ten black-and-white glossies.

The next drawer contained mostly papers. There was the only song I ever wrote, the oddly prophetic "Wishing I Had Somewhere Else to Go," some of the floor plans I had drafted after finding my father's blueprints, my creative writing, including short stories with titles like "Cellophane" and "The Apothecary Jar," and the journal I had kept since moving to New York in 1977. I packed it all away with great care.

The top drawer contained my collection of some of the men that got away, as well as a few who—thankfully—ran away. When I had met George at the Wildwood, I wrote his name and number onto a matchbook cover, identifying him as *the Greek guy,* but had annotated it after our first date with *who ripped me off.* I scooped up his and the others' matchbooks into my hands, hovered over the wastepaper basket, but decided instead to drop them into the bottom of my box to keep for posterity. Same with the snapshots that I gathered up, including the one of Parris and me in our straw hats—all that was left of an affair that never got off the ground, much like the workshop of the doomed musical we had done together.

And finally there was the cassette tape containing my reading with Ernest the Psychic of Central Park West. The stranger had greeted me that day without words, though as soon as I hit the button on my recorder to tape our session, he looked at me as though he were seeing right into my soul and uttered in a voice that seemed to channel less swami and more Paul Lynde: "Music,

music, music." He warned that there would be a "crisis" in my family but said that I would live to be "very old and would always be taken care of." I wasn't convinced.

I tossed the cassette into the Pennfield Farms box with all the papers and books. The physical contents might not have required special packaging or Styrofoam insulation, yet everything in there was the stuff of my dreams, as fragile as the eggs I had unpacked from that same box just hours before.

There was room for one more item.

I took a sweatshirt out of the dresser and laid it out flat on the floor. Still on my knees, I reached for the statuette of Tevye the Dairyman, carefully laid him along the edge of the pilled cotton, rolled him up into the sweatshirt, and tucked him down into the last dark corner of the box before sealing it shut.

The closest I ever came to actually being in a Broadway show was when I got a call to understudy the lead in a play called *Gemini*. The curly hair and Roman nose that were prominent in my head shot, not to mention the vowel at the end of my multisyllabic last name, made me a natural for the comedy about a young Italian-American guy struggling with his sexual identity. The play had already been immortalized by a bit running in a TV commercial where a deliciously understated character actress spewed the play's take-home line: "Take *human* bites!"

Parris had been so excited for me, reading through the sides and drilling me on the lines in preparation for the big audition. He waited outside the stage door for me while I read through my scene with a stage manager two or three times and did a cold reading of another. "Congratulations, lover!" He hugged me and kissed me on the lips when I told him I'd been called back. "This calls for a walnut ring!" We gorged ourselves on cake and coffee at Éclair, the bakery on Seventy-second Street, and pondered all the possibilities.

I had felt so free and full of hope.

After yet another callback, I didn't get the role, but I remember how my confidence had begun to soar. The experience taught me that someday I might actually read my name over a Broadway marquee. Now I felt lucky just to get a mention in the *Asbury Park Press*. I hated feeling that way. It wasn't Dad's fault. But now Parris was gone and my dreams were slowly deflating, like they'd been run over by a wheelchair.

I left my apartment that day with my Pennfield Farms box and made my way around the block to my new car. I hadn't given up all hope. Amazing what I could now read into a license plate.

"How did you make out in New York today?" Dad asked as I followed him down the ramp to the driveway.

"All right, I guess. The important stuff is all boxed up."

"How was the Buick?"

"Drives like a dream!" I retorted with a used-car-salesman inflection.

Dad rolled into the garage alongside the new van. When he had taken his driving lessons, one of the first things Dad had to learn was to back the over-size vehicle into the garage that he had originally designed with a standard-size sedan in mind. Uncle Tony had solved the problem by bolting a large wood block onto the floor so that my father could not accidentally back the unwieldy vehicle into the wall.

"How's it going so far?" I sized up the big Chevy.

"Pretty good. I drove all around town today."

"Knock off any fire hydrants?"

"No, just a crossing guard."

I laughed as Dad opened a little hatch on the side of the van that housed a small panel of switches. The first one operated the side door that opened up to reveal the hydraulic lift resting inside the van. The next switch swung the lift out on a pivot. The third one initiated the mechanism to lower it to ground level, grinding noisily like an oil rig.

Dad closed the hatch then rolled himself forward onto the small metal platform where there was another panel of switches. He held on to the safety bar and flipped the first switch. I watched silently as Dad was slowly raised into the air, grinding to a halt when the lift was level with the interior van floor. He flipped the next switch to swing him into the van's interior, ducking his head to clear the arch of the opening. One more switch would lower the platform flush against the floor so that Dad could disembark inside the van.

He backed himself off the lift and pushed forward. There was no car seat in the driver's position, allowing him to pull the wheelchair right up to the steering wheel. A metal contraption locked onto his armrest, holding the chair firmly in place.

Dad put the key in the ignition and the engine turned over. The operation of the van was completely manual, with the brake and the accelerator built into the steering wheel. I stood back in awe and watched a man who was paralyzed up to *here* drive this formidable vehicle out of the garage.

This was one of Dad's first independent forays into the world since acquiring the special license. The trip would only be a mile or so to visit Irene, my sister's mother-in-law, to celebrate Judy and Charles's second wedding anniversary. But there was added significance, since this had been our original destination for dinner on Christmas Eve 1980.

Mom came out of the house carrying a cake, John following close behind with a Pyrex dish covered in foil. "Okay, we ready?" Mom climbed into the passenger seat as if it were routine, her days of packing the wheelchair into the trunk of the Pontiac already forgotten. John climbed into the back of the van and looked to see if I was following. I pulled keys from my pocket.

"I'm taking my own car." I nodded toward the street where I had parked my new Buick Special Deluxe. "I'd like to be in charge of my own brakes if you don't mind!"

"Steven!" Mom disapproved. But Dad chuckled.

"*Oh, Gesù mio!*" Irene came running out of the house when Dad pulled into her driveway. My sister's gregarious and outspoken mother-in-law had as much a flair for the dramatic as she did for cooking. "My God, Clint, it's only taken you eight months to get here!"

Judy was a little slower coming out of the house with six months of pregnancy under her belt. She and Charles joined Irene on the driveway to watch the hydraulic lift lower Dad to the ground. I had parked my car in the street and walked over to join them.

"Oh, honey!" Irene brushed back the shock of white hair that sprouted from her widow's peak. "Don't leave your car like that." She pointed to my Buick. "These *meriganz* fly down this street like their asses are on fire!"

"Mom!" Charles admonished her.

"*Oh, Gesù mio!*" Irene ignored him, running to hug Dad when he backed off the lift onto the driveway. She wiped tears from her eyes. "Come on, the steamers are ready!"

Not leaving anything to chance, I ran back to my car and repositioned it so it straddled the curb in front of the house, parking half on the street and half up on the sidewalk for maximum distance from the lane of passing traffic. I took one last look back at KICK!-128 before joining the festivities inside.

"Well, that deserves a toast!" Irene was reacting to my father's announcement that he would be returning to his seat on the borough council at the next meeting.

"Forget the wine." Dad slurped down another steamed clam. "I'll take some more drawn butter!"

"Here, Dad, take mine." I didn't have much of an appetite after my day in New York. I dropped one last empty shell onto my heap then pushed the leftover butter over to Dad.

"God bless you, Clint!" Irene was laying newspapers out on the table as we all lifted our plates and glasses in preparation for the crabs. "Save room for the stones!"

Mom helped Irene carry colanders of the red shellfish over from the stove and dump them right onto the arts section of the *Asbury Park Press*. Charles handed out the nutcrackers as the conversation turned to the fact that there was a baby on the way who would give birth to a table full of uncles and aunts and grandparents. Irene had been very superstitious about my sister announcing her pregnancy too early as she irreverently recalled her own miscarriages. "You know what happened to me?" she began as Dad sucked the meat out of a claw. "I lost two in the toilet and one in the driveway!"

"Ma!" Charles cracked up as Judy clutched her swelled belly and we all had the biggest laugh of the evening.

By the end of the night, Irene was scooping out the Neapolitan ice cream as Mom cut the cake and Dad—as usual—got the first cup of coffee and the last word. "Remind me not to park in your driveway!"

We were all laughing enough that night to make up for the lost Christmas Eve—until being struck dumb by the sound of a crash, the screeching of brakes, and what sounded like a second crash.

"What the hell was that?" Dad yelled, furiously wheeling himself into the living room to look out the window as the rest of us ran out the front door to see what had happened.

The yellow Chevy van sat untouched in its parking space in the driveway, but my Buick was no longer in its spot straddling the curb. There was now a white van at the far end of the lawn, having apparently smashed into my Special Deluxe, thrusting it nearly ten yards into a fire hydrant that now gushed water like a geyser from under the twisted wreckage.

The driver of the white van sat unscathed behind the wheel—chewing. His shoulder-length hair was almost as greasy as the half-eaten pizza slice he was holding in his right hand. He had the nonplussed expression of someone who addressed everyone as "dude."

"Oh, Gesu mio!" Irene raised her hands up to Jesus as if in repentance.

The rear of my car was jacked up into the air. Water sprayed out in all directions as if the car had landed in a fountain. And hanging there in the middle of it all, clear as a bell, I could see that my license plate had lost its KICK and was now just KYK-128, holding on by one bolt, swinging back and forth, as if for emphasis.

Uh, thanks, Gesù mio. I get your point.

24.
PARTY BOYS

Poplar Avenue was already lined with cars as I squeaked into a spot almost a block away from Borough Hall. I was about to slam the door shut when I realized I was still wearing my greasy red apron. There was no dress code at the borough council meetings, but this was definitely not the look I was going for.

When Uncle Tony had given me his old long black coat, I had been able to wrap it in some scarf and attitude to turn it into a fashion statement. But there wasn't much I could do with the old tan '73 Malibu he lent me. I appreciated the gesture but must admit that after "dude" had kicked my Buick ass halfway down Wall Street, I was feeling as neutralized as the borrowed car's colorless body and about as bold as the beige interior.

But what Uncle Tony lacked in automotive fashion sense, he made up for in the dizzying plaid blazer he had chosen for the special occasion. "Steven!" He waved to me as he meandered up the street. "How's she behaving for you?"

"Drives like a dream!" I patted the back fender while noting the bumper sticker he had affixed from his Italian-American Association: KIDS DON'T DO DRUGS! I tucked the keys into my pocket and felt the homegrown cigarette some kid from Monmouth College had given me as a tip that day.

"Heh . . . heh . . . heh . . . heh." Uncle Tony patted me on the back, each chuckle like a tidbit of wise counsel as we crossed the street. "That's my boy!"

"Thanks again, Uncle Tony," I said with a little guilt. "I should be getting my new car in a few days. I owe you like a million dollars or something."

"Forget it!" He adjusted the collar of his sport coat. "You can pay me back in eggs!" He started to chuckle again as Dad's yellow Chevy van made the turn onto Poplar.

"There he is."

We crossed the street as Dad pulled the van into the handicapped parking spot in front of Borough Hall. I was both excited and nervous about Dad's return to his seat on the borough council, but this wasn't the first time I had accompanied him to one of these meetings.

When I was fourteen years old, the newly celebrated Earth Day on April 22, 1971, had inspired me to form an activist group called Youth Against Pollution, though our acronym more aptly described our spirit: YAP! With the help of eighteen friends and Mrs. Spiegel, one of our teachers, who acted in an advisory capacity, we procured a kit to collect water samples from Franklin Lake and all its creeks and feeder streams around West Long Branch. Each week we would run the fresh samples over to Brother James Farrell, a biologist at the Christian Brothers Academy, who tested them for levels of *Escherichia coli,* bacteria that could cause serious illness—or, at the very least, major diarrhea. God, did I feel important in those days!

The results of our tests showed staggering levels of E. coli in many of the locations. This might have indicated sloppy compliance by some of the borough residents as the town was being weaned off septic tanks and connected to the new sewer system. It was decided that I, as chairman and founder of YAP, should attend the next public meeting of the West Long Branch Borough Council and present our findings, hopefully heading a local pandemic of the runs off at the pass.

My father was at my side as we climbed the twelve steep steps that led to the entrance of the meeting hall on Poplar Avenue. The double doors at the top of the staircase opened into a large room with lots of blond wood paneling and beams reaching across a cathedral ceiling that made me feel like I had just walked into the Supreme Court. Chairs were set up on either side of the room to accommodate fifty or so spectators, though Dad said these seats were rarely filled. At the front of the room was a wrought-iron railing protecting the sanctity of a dais that supported a long wooden table fit for a Last Supper. Overhead, a clock hung on the wall just above a bronze plate depicting the seal of the state of New Jersey.

There were seats at the table for each of the six Republican councilmen, the Republican mayor, and their appointed clerk and attorney. A gavel rested on a marble block, indicating the mayor's place at the center of the table. Mayor Shaheen was absent from this particular meeting. Council president Fred Martinson would preside that night.

People were yawning through the submission of minutes, approval of budgets, and other old business as I sat next to my father, waiting to save the world from certain destruction; hopefully my stomach cramps were not an indication that the siege had already begun.

Finally it was my turn to speak. Mrs. Spiegel helped me set up an easel off to the side of the room in full view of the councilmen's dais and the peanut gallery. I had carefully charted the results of our tests on a large sheet of poster board with photographs of each of the sites. A reporter from the *Daily Register* hung on my every word as I rattled off the alarming numbers and pinpointed the specific locations in the borough where the water pollution was at its worst.

"Great job!" Dad leaned over and whispered to me when I was finished with my presentation and took my seat. Council President Martinson squirmed for a minute or two as the roomful of spectators waited to see what the official reaction would be to this rather shocking report by some zit-faced eighth grader.

"We appreciate all your efforts," Mr. Martinson said as if he were about to pat me on the head like a good little boy. "You just keep us apprised of any changes in the situation. Now I think it's time to—"

"But, sir." I stood up again like Oliver Twist asking for more. "We're just kids! There is nothing more *we* can do—that's why we brought this to *your* attention." The spectators seemed to hold their breath, as if the proceedings were highly unusual, but I continued. "Maybe the borough needs to crack down on some of its residents!" There were murmurs from the crowd as the reporter scribbled down my words for the next day's paper, where he would quote me generously while referring to me as "the Sorrentino youth."

I've never forgotten the gleam in Dad's eye that night.

He had that same look five years later in November of '76, when he garnered the most votes in an election that would place a Democratic majority on the West Long Branch Borough Council for the first time in its history. It was a barrier that few in the conservative town thought would ever be broken. When Dad was reelected in 1979—just one month before buying the luncheonette—he could not have imagined what other barriers there would be to break.

On Thursday, August 20, 1981, Dad arrived for his first borough council meeting in eight months. Uncle Tony and I watched him swing out of the van on his hydraulic lift, then flip the switch to lower it to the ground. The surface was uneven, making it impossible to get the lift flush with the pavement so he could roll off safely. I stepped forward to help out, but Councilman Paolantonio got there first.

"I got him!" he said as I stepped back. A photographer from the *Asbury Park Press* had also been watching, and now caught the shot of Dad's fellow Democrat helping him off the lift.

"Hey!" Angelo had walked from up the street and took the cigar out of his mouth. "Why didn't you wait for me before you took the picture!"

"You gotta be quick, Angelo," one of the other councilmen chimed in. "There's lots of politicians here tonight!"

I dropped back farther into the periphery as a group of men clustered around my father, contemplating the best way to get him up the flight of stairs.

"Tony, no!" Dad held his arm up to his brother-in-law, who had limped his way into the fray and gotten one of the central grips on the wheelchair. "Thank you, but you shouldn't be doing this!"

"Ehhh!" Uncle Tony didn't like to admit his own physical limitations but heeded my father's words and backed away to where I was standing.

"We've been replaced," I whispered to him as the group of men grabbed onto various parts of the wheelchair and took one final look up at the top of the stairs.

One of them gave the count—"One, two, threeeee!"—as Dad and chair were lifted off the ground.

"Wait!" Dad stopped them momentarily in their tracks. "One thing I have to know before we start up the stairs—are you Democrats or Republicans?"

The Republicans laughed the hardest as they all hoisted Dad and chair up the twelve steps to the meeting hall.

It was like a scene out of *To Kill a Mockingbird*. The first time Dad and I watched the film together on *Saturday Night at the Movies,* we didn't dare look at each other during the parts that choked us up—like when the townspeople filled the courtroom to capacity, practically hanging from the rafters, as they waited to hear Atticus Finch and the hope he represented. Just like the judge in that scene, Mayor Shaheen looked out at the standing-room-only crowd and banged his gavel.

"Before we get to the business at hand, I'd like to take this time to welcome back Councilman Sorrentino." He looked at my father. "Would you like to say a few words, Clint?"

"Thank you, Mayor." Dad had wheeled himself into the spot where his slatted wood seat had once been. "You know I've always been one to be budget-conscious." He paused as the crowd sat hushed. "So I decided to bring my own chair!"

The crowd was totally caught off guard, roaring with laughter and seemingly put at ease as Dad continued.

"I want to thank Mayor Shaheen and the council for its patience with me these past eight difficult months. And I'd like to thank all of the residents for their support." Dad had never fully recovered from the effects of the tracheotomy, not to mention his compromised breathing capacity that left his voice chronically hoarse. He paused to take a breath as he looked out across the sea of familiar faces crowded into the meeting room, his voice beginning to break as he choked back tears. "I never would have made it without you."

The room burst into applause. And the more Dad broke down, the harder they clapped.

The new hot-button issue in town was the controversy over a proposal to build a new first-aid-squad headquarters right across the street on Poplar Avenue. The squad had been sharing the firehouse across from the luncheonette, but now needed additional space for training or they would lose their state accreditation. Residents worried about their children's safety around the emergency vehicles that would be using the street, not to mention a threat to the calm of the residential area. To complicate matters, the upcoming November election was right around the corner and two seats on the council were at stake. Democrats and Republicans alike were very uncomfortable taking sides on the issue.

My father was assigned to the committee charged with resolving the matter. The chairman of that committee was Republican councilman Robert Shirvanian, one of Dad's political adversaries whom he had not seen since the cocktail party at Squires Pub. The two men had comparable résumés regarding volunteer and elective public service, but it was striking now to see the physical contrast between them. Shirvanian carried himself solidly, maintaining the stature of his athletic past. Dad, on the other hand, still looked somewhat haggard from the ravages of his illness and all the complications that had followed.

But something was happening that night.

A heated discussion ensued around the issue of the new first-aid-squad building while reporters from the *Press* and the *Register* recorded notes for their stories.

"I'm not sure how long it will take to come up with recommendations." Shirvanian spoke in his clear and steady voice.

Joyce and Sonny, who had answered our emergency call on Christmas Eve, listened intently from their seats along with other members of the first-aid squad as Dad spoke with his rasp.

"It's incumbent on the borough council to reach some sort of compromise. It probably will be less of a problem than everyone imagines." My father was almost a head shorter than everyone else on the dais, but he delivered a tall order. "There are sensible people on both sides. We'll reach an agreement. Don't worry."

Councilman Shirvanian seemed to caution my father, engaging him in a verbal yet oh so friendly tug-of-war.

"Whether or not we can develop a plan before the election depends on how deeply we have gotten into it." *Darling.* "I would not even venture to guess how long it would take."

"Well, if it's up to *me*"—*sweetheart*—"it will be settled very, very soon. I don't want to see this matter drag on until Election Day."

"Well, that only leaves us three months." *Sugar.*

"But all these people are very nervous and excited and I don't think it should be strung out that long." *Dumpling.*

The residents who lived near the proposed site murmured and nodded from their various spots in the room—feeling all the political love.

After the meeting, Jon Healey from the *Daily Register* rushed the dais. "Are you happy to be back, Councilman?"

"I sure am."

"How are you feeling?"

"Well. That wasn't such a bad hour and a half—I'm still standing!"

Healey's jaw dropped. He stopped writing and looked up as I tapped him on the shoulder. "Close your mouth, Jimmy Olsen—it's a joke."

"I'll tell you how *I'm* feeling." Mayor Shaheen interrupted the impromptu interview. "It feels great to have Sorrentino back on the council. He's really been missed and I expect things to run much easier and smoother with his return." Healey jotted down the quote then pressed Dad.

"Do you think you'll be up for running for reelection next year?"

Dad hesitated for a moment, a wry smile coming over his face. "I hope I'll be able to make a contribution to the council for the rest of my term."

That was all he had to say on the topic—but I recognized that gleam in his eye as he noticed me in the outer circle and smiled.

Once again, I stood back with Uncle Tony as the Republicans and Democrats swept Dad up, jockeying for the best grips on the wheelchair and carrying him back down the twelve stairs. As they helped Dad onto his hydraulic lift, the reporters from the *Press* and *Register* jumped into their cars and sped away. Their stories would cover the controversial building issue, but the headlines would focus on my father: OFFICIAL GRATEFUL TO RETURN and CROWD HAILS "CLINT."

I never expected to be mentioned in any of the articles—the "Sorrentino youth" wasn't making any news those days. But Dad was officially reinstated in his political life and was ready to move forward from there. I watched from afar as Angelo and Councilman Paolantonio waved him off as he manually shifted into gear. I walked back down Poplar Avenue to Uncle Tony's tan Malibu and drove away from Borough Hall, going nowhere in particular, trying to remember what it felt like to want to save the world.

25.
Ah YES,
THE OLD PIE IN THE FACE

"I don't want this!" Herck the Jerk pushed away the Knipp's roll and picked up his Lucky Strikes. "Gimme a porkroll-egg-and-cheese!"

Martin Leslie Pembrook looked halfway up from his crossword puzzle.

"I—I—I'm so sorry, Mr. Herck," Norma stuttered as she took back the plate. "I—I—I thought you usually got a buttered roll."

"Well, not this morning, sister!" He looked half-starved as he lit the cigarette, though not even the prolonged draw of smoke added any volume to his deflated bag of bones.

"Yes, well, I'm sorry," she said again, looking to make sure I had heard the order then retreating to the safety of a sink full of dirty dishes.

I could usually ignore Herck's comments, but it seemed harder for the women. Dolores, being the stronger of the two, approached Norma at the sink, offering an expression of female solidarity. "Don't apologize to that asshole!"

Herck, oblivious, rumbled to no one in particular. "Have the Syrians been here yet?"

"About ten minutes ago," I responded while tossing three slices of porkroll onto the grill—*un*scored—so they would curl up and make a shitty sandwich.

"Thank God!" He exhaled the smoke, looking like he'd been run down by a steamroller—twice.

Googie the Gizmo was all that separated Martin Leslie Pembrook from Herck the Jerk. He leaned back just as Martin's eyes rose above the horizon of his tea and cast a slow take toward the skeletal heap of misery sitting two stools down—no comment necessary—before turning his attention to me.

"And speaking of *accidents*"—Martin let his double entendre hang in the air for a second—"did you ever buy a new car, Steven?"

"Well actually, uh, uh, uh," I stuttered, wanting to avoid the issue as I finished concocting Herck's lopsided sandwich and dropped it down on the counter in front of him.

You're welcome, asshole.

"Oh!" Googie had just connected the dots. "Is it that blue thing out back?"

"Uh, yeah. It's that blue thing out back."

"*Scusa* me!" Old Man Pascucci had reached between Googie the Gizmo and Martin Leslie Pembrook, pushing them apart so he could tap his half-empty cup on the Formica. Martin slapped his *New York Times* down on the counter, causing Pascucci to freeze midtap, but the old man just shrugged in his face. "I putta too mucha shoogah!"

Dolores poured Old Man Pascucci's refill then waited there. "Oh no you don't! You stay right here. I'm gonna watch!" She stood by as the old man measured out a single teaspoon of sugar, looked up at her, then stirred it into his coffee. He had been mowing lawns all morning. "Here, bay-bay, now wipe!" She handed him a damp paper towel to remove all the grass that was stuck to his forehead.

"Are you *quite* finished?" Martin recoiled from the sweaty landscaper, who then retreated to his perch at table four. "Christ!"

"Here, Martin, doll." Dolores poured more hot water, picked his used tea bag up off the counter, and plopped it back into his cup. "Steep this, bay-bay."

Herck the Jerk had taken a couple of bites out of his sandwich, leaving the rest for the garbage. "Well, thank God I don't need that old guinea mowing my lawn anymore," he said as Old Man Pascucci emptied his corncob pipe into an ashtray. "Now I got my faggot nephew to do it for free."

Dolores and I looked at each other and froze.

Cue the pie man at the front door.

"Mrs. Smith! You're here just in time!" Dolores licked her lips when she caught sight of the middle-aged truck driver in khaki pants and a short-sleeve polyester shirt. We knew him only by the product he peddled, not by his real name. He certainly wasn't a "Mrs.," although he had the oddest ability to stand with his feet tightly together and his knees far apart like a ballerina in plié. Dolores whispered to me, "You know I can't resist a bowlegged man!" She scurried past while yelling the order down to Mrs. Smith. "Gimme a nice fresh lemon meringue and a coconut custard! Nice and fresh, hon!"

"And a chocolate cream!" I added to the order. "Nice and fresh, hon!"

"Oh no, *boychick,* the lemon's a big seller and your father likes the coconut custard."

"So get all three."

"Oh no, *boychick.* When my Vern and I—God bless his bowlegged soul— had the Pickle Place, we never bought more than two pies on a Thursday before a holiday weekend. It'll go bad. I'm tellin' ya!"

"No, it won't, Dolores. Chocolate cream pie is comfort food." My eyes followed Herck the Jerk, who was now scuffing down to the cash register. "And trust me, I need *lots* of comfort today."

"Hey, you're the goddamn boss. Whatever you say." She threw up her hands and ran down to the register, stopping briefly at the sink. "Don't worry, Norma, I'll ring up the asshole."

Mrs. Smith swaggered out to his truck like an ole cowhand as Dolores argued with Herck over the price of a porkroll-egg-and-cheese sandwich.

"Ah, shove it, Dolores!" He slammed his money down on the counter, ignoring her extended hand.

"What's the matter, bay-bay, you ain't gettin' any?"

"I don't *need* any!" he squawked before exiting out the front door.

I joined Dolores by the register, her back to the rest of the customers, as she watched him cross the street to the cleaners.

"Nyeh dobsha," she whispered to me, still following Herck with her eyes. "Have a shitty day, bay-bay!" For punctuation, she lifted her Banlon shell and flashed her breasts toward the College Park Cleaners, though thankfully the super bra censored her exclamation points.

Cue Mrs. Smith, arriving back at the register just in time for the show, getting more than hard cash for his pies.

"Sorry about that," I apologized.

"All in a day's work, sir," he said calmly and professionally like Joe Friday. "All in a day's work."

I peeked into the box containing the chocolate cream pie as Dolores lowered the Banlon and paid the bill. He gave her an extra-big smile when he left, though a couple of singles would have been more appropriate under the circumstances.

"Now, Dolores, please don't take this too personally." I spoke thoughtfully, not wanting to offend her. "But I really don't want to see your tits in the luncheonette anymore. Okay?"

"Why, *boychick*? Did you have something else in mind?"

Well, actually . . .

. . . *my faggot nephew* . . . *Fuck you, asshole!*

At eleven o'clock that night, I gripped the wheel and sank down into the torn plaid vinyl of my 1972 Plymouth Duster as I headed toward Asbury Park. It was the beginning of Labor Day weekend. The summer was winding down, but I was on a mission—and I wasn't going quietly.

My new "new" car was loud—to say the least. Despite a big patch of rust eating into each side, the body shouted the gayest shade of electric blue I had ever seen. And I was told that a new catalytic converter would silence the periodic backfire, though nothing could muffle the double toot on the horn that seemed to blare out *HO-MO!* But at least it had been a bargain and my family had been polite and encouraging when I first pulled the ravaged jalopy into the driveway.

I stopped at the light just before Asbury.

The old regulars in my hometown community who had embraced me since I was a kid—with the exception of a jerk or two—were still there, offering their respect and admiration, but they only saw the chaste and dutiful son. Since moving to New York, I had been emerging as a more complete picture. I found acceptance there that I still wasn't sure I'd get in West Long Branch. Would that town accept me for *all* that I was? Seeing Dad glow in the spotlight of his community only made me feel lonelier and increasingly desperate to reconnect with my own—or at least some reasonable facsimile. That's why I decided to venture out and cruise for a little "community" of my own.

Fuck you, Herck!

I accelerated when the light changed, my rusted Duster backfiring once or twice as it begrudgingly gained speed. I crossed the railroad tracks and made the right onto Main Street in Asbury Park, and then a left into the old abandoned shopping district on Cookman Avenue where the bars now were, keeping my eyes peeled for the Odyssey.

Despite what the bar's name suggested, there wasn't a Greek sailor to be found, but I don't think any of the male patrons in the dimly lit establishment really gave a shit.

I knew I was downing my screwdriver a little too fast, but thought my eyes were deceiving me when I recognized someone who walked in the front door. I lowered my head and turned away when he sat on the bar stool right next to me and ordered a Bud.

How can this be?

My mind was racing to come up with a plan to escape without being seen, though it finally dawned on me that maybe I was taking the wrong approach. After all, *he* was there, too. I drew a deep breath, sat up straight, and turned to face the situation head-on.

When I tapped him on the shoulder, he spun around and locked his incredulous eyes with mine.

"Hey Steve-o!" Brent's voice pitched upward, his eyes darting over to the door as if he were anticipating a raid.

"Well, I have to admit," I said with a smirk coming over my face, "I'm *really* surprised to see *you* here."

"I was going to say the same thing about you." He took a quick swig of his beer then leaned in just close enough for me to smell the remnant of the day's cologne on his neck.

"Is that Grey Flannel?"

"Hmm? Oh no, no. Aramis."

"Does your wife know?"

"That I wear Aramis?"

"No, that you're—you know."

"She knows I'm seeing a client tonight." He cast his eyes downward and adjusted his tie, as if preparing for the fictitious meeting. "I can't stay out too late." He sat up straight and guzzled down half his bottle.

I was sipping my screwdriver through the little straw, trying to figure out how to keep the conversation going. "Well, like they say—the night is young!" *Ahem.* "You know, Brent, I've always, well—you know—really noticed you."

"Really, Steve-o?" The man I had pined for freshman year looked up at me, chuckled, and took another sip of beer. He raised his right arm for a trademark single-handed comb-through of his raven hair, then looked away again. My stomach began to ache with the stab of rejection until he turned back to me and gave me the second surprise of the evening. "Ya know, Steve-o, I've always had a little crush on you." He looked me squarely in the eye, patting my leg three times before his hand came firmly to rest on my thigh.

Hellooo!

The ache in my abdomen turned to heart palpitations. But I thought I would experience complete cardiac arrest when he lurched forward and kissed me on the lips.

"Let's go park somewhere." He cut to the chase when we came up for air.

"No!" I quickly nixed that idea. "I tried that once and ended up with a flashlight in my face. I want to be indoors."

"Well, that might be a problem, Steve-o." Brent patted my leg again. "I don't think Candy would appreciate us using the guest room and you still live with your parents, right?"

"Wait." I pulled the keys out of my pocket and singled out one in particular. "I have a better idea."

I cringed as Brent pulled his sleek 1981 SAAB Turbo Hetero into the spot next to my dilapidated 1972 Plymouth Fagster, made more conspicuous by its unnerving shade of blue and residual backfire after the ignition was shut down. But embarrassment was quickly replaced by excitement when my attorney stepped out of his car, having shed his blazer and tie. He adjusted the waist of the finely tailored slacks that draped his long legs as he sized me up with hungry eyes that were glazed by a Bud or four.

"How tall are you, by the way?" I fumbled with my keys as we walked around to the front of the building.

"Six-one or two."

"My favorite height."

"Oh, Steve-o!"

The busy intersection was quiet this time of night, but Brent still scanned the road for familiar cars as I unlocked the door. Taking a final look around, confident that we had not been seen, I felt Brent's hand on the small of my back as I opened the door and we stepped into the dark luncheonette.

The only source of light in the kitchen spilled in from the street through the service window. I looked around for some cushioning, but all I could come up with was a little multicolor woven kitchen mat from Kmart that I moved to the middle of the concrete floor. Brent leaned back, tall enough to rest his granite-hard glutes on the edge of the marble slab where Aunt Mary and Aunt Angie had rolled the meatballs. He was practically in shadow, but I could still read the whites of his eyes and the glimmer from his wedding band as he folded his arms and cocked his head slightly to the right.

"Strip."

"What?"

"Take off your clothes." Brent started unbuttoning his shirt, speaking with the same commanding tone that he used when ordering a bowl of chili.

If we had been in a movie, the camera would then have panned over to the stove, where a pot bubbled over with tomato sauce and meatballs—and then cut straight to the afterglow, which in this case was stray light coming in from the service window, capturing my married Republican as he wordlessly scrambled back into his suit.

Despite Brent's offer to walk me out to my car—he hadn't said much else—I lagged behind in the darkness of the luncheonette, listening at the back door as the smooth engine of his SAAB turned over and faded away on its trip back to Candy Land.

Cue Mrs. Smith.

I opened the refrigerator door, squinted at the harsh light, and pulled out one of the cardboard boxes. I placed it on the marble slab in the kitchen and grabbed the pie server and a fork and plate. We had served only two slices of the chocolate cream pie during lunch that day, leaving three quarters of it untouched.

Cutting through the rich topping and silky filling, and right down into the flaky crust, I scooped out a large slice and plopped it sideways onto my heavy blue plate. I assume it was delicious, though the taste barely had time to register on my palate as the pie disappeared in a rapid series of forkfuls.

Maybe I'll have another—just a sliver.

And another.

Finally, forgoing the plate, I continued to devour the Mrs. Smith's Chocolate Cream Pie—until the box was completely empty.

26.
IN THE NAME OF THE FATHER, THE SON, AND THE WHOLLY TOAST—AHEM

"Howdy, Mr. Steve!" Stanley's Bermuda shorts revealed a pasty set of shins set off nicely by the black socks.

"Beautiful day, huh?"

"Yep. You comin' down to the lake for the festivities?"

"Wouldn't miss it for the world!" I fanned grill smoke away from my face. "Are those your running sandals?"

"Yep." He climbed onto a stool and spun around once. "I'll have a fried egg on a Knipp's."

"Sold out of rolls. Only toast this morning."

"Like I said, fried egg on toast—and don't forget to harden the yoke, I don't want to dribble on m'good shirt!" He tucked his thumbs under his armpits like he was showing off a vest, but he wasn't the only one in the place wearing the bright red T-shirt.

It was Sunday, September 13, 1981, and over two hundred people had signed up to participate in a five-mile race that would originate at Franklin Lake, wind through the streets of the borough, cross the Monmouth College campus, and finish back at the little park near the water. And whoever wasn't participating would be lining the streets to cheer the runners on. That sunny day, it seemed like the whole town was wearing the bright red T-shirts with CLINT SORRENTINO BENEFIT RUN emblazoned across the front, next to a big heart containing the words WE CARE CLINT, placed over the real thing.

"Ahhh, shoot!" Aunt Angie grumbled while unloading the groceries onto the marble slab, the large red T-shirt pulled over a lumpy blouse and a Salem hanging out of her mouth.

Mary was squashing wet bread and eggs into the chopped meat. "What, Ange?"

"Tony!" she yelled out the service window to her husband, who was perched on a stool, resting his bad leg on the footrest, his red T-shirt pulled to capacity across his belly. "I need you to run quick to ShopRite!" She coughed. "I forgot the parsley!"

"No, no!" I yelled over my shoulder while stacking the porkroll-egg-and-cheese sandwiches for the three Palladino sisters. "There's a shaker of the dried stuff—John will show you where it is!"

John was pouring coffee for the two Palladino parents and looked up. "I'll get it."

"Thanks, John." I looked at him. *What a great kid,* I thought. I hated that my responses to him were as unpredictable as the weather, and that he'd become my mood barometer. I'm sure he saw his role more as Punching Bag.

"Sure." He smiled back, no doubt pleased with the unusually sunny day.

"Besides," I yelled back to the kitchen, "I know you wanna get to the lake on time!"

"I can be back in ten minutes!" Uncle Tony dropped his other foot to the floor and attempted to stand, still stiff from collating all the Sunday papers with my brother.

"Uncle Tony, sit!" I commanded. "How 'bout some breakfast?"

"Ehhh!" He raised his two arms then released them toward me in a broad dismissive gesture.

"I'll make you sunny-side."

"Scrambled," he grunted, and sat back down. "White toast."

"I'll have the same," Coz the Cop said, just coming in from Mass, though his Sunday best was full uniform. "Big day for Dad, huh, Steven?"

"You're not running?" I asked while dropping four slices of Wonder bread into the toaster.

"Oh no. We're all on traffic duty today. Half the town is shut down."

"Somethin' smells good—oh shit!" Dolores had swung open the back door so hard that it gonged against the metal fountain tanks and rebounded into her face. "Steven, you better do something about this door!" She slammed it shut behind her, then noticed my aunts working in the kitchen. "How ya doin', girls? Fry up lots of extra now, them meatballs are big sellers!"

"Dolores, today's your day off—I'm not paying you for the free advice."

"You can afford it, looks like you're doin' a nice business today, hon."

"Well, between the Catholics and the runners—"

"I didn't know so many goddamned people still went to church." She scanned the room, waving and blow-kissing. "I'm gonna have a quick bran muffin then go pick up Vivian. We wanna get a good spot at the lake."

"Out of muffins. Just toast."

"Shit! Toast, then. And coffee." She noticed Coz the Cop stroking his mustache and reading the *Register* two stools down. "You ain't runnin' like that, hon. We gotta get you out of that uniform!"

"You're doing a pretty good job filling out that T-shirt!" he joked, looking up from the sports section.

"Actually, Dolores," I piped in, "the red cotton is very becoming on you—I think it's the first time I've ever seen you in natural fibers." The *un*natural thing, however, was the way the T-shirt stretched across her bosom, distorting CLINT SORRENTINO like a funhouse mirror.

"Here you go, Dolores." John poured her a cup of coffee. "I'll get your toast."

"Thanks, doll." She lit a Pall Mall.

"Thanks, John!" I added.

"You runnin' a fever, *boychick*?" Dolores asked when John stepped away.

"What do you mean?" My eyes drifted over to the customers walking in the front door, most notably the one with the silky running shorts and white Adidas.

"You're bein' so nice to your baby brother. It ain't like you."

She turned to see where I was looking.

"Yeah, well, the night is young."

I watched Brent Jamison and party settle in at table two. Dolores gave them a fingery wave as John picked up the order pad.

"That's all right, John." I grabbed the pad from him. "Keep an eye on the counter—I'll get their order."

"Um-hmmm," Dolores purred suspiciously as she drew on her cigarette and watched me venture out onto the floor.

"Well, good morning!" I bubbled when I got to Brent's table.

"Hey Steve-o! I haven't seen you for a while."

"Yeah. Two weeks!" I cleared my throat. "Coffee?"

"Uh, yeah," Brent mumbled, squirming around in his seat, then waved to Dolores, who had spun around on her stool for a better view of the proceedings.

"So sorry I don't have a booster seat for the baby." I cooed at the little girl.

"That's my little Amanda," Brent crowed, "and Steve-o, this is my wife—Candy."

Don't remind me.

"Of course! We met at the cocktail party—remember? How are you, Candy?"

"I'm starving." She rested her extended chin on the baby's head and hugged the child tightly, rocking side to side.

Dear, sweet, starving Candy.

"So am I," Brent said in a high-pitched voice while making faces at his nine-month-old daughter.

"No, you're not, Brent!" Candy interjected. "You're running five miles today—you'll get cramps!"

"Wow, impressive." I patted him on the back. "I bet you run pretty fast!"

Brent cleared his throat and dropped his pitch a little lower than normal. "I'll just have an order of rye toast."

"Just Wonder bread this morning. Sorry."

"White, then, I guess. It's not my favorite, but you always arrange it so nicely around the plate into a little star!" he said, patronizing *me* more than the business.

"Yeah, it's all in the presentation."

Brent took the baby from Candy's arms and lifted her up over his head. "That's my girlie, that's my girlie!" he gushed until she squealed.

I was genuinely moved by the fatherly affection, but had to look away. Unfortunately, I caught sight of Carmen, who'd just barreled up to the counter, his red T-shirt pulled north of his pants with a healthy serving of crack displayed off the back of his stool.

I wrote down Brent and Candy's orders, tore the check from the pad, and slapped it on the table. But when I went back behind the counter, I stopped briefly by the register and scribbled a note, tore the check from the pad, folded it, and stuck it in my pocket. I looked over at Brent and felt the barometric pressure begin to change.

"Three eggs over, extra ham, extra potatoes, and a toasted bagel," John relayed to me officiously while grabbing the silver for Carmen's setup.

Okay, sonny, the party's over.

"John! Hellooo!" I thundered. "We're out of bagels in case you didn't notice! *Think,* for God's sake!"

"How about eggs?" John snipped back. "Are we out of them, too?"

I knew that I could still open up like a late-summer storm cloud, but I swore that kid had been recently weatherproofed.

"Ehhh!" Uncle Tony bleated as he began to lift himself off the stool. "Why don't I run down to Eli's and pick up a dozen bagels? I can be back in five minutes."

"Sit!" I commanded.

"Hmmm." Dolores was staring at me as she drew in one final puff before snuffing out her Pall Mall in the ashtray. "I gotta go pick up Vivian. I'll see you down at the lake, *boychick.*"

"Yeah."

When everyone was fed and toasted, I retreated to the kitchen to see how the ladies were doing. Aunt Mary slapped my hand when I gobbled down one of the meatballs that she had just pulled from the frying pan and placed on the towels to drain. Aunt Angie pushed me aside so she could protect her morning's work, quickly dropping the rest of the meatballs into the pot of sauce that bubbled on the stove. I watched the two sisters round their backs and work feverishly to finish in time for the race. They stood side by side on the small woven kitchen mat from Kmart, oblivious to the wear and tear it had endured since the last time they made meatballs.

Everyone seemed so excited. I could literally watch the momentum building in my father's life when I looked out the service window at the sea of red T-shirts with the heart emblem that bore his name. There was no shortage of love in that place for him.

And there was Brent, sitting tall and handsome with his family, eating toast and harboring our shared secret. Not since high school, when I watched him playing basketball, had I had the opportunity to see him in a pair of Adidas shorts with the sides cut high on the thighs. I was so drawn to those powerful legs.

When he swiped the check from his table and stood up, I rushed out of the kitchen and down to the register to meet him.

"So, Steve-o, what's new with you?" Brent handed me the check, shuffling back and forth like he had to pee.

"Well, actually, I'm finally moving into my own pad."

Did I really just say pad?

"Good for you!"

"Yeah. Right." I reached into my pocket where I'd placed the folded kitchen check with the note on it and handed it to him with his change. "It's my new phone number," I whispered.

"I'll see you down at the lake, Steve-o," Brent declared in stilted speech like a bad actor, averting his eyes, quickly stuffing the paper into his wallet.

"Good luck!" I called after him as he hurried back to his table and scooped his daughter up into his arms.

"That's my girlie!" he repeated on his way out the door, ignoring me.

"Run a good race!" I added. He still wouldn't look back.

Something told me that *I* was the one getting the runaround.

★   ★   ★

The next day's *Daily Register* captured the big event in one of its headlines: OVER 200 RUN AROUND TO BENEFIT SORRENTINO. It told how local businesses and friends had sponsored the event, including ShopRite and Angelo Valenzano and Martin Leslie Pembrook and the Larchwood Bar and McDonald's. Runners had entered from around West Long Branch and neighboring boroughs like Wanamassa and as far away as Newark. Apparently, everyone was there. It said that Councilman Frank "Clint" Sorrentino "was heartened to see such a large turnout."

It must have been nice—though I wouldn't have known.

"We missed you down at the lake," Mom said, peeking into my room. "Are you all right?"

"Yeah, I needed to do some stuff for my move," I lied, staring at the ceiling.

"Your father was asking for you." She looked around suspiciously.

"Oh." I pulled the covers right up under my chin. "Who won?"

"The Gallirio boy from Whalepond Road."

"Oh."

"Such a gorgeous day out there. Are you sure you're all right?"

"Yeah, just tired."

Mom closed the door again as I pulled the covers back up over my head.

27.
ALL THE WRONG MOVES

The day I moved into my new apartment on Franklin Avenue, I knew that my ties to New York City had been completely severed. But at least the location was convenient. I was right around the corner from the Long Branch passenger station, barely two blocks from Monmouth Medical Center, and right down the street from the Damiano Funeral Home. Basically, I could get hit by a train, be DOA at the hospital, and get embalmed without ever having to leave the neighborhood. Who needed proximity to the Broadway theaters when you could get something near a funeral home in New Jersey?

The move wasn't too involved. The only furniture I took from my parents' house was a twin bed, a kitchen table, Dad's old recliner, and the Hoover hutch from the basement.

"Careful, John. Easy!" I directed my brother as we slid the old relic into the back of Dad's van. "I don't want to scratch the new paint job." Once I removed the stack of 78s and blueprints and tools and coffee cans, and threw a coat of glossy paint on the outside and lined the inside with Con-Tact paper, it was transformed into a functional piece of furniture for my new apartment.

"But, Steven, there's one little problem—" John started to say.

"Reggie! Quiet!" The dog was whimpering from inside the house, scratching at the door that opened into the garage. "What, John?"

"How is Dad supposed to get into the van?"

"Oh shit!" We had blocked the hydraulic lift. "Let's pull this out again—careful!"

"What are you doing?" Mom slid sideways through the door, then slammed it shut with her foot before the dog could escape. She was carrying a small but weighty bag against her chest like a baby.

"Dad has to get in first," I explained as John and I slid the hutch back out of the van. "Where is he?"

"Here I am!" Dad said cheerily as he rolled off the concrete ramp out front and turned into the garage. "Sorry, I had to catheterize."

"Oh, excuses, excuses."

"Reggie, shut up!" Mom yelled at the mutt, whose wet nose pressed against the small window on the door. "Here, Steven, this is for you."

I opened the bag as Dad rolled forward onto the lift and engaged the grinding gears that began to elevate him.

"Oh wow, I remember these!" I shouted over the noise while pulling out one of the ornate silver-plated forks. I hadn't seen the once-brilliant flatware since the late sixties when we made the switch to stainless.

"At first, I was thinking why not wait until you get married—"

Because we'd all drop dead waiting. That's why.

"But it's your new apartment, I thought."

"Thanks, Mom."

Once Dad had locked himself into the driver's position, John and I reloaded the Hoover hutch into the van.

"You better get going. My mother and father are probably down at South Broadway already." Mom kissed me on the cheek. "I'm sure they have lots of stuff for you. Good luck."

"Thanks, Mom."

She walked back through the garage, keeping the dog at bay as she carefully slipped through the doorway. "All right, pup, it's okay, pup."

"I guess that's it," I said as John climbed into the van with Dad. "I'll meet you guys at Nonny and Poppy's."

I carried the bag of silverware out to my car, where I had already stuffed my clothing into the backseat, along with the sealed-up Pennfield Farms box that I had packed weeks ago in New York.

"Wait!" Mom came running out of the house with her old green Eureka canister vacuum cleaner in one hand and a shopping bag in the other. "Here—you'll need this."

"Oh my God, Mom! Are you sure?" I took the large contraption by the handle. "Isn't this one of your prize possessions?"

"Oh, go to hell!" she barked before kissing me one more time on the cheek. "Good luck in your new place." Apparently, though, she had not closed the door all the way. Reggie came bounding out of the garage like he was running from a tidal wave and took off down the street.

"Reggie! Reggie!" she yelled after him. "Damn that dog!" She handed me the shopping bag. "Here, it's got all the original attachments."

You would have thought I had just been entrusted with a precious family heirloom, and as I gingerly packed the old green Eureka canister vacuum cleaner—with all the original attachments—into the backseat of my 1972 blue Plymouth Duster, I got the eeriest feeling.

My grandparents were waiting in their car when we pulled up to their abandoned residence on South Broadway. They had been among the last to leave the decaying neighborhood, reluctantly moving to a new condo in the West End section of Long Branch, but they still maintained ownership of their two brick buildings. Poppy, in particular, wanted to hold on as long as he could to the place where his bakery, grocery store, and hotel had once flourished in the bustling community. But Commander's Bar had had its last call years ago, about the same time Pedone's market gave up trying to compete with Foodtown. Mr. Caputo had packed up his pastries and lemon ice and moved to a strip mall in North Long Branch, and Rex Pizzeria closed long before Uncle Freddy became too ill to run it. Even the trains had been rerouted to new tracks, no longer running through the "Little Italy" section of Long Branch where the Mayor of South Broadway had once reigned.

My grandparents had left behind many of the furnishings in the large second-floor apartment where they had raised my mother and her four siblings. Remnants from the family's businesses were scattered about in the labyrinth of basements and secret spaces that Poppy had helped design during the days of Prohibition. We even suspected that a distillery remained hidden away under a removable staircase leading up to the kitchen.

South Broadway may have been Poppy's last hurrah; it was also my last stop before moving into my apartment on Franklin Avenue. I think he was thrilled to see me blow some of the dust off of his treasured past and said I could take whatever I wanted. But there was no getting around it: Everything old was old again.

"Joe, you wait out here with Clint," Nonny directed. "I don't want you climbing the stairs!" Poppy raised the back of his hand to her in a furious gesture but complied nonetheless, mumbling on his way over to the van to talk to Dad through the window.

"Ttt." Nonny looked at me with all the confidence of a woman who inexplicably kept her knee-highs rolled down around her ankles without a hint of self-consciousness about her varicose veins. John and I followed her through the front door.

We made several trips in and out of the building, loading up the van with a few "new" things for my apartment. The furniture wasn't in the best of shape, but at least I could throw a cushion over the tattered cane seat of the armchair I found and set out some of the Depression glass and old photographs for show.

On each trip, I heard the quiet blend of Poppy's broken English and Dad's raspy tones as they reminisced about the old days. When I stood at the back of the van and wrapped some dishes in newspaper, they seemed oblivious to my presence, gazing and pointing at the graffiti. Where SWEET FAMILY BREAD had once been stenciled onto the window, there were now wooden boards to keep out vandals. It was hard to believe this had once been the thriving flagship of Joe Tarantolo's family businesses.

I'd heard so many stories over the years about turbulence within the family after Dad took over the bakery. I wondered whether or not he had actually been pulled into the family business of his own accord.

Hmm. I wonder what that feels like?

John hadn't been born yet, and Judy, Michael, and I were oblivious to whatever had gone on. We used to spend Saturday mornings there, climbing the flour bags while Dad slid pallets of hand-shaped dough into the brick oven—singing—as Poppy patrolled the premises. Dad crooned old standards like "The Very Thought of You," and unbeknownst to us, Poppy's meddling was slowly driving him nuts. But Dad let it pass. He never spoke up when he knew he wouldn't be heard.

Years later, when Poppy lent Dad half the down payment for the luncheonette, I'm sure he legitimately wanted to help—as much as he also wanted to be the big shot. I really loved my grandfather, especially when I pictured him in his heyday, strutting down South Broadway like he was Mr. Long Black Coat from New York.

But now it was rumored that the neighborhood would be razed to make way for a Hilton. Poppy held on stubbornly, determined to be the last to sell. As long as those buildings stood, the glory of the past they represented still seemed alive. But once they fell, there would be no choice but to surrender to the uncertainty of the future, move on—or just call it a life.

"Thanks again, Nonny." I leaned over to give her a hug.

"Stop by the house, dear," she said, holding my arm and slipping me a fifty.

"Nonny—"

"Shhh!" She looked over her shoulder to see if Poppy was watching. "I breaded some *gootalettes*."

"I love when you do the chicken like that, Nonny—"

"Veal today, dear."

"Oh?" I reconsidered for a second. "No! I have to get this stuff over to Franklin Avenue."

"And some nice stuffed artichokes—and fresh fruit, all cut up."

"I can't. I'm fat. Now get the hell in the car!" I helped her into the front seat then shut the door. "Thanks!" I mouthed while slipping the fifty into my pocket.

She blew me an extra kiss from the front seat as I walked around to say good-bye to Poppy.

"Drive safe." I tried to hug him but he grabbed my arm and stuffed a wad of twenties into my hand. "But Poppy—"

"No, you take!" He pushed my hand away, still in charge, still the family protector, still the big *goomba*!

"John, careful!"

He stopped and threw me one of those looks that I'd come to love, then held the stack of dishes out in front of him like he was going to smash them in the street. *Better than in my face,* I thought, backing down as he disappeared into the house on Franklin Avenue.

"What are you going to do with that old thing?" Dad watched me unload the Wonder-bread rack from the old grocery store.

"I thought I'd sand it and repaint it for my stereo. You know, I haven't listened to any of my albums since Christmas."

"Yeah, I know." Dad looked out the windshield, his fingertips tapping out a steady beat on the armrest of his wheelchair. It was the only music he seemed to be making those days.

I put the rack down in the street and walked around to the window. "Do you ever sing anymore?"

"I can't."

Funny, neither can I.

"But have you at least tried?"

"Please, I'm still working on my Ping-Pong ball." He referred to the little device from rehab that he still used daily to strengthen his breathing.

"Do you remember that Roger Miller album?"

"Yeah." He sighed. "You knew every single word."

"We played it twice a day when you first brought it home. Remember?"

"Sure. 'King of the Road.' "

"Can I have it?"

"Take it! I don't even know where it is anymore."

"It's in the back of the van. I packed it already."

"Ah, jeez."

I made another couple of trips in and out of the apartment, passing John going the opposite direction on the stairs. When we were done, John settled onto the front stoop with a can of soda while I climbed into the passenger seat of the van to rest for a few minutes and say good-bye to Dad.

"You got everything?" he asked.

I nodded. "Yeah. Everything." I looked out the window at my car, parked there in front of the house like a junkyard carcass.

"How the hell do you do it, Dad?"

"What do you mean?"

"How come you're not pissed off and depressed? I mean, how do you just sit there and take it?"

He shrugged.

"You've lost so much."

He lowered his chin and looked at me over the top of his wire frames. "I haven't lost *every*thing."

I'd seen that little smirk before and it made me want to smack him.

I was fifteen or sixteen and I'd had one of my rare arguments with my father. It was over something stupid like his disapproval of my "damn long hair," or he was forbidding me to go on a camping trip with some friends that included a couple of (gasp!) girls, or whatever. It wasn't important. All I know is that we were standing face-to-face, arguing in the living room. I was so angry with him, fueled I'm sure by adolescent hormonal tidal waves, and before I had a chance to think, the venom just flew out of my mouth. "I hate you!" I screamed into his face. That was the only time I ever remember trying intentionally to hurt my father.

But Dad just stood there. His shoulders dropped like he had been wounded, but he didn't say anything. That's when he gave me that look. He dropped his chin to his chest and looked out over his glasses (they were black horn-rims then) and gave me that smirk. I couldn't tell if he was embarrassed or maybe afraid to fight back. He was silent. Was he being a wimp? He walked away and never brought it up again. I knew I had been forgiven but I didn't understand. Was it really forgiveness or was it denial? Was it strength? Or was it spinelessness?

I hated that fucking look then because I couldn't read it, and I hated it now.

"Why aren't you angry?" I asked angrily.

"Why should I be angry?" He seemed genuinely perplexed.

"You can't walk. You can't run your business. You can't sing, for God's sake. You *love* to sing."

"Other things are more important."

"But you're paralyzed!"

"But I can't do anything about that. You just do what you can do."

"Christ!" If ever I needed the father–son talk, it was then. "Make me understand."

"What do you want me to say?"

"Oh, nothing. Just go home and blow on your Ping-Pong ball thingamajig!"

"You're not taking any of my Bing Crosby albums, are you?"

"You call him a *singer*? Sheesh." It was the best dig I could come up with as I stubbornly stayed on topic. "Dad, don't you ever ask yourself: 'Why me?' "

"Yeah." Dad turned to me and smiled like he already knew the answer to that question.

"Well?"

The way he looked at me with that smirk—I just wanted to kill him.

"I dunno"—he smiled—"maybe you have to be a father to understand."

I thanked Dad and John for helping me move and waved as they drove off down Franklin Avenue. Other than the fuel in that van, I still didn't understand what kept that man going.

I looked up and down the street.

That was it. I was no longer a resident of New York City. But at least I was independent again. I had my very own three-room apartment on a beautiful block down the Jersey shore, extra peaceful in the presence of the stately Damiano Funeral Home a few doors down. I guess this was my chance to jump-start my life again—so why did I feel more like I was being laid to rest?

28.
CLOSED
FOR THE HOLIDAYS

On the morning of December 24, 1981, I could barely get out of bed—but I did.

I showered and shaved, forced on the ever-tightening restaurant pants and matching smile, grabbed the Dutch Masters cigar box, tossed in the envelopes for Dolores and Norma, and fired up my old Duster for the short trip to the luncheonette at five-thirty in the morning.

Fuck Christmas!

"Oh Norma honey, you can't serve this to Half Cup Howard." Dolores mimed a gag reflex then yelled down to the old regular. "You don't want the ham today, doll—it's all slimy!"

"Dolores!" I cautioned as she stood there sniffing the block of processed meat in front of all the customers. "It's Half Cup *Harold*. And could you please be a little more discreet?"

Norma took a quick whiff on her way by. "Ooof!" She retched. "I'll get the coffee."

Tombstone's head slowly rose back into view, like a groundhog with a hangover, caught a glimpse of the outside world, and disappeared again into his hands.

"I'll fix ya up nice, bay-bay," Dolores yelled down to Harold as she shoved the questionable ham back into the Bay Marie, then yelled over to me at the grill, "Gimme a porkroll-egg-and-cheese for Howard—and ninety-six the ham." She cupped her hands around her mouth like a hog caller and shifted into a loud whisper. "It's all slimy!"

"Eighty-six," I muttered while turning to Half Cup Harold for confirmation.

"I guess I'll have the porkroll—before it gets ninety-sixed!" Harold grinned while waving to me from the end stool. "Merry Christmas, kind sir! How are you doing there?"

"Great!" *Shitty.*

"Dasha!" Vivian swept in the back entrance with freshly colored hair feathered forward for the holiday.

"Vwaj, doll. You look gorgeous! Got a big date?"

"Nooo!" She looked down, pushing her chin into her chest as she adjusted the bright holiday brooch on her lapel. "It's Christmas Eve, for God's sake!"

"So? You can still get some *yebotch* under the mistletoe!" Dolores gave her wig a triple little twist to accentuate the innuendo.

"Ahhh!" Vivian screamed, and beat her hand five or six times on an empty stool, startling Tombstone back to life. She finally sat down with a big sigh. "Oh, I'm telling you, Dasha, you ought to be in pictures."

"Damn right," Dolores gibed while passing me at the grill. "Then I'd make some real pay."

"Hi, Vivian." I smiled while tossing Harold's porkroll onto the grill. "Merry Christmas."

Before she had a chance to respond, Tombstone interrupted.

"DOLOOORES!" The blood vessels on his face could barely contain themselves.

"He lives!" she announced, bringing him coffee and calling out his order. "Twelve runny fried eggs—extra greasy!"

"Thanks, toots."

"Sure, doll!" She turned to Vivian and me, lowering her voice for the commentary. *"Nyeh dobsha."*

"Boy, that Dolores." Vivian primped the sides of her new cut. "How do you do it, Steven?"

"How do I do what?"

"How do you keep from laughing all day?"

"You think I'm closing early today because of the holiday?" I scooped up one of the slices of porkroll, flipped it over, and slapped it back down on the grill. "It's so I don't get cramps from all this laughing."

"Ah! You're a riot!" Vivian spun around on her stool. "Good for you, dear—coffee!" She waved at Norma. "You people deserve a break after last year. What a holiday for your family, huh? How's Clint?"

"You'll see him here shortly," I said while cracking the eggs for Tombstone and talking over my shoulder. "I'm taking him over to Angelo's for a Christmas party later."

"What a great kid you are!"

"I'll finish here." Dolores grabbed the spatula from my hand. "I think your lawyer wants a word with you."

"What are you talking about?" I noticed that Brent Jamison had just walked in the front door with his big dimple and a couple of work cronies. If Dolores suspected anything, at least she chose to play dumb, elbowing me away from the grill. "Okay," I said, "if you insist."

"Hey Steve-o. Merry Christmas!" Brent sat up straight with both hands flat on the counter—not the most comfortable position for him, but it did play up the shoulders. I noted that the wedding band was still snugly in place, but his dialing finger appeared to be free enough. "How's the new apartment?" he asked.

"All settled in," I said coldly. "You should see it."

Norma quietly slipped an order to me. "A toasted corn for Vivian." But her meek request didn't make it past Dolores's radar.

"No, no, Vwaj, you don't want them corn muffins! They're all dry and mealy today." Her face scrunched up like she'd just gotten a whiff of sulfur as she handed Tombstone his plate of eggs. "I'll fix ya a nice bran!"

"But, Dasha, I don't like bran!" Vivian looked to me for backup.

"Don't look at me, Vivian." I threw my arms up as Brent sat there in his holiday cable knit, camera-perfect as a spread in L.L. Bean. "Nobody around here gets what they want!"

"Aye!" Tombstone rumbled like a pirate who'd been out at sea too long as he slurped up his fourth or fifth egg. "Ya know, Dolores"—his tongue caught the yoke that dribbled out of his mouth—"ya got a nice shape on ya."

"Ya know, hon, my Vern told me somethin' a long time ago. Let me para-praise."

The old regulars knew by the tone of her voice that she was about to impart some wise words as they quieted themselves.

"It went somethin' like this," she continued as they leaned in a little closer. "Ass-lickers always get the shitty end of the stick!"

Brilliant, I thought as I grabbed a blank pad of kitchen checks and a pen.

"Steven, what the fuck are you doing down there?" Dolores saw me furiously scribbling away.

"I'm writing that one down for the screenplay."

"Oh!" She primped her wig like she was preparing to be immortalized.

"Here you go, Dolores. Merry Christmas." I discreetly slipped her the envelope as Brent looked up from his Diet Pepsi.

"Oh, you're a goddamn doll! Come here, *boychick.*" Without warning, Dolores pulled me against her bosom, knocking most of the wind out of me. "I hope this Christmas Eve is a happier one for your family than last year's." She let go of me as Brent offered her a napkin from a nearby dispenser to wipe the tears from her eyes.

"Thank *you,* Dolores." I lowered my voice and caught my breath. "And by the way, please keep it to yourself." I looked over to Norma at the sink. "I gave you a little more and I wouldn't want her to feel bad."

Our squishy moments were even shorter than they were rare.

"Well, you're goddamn right about that! I *better* be getting more than her—she don't move her ass around here!" Dolores started to tear open her envelope. "I been in this business a long time, ya-know-wadda-mean? When my Vern and I ran our Pickle Place, we gave out good stripends for Christmas. A good week's pay. Ya-know-wadda-mean?"

"Stipend," Brent corrected her as he winked at me.

Dolores sneered at the two of us then stuck her index finger into the envelope and counted the bills. "I got news for ya, Mr. Big Apartment of His Own in Long Branch, your father gave me *twice* as much last year!"

"Dolores, he didn't give you *anything* last year!"

"You're fulla shit!"

"Dolores!"

"You're fulla shit!"

"Oh really?" Just at that moment, Dad started tapping on the front window and beckoned to me to help get him in. "Well, here he is now—let's ask him!"

"Oh shit!" Dolores stuffed her envelope into her apron pocket and took off in the opposite direction. "Come on, Norma! We got a lotta work to do!"

I went to the front door and lugged my father up the single step into the luncheonette.

"Merry Christmas, doll!" Dolores shouted from the Corey coffee machine. "I'm makin' ya a fresh pot!"

"Merry Christmas to you, too, Dolores!" Dad waved as I rejoined her behind the counter. "I'll take a cheese sandwich!"

"Anything you say, doll. You're the best!"

Brent Jamison was the only customer sitting within earshot. He snickered until I threw a little barb at Dolores that came flying back at me like a boomerang.

"Ass-licker," I said.

"Cocksucker," she retorted.

I froze for a second, not knowing whether she had meant that literally or figuratively. I didn't dare look at Brent in that moment. Knowing that I might inadvertently reveal myself with the wrong reaction, I thought it best to be blasé, reacting nonchalantly, more like she had just called me *bird-watcher* or *philanthropist.*

"I'll get the sandwich," I said.

"I'll get the coffee," she retorted.

The family began to gather at the brick house around six. Mom's sister helped her in the kitchen while Nonny toddled around handing out the "envelopes" and Poppy sat unnoticed on the couch. Everyone cooed over Judy and Charles's six-week-old little girl and noted the irony that Dad's first grandchild had been born on Election Day.

Aunt Rosie weighed in about five pounds lighter and an inch shorter that year because of the osteoporosis. But you could still count on her to tell the truth when queried about her health. "Rotten!" she carped as John and I laughed at her frankness. Then she pinched her face into that little-old-lady smile, seemingly satisfied that she had played to her audience.

Dad rolled up alongside the table in the den, where Mom had laid out the appetizers. He looked so happy. I don't know if it was the shrimp cocktail that was contributing to his sense of well-being—or if it was the sheer satisfaction of his council committee finding an alternative site for the first-aid squad building—as promised. Or maybe he was just happy to have gone three months without a bladder infection.

Dad was now outfitted with a rubber device that slipped over his penis like a condom and allowed his urine to drip freely down a tube and into a bag that was strapped to his ankle. The entire operation was completely hidden and undetectable under his pants. And since it was noninvasive, it reduced the risk of bladder infections that came with frequent catheterization.

Whatever the reason, Dad seemed ready to celebrate.

Right before we sat down to dinner, the anniversary of Dad's paralysis was finally acknowledged in vague references and incomplete thoughts. "Can you believe it's been a year?" Judy switched the baby to her other shoulder, rocking back and forth and pushing Reggie's snout away.

But Mom was more fatalistic, bringing down her cleaver like she was pronouncing a life sentence. "Well, this is what it will be from now on." She hacked off the top portion of the *finocchio* and separated the stalks, breathing in the aroma of the licorice-scented vegetable. "Every Christmas Eve we'll stop and tick off another year."

She carried the dish into the dining room and placed it next to the salad. The table had been extended to capacity with extra chairs shoehorned in to accommodate the overflow of family.

"Okay, let's eat!" Mom commanded with a single clap as everyone squeezed into his or her place.

And now that the back porch had been converted into a den, there was an open archway where the dining-room windows used to be, allowing plenty of room for Dad to roll up to the head of the table.

"More coffee, anyone?" Mom came in from the kitchen holding the pot as I plucked another *taralle* off the tray of homemade cookies that were stacked up like icy golf balls in the middle of the table.

"Too much!" Nonny patted her chest and grimaced like she had heartburn. "I got agita!"

So did I, but that didn't keep me from gobbling down the traditional white sweet. "I'll have shum coffee," I answered with my mouth full of cookie. "Ish weird."

"Oh, I know," Mom defended as I washed the *taralle* down with some hot Maxwell House. "The icing didn't come out right this year."

"No, I mean, it's weird. Last year at this time—well, everything's so normal. It's just weird."

"I'll have another cup!" Dad ignored my comment while locking his arm around the handlebar of his wheelchair so he could reach across the table for another slice of cheesecake or whatever else was on the table looking festive and delicious.

My mind insisted on dipping below the surface, however, where Dad's urine flowed freely down the hidden tube and into the calibrated bag strapped to his ankle.

How do you do it, Dad?

"Let's open that bottle of anisette that Angelo gave me today," Dad prompted. I went to retrieve the box from under the tree and Judy went for the little glasses. "Did I tell you what happened the first time I took the van to Bricktown to see the baby?"

Dad recounted how he had become quite adept at maneuvering his van around the local streets of West Long Branch, but that his first attempt at an exit ramp off the parkway had sent him toppling over from the centrifugal force. He had managed to keep one hand on the wheel, steering blindly, until decelerating enough to pull himself back up in the wheelchair. Gasps gave way to laughter as we all imagined the sight of it.

"Reggie!" Even the dog was excited by the story, nuzzling crotches from under the table as Mom jumped up and swatted his snout. "Oh my God, Clint, that's not funny! Honestly!"

She disappeared into the kitchen to start frying up the dough.

"So, Clint, you running for reelection next year?" One of my uncles turned the topic to local politics. "Your term is up, right?"

"I'm thinking about it," Dad dodged the question like a true politician.

"Here's to Clint!" My uncle raised his glass of anisette. "And may he be reelected and stay the hell off the Garden State Parkway!" Another roar of laughter filled the dining room.

When Mom returned with the tray of *zeppoli,* I couldn't dig in fast enough. I was shocked to hear Dad say that it had been a "good year" but was downright uncomfortable when he shifted the attention to me. I cringed at any reference to the good and dutiful son who had dropped everything to take over the family business.

"To Steven!" Dad toasted me, citing my dedication to the luncheonette, though my smile was as leaden as fried dough.

I was smiling on the outside, but resisted letting in the sentiment. I wasn't ready to hear my father's words. If anything, I felt more in tune with Poppy, sitting grimly at the other end of the table, sighing.

29.
CORN FLAKES
AND A
NOTABLE PASSING

Get me outta here!

Most of the old regulars from the luncheonette were completely unaware of how miserable I had become. I think they relished my sunny facade—even cheered it on—coming to rely upon my smiley rendition of Good Kid. I think it made them feel nurtured and safe, like the familiar aroma of fresh-brewed coffee that filled the air at Clint's Corner.

But by the spring of 1982, the facade began to crack.

I don't remember exactly what got to me first, but it may have been the morning I looked up from my grilling to find Old Man Pascucci sitting bare-foot at one of the tables, whittling away at the side of his right foot with a pocketknife, flicking dead skin onto the floor of the luncheonette.

"MR. PASCUCCI!" I shouted as all conversation and spoon clinking came to a screeching halt.

The immigrant landscaper was about to flick off another one when he looked up and fired back at me defiantly. "I GOTTA CORNS!" *Flick.*

"Well—FUCK!"

Stanley was not used to me losing my temper. He pulled his cap down over his eyes and brought one hand to his face like Jack Benny. Customers from Half Cup Harold clear down to Googie the Gizmo shuffled uncomfortably on their stools like they were attending their first ACOA meeting. For several seconds, everyone had shut the fuck up except for Peggy Lee, who continued to belt out "I Love Being Here with You" from the safety of LITE-FM, oblivious to the mood swing in the luncheonette.

Old Man Pascucci pulled on his right sock as Dolores came barreling in for the save like Molly Pitcher at the Battle of Monmouth. "Here ya go, bay-bay, this one's on the house!" She lowered her head and threw me a rare direct look over the top of her Coke-bottle glasses.

Martin Leslie Pembrook went back to his *Times* crossword puzzle and Stanley started to whistle again as Old Man Pascucci approached the counter with one bare foot and an empty cup to claim his free coffee. He looked at me.

"No you worry. Everyting a-good."

"*Rrranny bozke!*" Dolores commented. "How long you been in this country that you still don't matriculate good English? Jesus!" She poured his coffee. "Here, I'll even let you do your own sugar."

"Fuck." I muttered another little one for good measure.

"Whoa, Steve-o!" Brent Jamison stood at the counter applying lip balm with his pinkie, having arrived just in time for my outburst. "Late night?"

"I wish."

"Hey, doll! I know just what you want!" Dolores stopped on her way back to the coffee station to tell Brent what he was having for breakfast. "I'm gonna make ya some nice sunny-side with bacon."

"Maybe something quicker, Dolores—"

"Off to see a *client*?" I interrupted.

"Well, actually, Steve-o, we're on our way to the travel agent to pick up our tickets." He turned and waved to his wife, who was glowing over at table three, a big smile on her face for a change. "Candy and I are going to Florida next week for Easter. You know she's pregnant again?"

"Congratulations, bay-bay!"

"Yeah, Brent. Congratulations."

"*Boychick,* make that two orders of sunny-side with bacon—we're havin' a bay-bay!"

"No, Dolores—" Brent tried to protest, but Big Bobby and Flip had just walked in the front door and drawn her attention.

"And two porkroll-egg-and-cheese sandwiches for my Jersey Central boys. Come on—move your ass!" She gave me an openhanded slap right across my *poyzladki* as I whirled around, the blood rushing to my face, not to mention my sore buttock.

Dolores shouted to the customers. "I know what ya want, boys!" They hadn't even put their hard hats down on the empty chairs and she was already dashing over with two cups of coffee.

"Do me a favor, Steve-o." Brent hooked both thumbs onto his belt and tugged like it was getting too tight. "Could you please hold the bacon?"

"Already starting to show?" I sneered.

Brent huffed at me before returning to his table, where he and Candy leaned in and tapped foreheads, giggling like a couple of schoolgirls.

"*Today* they decide to switch to Yoo-Hoo," Dolores muttered on her way to dump Big Bobby and Flip's coffees in the sink. "And make me a half a number four—extra spiced ham—to go!"

"Who the fuck eats *gabagool* at ten-thirty in the morning?" I groused to the slicer as one of the two Anitas waved from the register.

"Extra onions! Thanks, babe!"

Grrrr.

"What a crank ass you are today!" Dolores came up behind me at the Bay Marie.

"I am not!" I whined, turning just in time to catch Old Man Pascucci whittling away at the other foot. "Mr. Pascucci!"

He looked up at me and shrugged. "I no finish the *lefta* one!" *Flick.*

"Well—fuck!"

"I'll stone the grill today—you can sweep up the dead skin."

"What?" John was incredulous when I told him what Old Man Pascucci had done that morning. "How come I always get the shitty jobs around here?" he joked.

But I remained staunchly humorless as we served the final customers of the day and started to clean up.

John had gotten the first dose of my foul mood when he arrived at about noon to work the lunch rush and took an order for a baloney sandwich. "Think!" I cross-examined him. "Do we now, or have we *ever* served baloney in this fucking place?!"

Dolores had jumped in for the save when she zoomed past on her way to the Bay Marie and walloped me on the side of my head. "Give 'm salami with a shitload of mayo—they won't know the difference."

John had pretty much steered clear of me the rest of the afternoon until I broke the ice with the dead-skin story.

But Herck the Jerk didn't give a shit about Old Man Pascucci's corns. "Gimme a rare hamburger—and another one to go." He drew deeply on his fourth Lucky then exhaled in our direction. "I have to feed my faggot nephew," he complained.

Dolores had already counted her tips and was about to leave when she saw that I was ready to blow again. She tossed her pocketbook under the counter and jumped back into active duty. "I'll get ya a fresh cup of coffee, hon."

"Gimme a Pepsi."

"I know, hon," she said, running down to the fountain while I threw on the burgers and took cleansing breaths at the grill.

The luncheonette had emptied out and John was starting to sweep the floor.

"Why don't you get going, Dolores? John and I will be fine." I had plopped the burger down in front of Herck and placed the to-go order in a bag next to his Pepsi.

"Okay, then. I'll get goin'." Her grandsons were visiting from out of town. "We're gonna color Easter eggs!" Dolores bubbled as she swiped a bottle of vinegar from the shelf over the Bay Marie, grabbed her pocketbook, and ran out the back door.

I was stoning the grill when Herck dropped his half-eaten burger onto the plate and walked over to the bathroom, tripping up the small step that led inside. "Goddammit!" He shut the door behind him.

He emerged a few minutes later, darted over to the counter to grab his hat, and scurried down to the register. I noticed how gaunt he had become in the past few months, his skin hanging off his bones like wet rags slung over a towel rack, the rim of his fedora practically wide enough to cast a shadow over his hollow face and slip of a body. But for a change, there was no protest over the cost of his order as he quickly paid me and vanished out the front door.

When I went to clear the counter, I saw that Herck the Jerk had left behind the brown bag containing his faggot nephew's hamburger. "John, see if you can catch the asshole before he gets to his car." I held up the bag as John emerged from the bathroom with a funny look on his face. "What?"

"Steven, you have to come see this, you won't believe it." He giggled. "It won't go away!"

"What? What do you mean?" I was annoyed.

"Just come look for yourself!" He put his hand over his mouth to suppress his laughter. I followed him into the bathroom, where he pointed into the toilet bowl at a gritty bowel movement that was about the same size (and apparent density) as a small house pet.

Disgusted, I immediately flushed. The water *whooshed* down the drain, but the unwelcome visitor bobbed around, not going anywhere, as the bowl refilled. I flushed again and again. But each time, it just shifted around a little bit until settling back down like a beached whale.

John was laughing so hard at this point that tears streamed down his face, but I was stubbornly controlled. I stormed out of the bathroom to get something and returned a minute later.

"Here, John, use this." I handed him a wire hanger. He stopped laughing. "Well?"

Mock horror came over his face when he realized the task I had just placed before him; the three of us—John, me, and the big BM—locked in a standoff.

"No way I'm touching that." John put up both hands in self-protection and started to laugh again. "That has to be Mr. Herck's!"

"John," I stated with all the uptight authority of a man of science, "that can't possibly have come out of him!"

John looked at me, incredulous.

Once I started to laugh, I couldn't stop. It was as though the dam holding back fifteen months of tension had finally given way. But I hated losing control in front of my brother—or anyone else, for that matter. It frightened me.

They might see that I was not perfectly up to the task of Good Son, Family Savior, Mr. Long Black Coat from New York, or whatever. Pick a role.

What if the laughter were to give way to crying, and all the fear and anger and frustration I was harboring were to be exposed for everyone to see? I was ashamed to feel this way, for surely it was my father who had made the real sacrifices. Mine, after all, were inconsequential. I was inconsequential.

But at least the laughter felt good.

John smiled at me, looking happier than I had seen him in a year, as I momentarily traded one role for another: Attila the Luncheonette Manager was just Big Brother again.

I ran to answer the phone.

"Oh, hi, Dad! What's up?" I could hear the wire hanger clinking against the porcelain as John guffawed from behind the bathroom door.

"Your mother wants to know if you're coming to dinner tonight?"

"What are we having?" I was still tittering.

"What's so funny?"

"You had to be there," I puffed, still catching my breath. "We missed you at lunch today."

"Were you guys busy?"

"The place was a madhouse." I sighed. "But the cigar box is full!"

"Yeah, the business has been pretty good. I was hoping to finish paying Poppy back for the down payment, but you know him, he won't hear of it."

"Not such a bad battle to lose."

"Listen, Steven, I know you don't want to do this forever, but you know the luncheonette is yours if you want it. Otherwise—it may take a while—but if you want, we can talk about selling it."

My heart started to pound.

Strangely, I felt the same fright I'd experienced on Christmas Eve 1980 when I'd watched my father falter. It was so swift and unexpected—plucked out of one life and dropped into another. I just wanted to be in control again. *What's going to be taken away next?* I had thought.

Shit! I was losing my confidence. I didn't know if I could change directions again. I was so disconnected from my life in New York and the dreams that had gone with it, that the luncheonette—bad days and all—had become more of a sure thing. Safe. I think I was afraid to leave. If only I could really believe that Dad was going to be okay. That *I* was going to be okay. If only I could reclaim my nerve.

"Dad, let's talk about this later," I said abruptly.

"Okay."

"So where were you today? How come you didn't come in for lunch?"

"I had a private meeting with Patsy and Jim and a few of the other Democrats."

"Really?" I sensed that something was up. "What was that about?"

"Well"—he started slowly—"you know that my term on the borough council is up at the end of the year."

"Yeah, so have you decided to run for reelection in November?"

"Well, not exactly," Dad explained. "You know that Henry Shaheen has decided to step down?"

"Yeah?"

"So . . ." He paused before breaking the big news to me. "I've decided to run for mayor of West Long Branch."

"Oh my God, Dad. Congratulations! Oh shit! Has this town ever elected a Democrat for mayor?"

"Not since the twenties."

"Wouldn't it be safer to just go for your old council seat? Isn't that more of a sure thing?"

"Well, sometimes you just have to take the chance."

I could almost hear the gleam in his eye.

"That's incredible, Dad. I'm so happy for you!"

Really.

I felt a twinge of sadness deep inside.

Guest Check

TABLE	SERVER	240128	GUESTS

PART III

TAX

PLEASE CALL AGAIN

30.
OUR FATHERS

On October 6, 1982, the race for mayor was still one month away—though some of the old regulars were campaigning for attention like there was no tomorrow.

"DOLOOORES!" Tombstone held on to his temples for dear life, his headache intensified by the sound of his own voice. "This is a special occasion, so listen up!"

"Yeah, a special occasion—for your *wife*—now that she chucked you out on your ass!" Dolores snarled on her way down to Carmen with a three-egg omelet—extra cheese, double ham, toasted bagel, but hold the potatoes.

"So what'll it be, Tombstone." I yawned. "A dozen runny eggs, extra greasy?"

"Ooooh!" He groaned into his palms.

Half Cup Harold sat politely to the gravedigger's left, raising his hand like a schoolboy. "I'd like a refill, if you please—thank you, kind sir!"

"Mornin', folks!" Stanley squeaked like the hinges on the back door, caught a glimpse of the company, then dropped his voice several registers. "Mornin', Tombstone."

"Rrrrr," he growled back as the front door flew open and the Syrians rushed inside about ten minutes behind schedule.

"Two regulahs!" Isaac demanded.

"And a poppy bagel with a schmeah—and scrape off half the seeds!" Elliot waved to me. "Steven, when ah we going to tawk about yaw new stereo?"

"Don't be pissed," I said, scooping cream cheese out of the Bay Marie. "I already got one on sale at the mall."

"Schmuck! I coulda gotten you a deal!"

"Sorry, I'll go to confession!" I handed the bagel off to Dolores, whose wig started to inch up when she darted down to the front with their orders.

"Speakin' of specials," she hawked like a carnie, "we got somethin' special for *you* this morning!" Dolores dug deep into an apron pocket that was large enough for a small kangaroo, and sifted through kitchen checks, Pall Malls, and some emergency cosmetics. "Here we go, hon!" She handed Elliot a clump of SORRENTINO FOR MAYOR bumper stickers. "Hand 'em out to the boys!"

"Fantastic!" He waved them in the air as he rushed out to the bus to New York.

"There you go, *boychick,* a whole shitload of Syrian Jews! If they're votin' for your dad, he's definitely gonna win!" She gave her wig a sharp yank down to punctuate the point, but I was uncomfortable.

"Dolores, my father was very clear: no electioneering at the luncheonette!"

"I ain't electioneerin', I'm just trying to get 'm some votes!"

Stanley whistled at us from the other end as a reminder that he hadn't placed his order yet. "I'll take a coffee, a Knipp's, and one of them bumper stickers, if ya got any left."

"One *SORRENTINO FOR MAYOR,* comin' up!" Dolores vaulted down to the other end of the counter, where the campaign materials were stacked on the bottom shelf. Tombstone leaned forward to watch her bend over.

"Ya got my vote!" He settled back onto his stool, unfazed by the finger she shot back at him. He howled at her again, "DOLOOORES!"

"Christ! They can hear ya over at Mount Caramel Cemetery! Don't you have to get to work soon?"

"Listen, buttercup," he flirted, his voice still drowning in morning phlegm, "I want a dozen poached eggs in a bowl with a lotta melted butter on top."

"Ugh!" Dolores looked at me. "No wonder Brenda threw 'im out." She put her hand to her throat and grimaced like she was going to puke. "I'll fix the prick up." She handed him a bumper sticker before bending over to pull a dozen eggs out from the fridge under the Bay Marie.

"Hmm." Tombstone looked her up and down. "Dolores, toots, I just thought of a great idea!"

She stood up, wielding the carton of eggs like she was going to bop him with it, the refrigerator door still ajar. Half Cup Harold sat by primly, folding his hands on the counter like he was attending a Communion breakfast, as the gravedigger continued.

"Listen, Dolores, you got that whole three-bedroom ranch all to yourself over there." He rubbed his three-day stubble as a nasty smile came over his face. "Why not take in a nice boarder?" Tombstone flexed his eyebrows at her like Groucho Marx.

"Because," Dolores replied swiftly and without calculation, "I'd rather jerk off than let the likes of you in my house!" Beat. Snap bra. Kick the fridge shut. Exit counter left.

Half Cup Harold's reaction might best be described as a model for the classic Hollywood spit-take, though I began to bellow. I hadn't laughed that hard in five months, not since John and the Battle of the Bowel Movement.

I barely noticed that the phone was ringing.

"Oh hi, Dad!" I was still composing myself, standing near the cash register, listening to my father deliver some news on the other end of the line. "Yeah . . . yeah . . . oh shit." I could see Dolores through the service window back in the kitchen, dropping a dozen eggs, one at a time, into a pot of boiling water. I looked down the row of customers hunched over their coffees and rolls, all satisfied for the time being, except for the gravedigger, who waited impatiently for his breakfast to come and his hangover to pass.

I hung up the phone and just stood there for a minute, unable to move.

Poppy was dead.

I was scared to death the first time I attended a wake at the Damiano Funeral Home. I was thirteen and Aunt Mary's dearly departed husband was slated to be my first "body." Nervously stalling for time when I entered the ornate foyer, I etched my name neatly into the guest book. All I could hear was my aunt Rosie's voice in my head from the night before, complaining about having to go to the wake: "I can't stand that smell!" Grateful for the warning, yet terrified, I held my breath as I approached the casket, trying to stave off the formaldehyde fumes or the sinister odor of human decay—or whatever it was that had repulsed her. It wasn't until I took a necessary breath in front of my dead uncle that I realized Aunt Rosie had been referring to the gladiolas, not the corpse.

I quickly outgrew that childhood fear of death, and had attended many wakes at Damiano's since. But when Poppy finally succumbed to congestive heart failure, I discovered that I had developed a much more grown-up fear.

I walked the half block from my apartment to the funeral home, avoiding the embarrassment of parking my beat-up 1972 blue Plymouth Duster alongside the coiffed gardens and meticulous landscaping that framed the stately structure. Vida Damiano and her son, Buddy, who was also heir apparent to the family business, stood stoically on either side of the large front porch outside the main entrance, welcoming visitors into their parlor of death.

My father's Chevy van sat conspicuously out front in the handicapped parking space. The visitors pouring in to pay their final respects to the Mayor of South Broadway couldn't help but notice the SORRENTINO FOR MAYOR bumper stickers affixed to the chrome on the front and back of the vehicle. I'm not sure that Dad had intended to use the occasion to pick up a few votes, but I *am* sure that Poppy would have insisted.

I signed the guest book in the foyer and made my way into the large anteroom, where rows of cushioned chairs were set up for the overflow from the main room. My brother Michael squirmed uncomfortably in one of them, having already announced that he would not be viewing the body and declaring the whole process to be maudlin. John stood off to the side with his hands in his pockets. I nodded to my brothers and a few of my cousins before entering the main parlor.

I tapped Dad on the shoulder as I passed him, avoiding any eye contact while skirting my way through aunts and uncles before kneeling in front of the casket. I whispered a stilted Lord's Prayer then leaned over and kissed Poppy's cold forehead.

The hand I felt on my shoulder was my mother's. Despite all the stories of her father's despotic reign over his family and businesses, Mom had always said, "He was like a different person when the grandchildren came along." I was relieved that she was dry-eyed at the moment, not knowing how to offer her comfort and afraid to ask for some for myself. I hugged her stiffly. Behind her, Nonny stood a little taller than usual with the help of a fresh bouffant and a rare foray into heeled shoes that must have pressed painfully against her bunions. Despite her seventy-five years, the only wrinkles on her face formed when she smiled. I approached her, leaned over, and cried in her arms.

Within a half hour, both rooms were filled to capacity as a long line formed to the right, at times reaching all the way back to the foyer. The mourners made their way up to the casket, then circled back along the front row, where they greeted Nonny and her children and their spouses. A seat had been removed at the end of the row for my father in his wheelchair. I didn't leave his side the entire night. In fact, I clung to him.

Meanwhile, Vida and Buddy had come inside and were monitoring the proceedings like proud party planners at a black-tie affair. We all watched Great-aunt Fanny slowly wobble up alongside the coffin in all her mourning glory. Her daughter tried to dissuade her from kneeling, probably worried she might not be able to get back up, but the large old woman insisted. I hadn't seen her since Great-uncle Freddy's wake two years before in that same room, when Poppy had stood by his brother's casket wailing at the heavens. That night, Great-aunt Fanny had fumed at him like Mount Etna. But now she respectfully leaned in—probably checking to make sure that he was really dead—before her daughter helped her to her feet so she could greet the family. The big widow embraced the little one, then made her way down the line. Two years ago she had asked me, "How's that New York goin', dear?" I'm not even sure she recognized me this time.

But everyone seemed to recognize my father. Whoever was left of old Long Branch shook his hand, nostalgic for the section bread from Tarantolo's Bakery. The newer generation, who had migrated the couple of miles into West Long Branch, knew Dad more currently through the luncheonette or the borough council. They lined up, too, to offer their sympathy—and some additional messages.

After swinging by the casket and circling back, each visitor stopped and took Nonny's hand. "I'm so sorry, Mrs. Tarantolo" was followed by multiple choruses of "I'm so sorry . . . I'm so sorry," one each for Mom and her four siblings, as the mourners made their way down the line, finally ending at my father with "Good luck in the election, Clint!" When Ted Kander, a prominent West Long Branch Republican, paid his respects to the corpse then came through the line, he shook my father's hand and said, "Good luck, Clint. I'll be rooting for you." As he walked away, Dad turned to me and whispered, "Bullshit!"

Once the entire procession of mourners had passed by the casket and greeted the row of family, Vida nodded to Buddy, who stepped forward among the towers of gladiolas and elaborate sprays, cleared his throat, and read from the Scriptures: "Father, God of all consolation, in Your unending love and mercy for us You turn the darkness of death into the dawn of new life."

Through it all, the family patriarch lay in his coffin, his gold tooth hidden forever behind sewn lips. I didn't realize it till then, but my grandfather had always served as a buffer around my father's mortality. As long as Poppy was alive, I felt protected from the prospect of my father's death. But now Dad had notched up into a place where I could perceive him to be "next." *And then who?* I hadn't even begun my life at twenty-five, and already the line of succession was catching up to me. And worse, the two men on whom I could always count for strength and protection were now a dead man and a paraplegic.

At the end of the reading, I noticed that Dad had tears in his eyes.

When we buried Poppy the next day, I began to feel like one of the living dead. It seemed that life was becoming defined only by what could be taken away. The dreams and optimism that had once driven me into the city to grab the brass ring were becoming buried by the fear that I had to give it back. I thought about Parris. He must have finished his tour by then and moved on to something new.

I hated how stagnant the days felt.

For the next few weeks, I found myself going through all the motions of scrambling eggs and shredding lettuce, keeping a watchful eye on that man in the wheelchair over at table one. Some nights, I joined Dad and his campaign workers stuffing envelopes and making phone calls, while other nights I drove into Asbury Park and paced the perimeter of the center bar at the Odyssey or searched the faces around the pool table in the back room for signs of life.

I got home one night around eleven, still weary and numb, and feeling as empty as the two hang-ups on the Emerson answering machine that Elliot the Syrian had gotten me wholesale. I walloped the "erase" button to clear the tape, changed into a pair of sweats and a T-shirt, and collapsed onto my love seat in front of the television.

I jumped when the phone rang a few minutes later, but was more surprised to hear the sad voice at the other end.

"Hi, Steve-o."

"Brent?"

"Yeah, that's me," he slurred.

"Well, it's only taken you like a yeeeeear to call."

"I still come to see you at the luncheonette," he whined.

"You sound like shit. Where are you calling from?"

"I'm at a phone booth just around the corner by Fine Fare." Silence. "Do you think I could come over?"

"I don't know," I said, wondering if Brent had forgotten at that relatively late hour that he had a wife at home about to give birth to their second child. But I didn't give a shit. There was a pit inside me that ran deeper than a grave at Mount Carmel—and just maybe I could fill it up with something that felt like love.

"Yeah," I relented, "come on over."

31.
ONE FROM COLUMN A—
NO SUBSTITUTIONS

"I'll tell you what kind of mayor your father will make!" Gertie pulled a serrated knife and a grapefruit out of her pocketbook. "Hand me a bowl, dear."

"Who asked for this, sister?" Herck the Jerk pushed his glass of Pepsi back toward Norma. "Gimme a coffee!"

"I'm trying to tell a ssstory here, you old coot!" Gertie swung around to Herck as he started to light up a Lucky. "Let me bum one of those."

"Fffff!" He even offered her a light as Dolores muttered to Norma and me over by the grill.

"One of these days I'd like to slip a little somethin' into his coffee. Ya-know-wadda-mean?"

Yeah, a stool softener.

Gertie exhaled an airy combination of spittle and smoke as she tried to continue with her story. "Ssso anyway—"

"Dad's here!" Flip dropped his porkroll-egg-and-cheese sandwich onto the plate, but Big Bobby had already run over to hold the door.

"I got 'im!" I called, handing my spatula off to Norma.

Gertie spun halfway around on her stool, crossing her legs like Shirley MacLaine on a grand piano. She watched as I leaned the wheelchair back and hauled my father up that single step into the luncheonette—just one of the obstacles he faced on that election day.

"Hello, sssweetheart!" She blew him a kiss.

"Hi, Gertie . . . hi, hi . . ." Dad waved to the other old regulars as he pulled up to table one and adjusted the patterned tie he had chosen for the big day.

"Gimme a hamburger!" Herck the Jerk barked to no one in particular.

"Ssso anyway!" Gertie continued when I got back behind the counter. "Let me tell you what kind of mayor your father will make."

"I'm listening," I assured her while tossing Herck's patty onto the grill.

Gertie was precutting all the sections of her grapefruit before eating it, reminiscing about her days in the school system back in the late sixties when my father sat on the local board of education. "Remember when I was sssubbing for Bea Lippel in the sssixth grade? You were in that class, did I ever tell you this ssstory, dear?"

"Uh, no," I said cautiously, eyeing my father at table one, where Angelo had just joined him. Norma was within feet of taking their order, but she never had a chance. Dolores had headed her off at the pass by running out from the north side of the counter.

"I got it!" Dolores claimed her territory, leaving Norma to tend to the Jerk.

"Where's my goddamn burger?"

Gertie rolled her eyes, dropped her serrated knife back into her pocketbook, picked up the cigarette that had rolled away from her ashtray, and took a drag. "Well, back then, a sssubstitute teacher at the Frank Antonides School got a lousy fifteen bucks a day. Ha! I must've been nuts!"

"Steven, your father wants American cheese on white with mayo—I'll get his coffee—and a pepper and egg on sub bread for Angelo—I'll get his iced tea—I made it fresh today—and quit talkin'!"

"Ssso anyway." Gertie spooned out a section of grapefruit and put it in her mouth, wincing at the sourness. "I corner him one day back when this place was still Gallo's—your father was sitting right there—and I say, 'Clint, dear, do you know I'm only getting fifteen dollars a day to substitute-teach and that I have to pay my own cleaning lady twenty dollars a day?' " She looked over her shoulder to make sure Dad was in earshot. "And do you know what he had the nerve to say back to me?"

"What?" I dared prompt.

"He said to me, 'Well, Gertie, then why don't you just ssstay home and clean your own goddamn house!' " Her face reddened as she wheezed with laughter. "So that's why I'm going to vote for your father for mayor!"

"Huh?"

Dolores had returned at this point to grab some place settings and make sure she wasn't missing anything. "Why's that, bay-bay?"

"Because he's fiscally responsible and I loooove 'im!"

"There you go, *boychick*, she's the biggest Republican in town. If she's votin' for your dad, he's definitely gonna win." Dolores adjusted her bra with a particular twist performed only when she wanted to appear authoritative.

Herck slithered off his stool with a cynical scowl and walked down to the bathroom, ignoring my father's nod as he passed by.

Well, so far, we're one for two.

Gertie may have been the biggest Republican in town, but even with her vote, Dad still had an uphill battle to overcome the lasting affects of acute transverse Democrat-*itis*.

But if Dad had had a rocky year or two, so had the local Republicans. After an investigation of one of their councilmen, a grand-jury presentment stopped just short of filing criminal charges, finding that the elected official had violated a conflict-of-interest law through a personal business transaction with the borough. Although Republican mayor Henry Shaheen had not been implicated in any way, he was no doubt worn down by the scandal and his own many years of service, and decided not to run for reelection. His obvious successor was council president Robert Shirvanian. Some thought that Dad's popular Republican opponent was a shoo-in since the borough had not elected a Democrat for mayor since Frank Antonides back in 1926.

Laura Quinn from the *Daily Register* would note in an article: "A member of the council for fifteen years, Shirvanian often directed council meetings with a sure voice and authoritative style when outgoing Mayor Henry Shaheen was not present." In that same article, Dad had been described as "soft-spoken and undemanding—a seemingly background figure."

"I never talk unless it's really necessary," Dad responded to Quinn's assertion in that same article. "My nonaggressive approach is needed in a town often rattled by partisan feuds. My primary concern is to see that everyone works together. I've never been a political animal."

Shirvanian's background was comparable to my father's years of elected service on the board of education and the borough council, as well as volunteer activities with the West Long Branch Sports Association and Community Center. He was also a handsome picture of athletic health with the arguable advantage of walking the town door-to-door in the weeks leading up to the election.

Unlike he had done in his past bids for council, my father had not been able to campaign like his opponent. He had had to rely on the lunchtime buzz and a plethora of flyers and mailings. Even then, some of the "Old Gatekeepers" (as Dad referred to the oldest and staunchest members of the Republican Party) were overheard criticizing him for appearing in campaign photographs in his wheelchair, saying it was "manipulative." Mom defended the pictures: "What were we supposed to do, prop him up against a tree?"

On election night, the large message board outside the Squires Pub restaurant, which had proclaimed WE CARE CLINT for the fund-raiser sixteen months earlier, touted a different greeting in large block letters: WELCOME WEST LONG BRANCH REPUBLICANS AND DEMOCRATS. As usual, the two parties would gather in large rooms at opposite ends of the complex that night to wait for the results. Part of the ritual called for the losing candidate, after a few Scotches, some miniature Reubens, and a swallow of humble pie, to cross the restaurant to the other camp and congratulate the winner. In this case, no one knew if that man would be walking or rolling.

Members of the family paced nervously around the large banquet room where Dad's supporters were waiting for the polls to close.

"I don't even want to think about what I'll do if he loses," my brother Michael said while hitting his right fist into his left palm as John fidgeted nearby. Judy distracted herself with calls home to Charles to check on the baby, and Irene wrung her hands and muttered nervously in Italian, "Oh, Gesù mio!"

The crowd dwarfed Rosie, Mary, and Angie, who contemplated their baby brother's success or defeat, holding soft drinks, their black pocketbooks dangling from their wrists. Nonny sat alone at one of the tables looking lost and disoriented without Poppy to watch out for anymore.

A waiter delivered a cup of coffee to Dad, who was at the front of the room with Uncle Tony leaning on his wheelchair and Angelo on the other side looking like W. C. Fields in profile, his unlit cigar held for effect. Someone was snapping a picture, but the three smiles looked forced and nervous.

"*Boychick!*" Dolores had gone extra heavy on the pancake, applied like she'd gotten a makeover at Damiano's, as she appeared at my side and placed a calming arm across my shoulders. "You people must be gettin' ready to shit yourselves!"

"Nice mouth."

"It's the new lipstick, doll. Come with me, Vivian's gettin' us some drinks."

"Not right now, Dolores." I held up my amaretto sour, the second in fifteen minutes. "I want to grab a spot with a good view."

The focal point of the room was a large easel-mounted chart with SORRENTINO and SHIRVANIAN listed alongside eight blank columns, one for each of the borough's voting districts. Both parties had a "challenger" posted at the eight polling places to watch the proceedings during the day. When the polls closed, members of the election board would open the machines and read off the totals next to each candidate's name. The Democratic and Republican challengers would scribble the totals down on a piece of paper, then run out to their cars and speed over to the Squires Pub to deliver their respective results to their respective banquet halls.

Jim Flanagan, one of Dad's friends and campaign workers, stood by the chart with a large black Magic Marker, pulling anxiously at his reddish beard and compulsively adjusting his horn-rim glasses. The stress of Election Day was wearing on him, but not so on Patsy Delehanty. The handsome woman was an exaggeration in word and look. She was Dad's campaign manager, standing guard on the other side of the chart, as unflappable in that role as she had been in raising more kids than anyone else in West Long Branch. Patsy checked the power on her calculator as Jim mulled over the blank boxes on the chart.

It was eight o'clock. The polls were just closing.

The decibel level of the crowd was rising like horns and sirens in a city traffic jam. I saw Dad gulp down the rest of his coffee and beckon to my mother to join him as he looked around for Judy and Michael and John. Whatever happened, he wanted his family around him. I tapped him on the shoulder. "We're all here, Dad." He smiled.

I checked my watch again: 8:05. The noise in the room intensified.

8:09 . . . 8:14 . . . finally, an unidentified voice shouted from the back of the room.

"Gerry's here with district eight!" About a hundred people had clustered near the front of the room, blocking access to the chart.

"Stand back!" Patsy Delehanty took charge as Jim Flanagan uncapped the black Magic Marker and assumed his position over the blank boxes. "Give him room!"

Gerry Warner from district eight was the first challenger to arrive. At first he looked confused by the crowd, as if he had come upon the scene of an accident. A path was finally cleared and Gerry's expression now held the smugness of a kid with a secret. He calmly made his way to the front of the room so he could read the tallies to Jim.

"Quiet!" Patsy fish-eyed the crowd and readied her calculator.

"Shirvanian—one seventy-two." He paused as Jim filled in the box. "Sorrentino—one ninety-eight."

The crowd roared its approval, but my father was surprisingly sedate and unenthusiastic.

"It's not very decisive." Dad spoke authoritatively to the few of us who were close enough to hear him. "District eight is where all those new homes are, lots of Democrats. We usually win it real big."

"But, Clint," Angelo chimed in, "that's where Shirvanian lives. You beat him in his own district!"

"I don't know what it means yet," Dad said. "Let's just wait."

My brother Michael looked at me and rolled his eyes, continuing to pound his fist into his palm.

Lucy Zambrano was the next challenger to appear breathlessly at the door. She stopped momentarily to get her bearings, then headed down the center of the room like she was walking the plank. She was stingy with her facial expressions, but the crowd clamored for any hint of how the numbers played out in her district.

"Shhhh!" Patsy scolded the impatient throng. "What have you got from six, Luce?"

Lucy brushed the hair away from her face. "Shirvanian—one sixty-eight." Her voice was shaking as Jim filled the number into the blank box. "Sorrentino—one fifty-three."

"Shit!" Angelo led a chorus of expletives throughout the room. Uncle Tony moaned. Michael looked up at the ceiling and gritted his teeth.

I looked at my father for a reading and was surprised to see a big smile come over his face. "Dad?"

"This is a good sign," he explained. "District six has the biggest block of Republican voters in town. We should have lost bigger. This is a good sign," he repeated.

For the next ten minutes, the challengers from five then two then seven then three then four rushed over from their polling places and into the Squires Pub, each one feeding his or her numbers to Jim Flanagan, the subtotals shifting back and forth, favoring Dad and then his opponent in a numerical seesaw.

All eyes in the room were fixed on the numbers. Interpreting. Analyzing. Some of the onlookers turned to my father, trying to glean any piece of information from a facial expression or an utterance that might predict the outcome. But the fact was, the votes were cast and now it was just plain old math.

By about 8:23, Dad carried a minuscule lead with seven of the eight districts accounted for. All that was left to report was district one. Traditionally, one had been heavily Republican, though it was also the district where my parents lived. People in the room looked to Dad for a call, but he only had one thing to say. "It's a toss-up."

"Dasha, I can't stand the tension," Vivian whispered to Dolores, her curves as smooth as the cocktail glass she held.

"Shit." Dolores was as lumpy as the bourbon on the rocks that rattled in her hand.

The crowd simmered anxiously in anticipation of either victory or defeat when the challenger from district one appeared at the back of the room. Bill

Diesinger's salt-and-pepper hair aimed slightly backward and up from his run across the parking lot. He was flushed and licking his lips, clutching the piece of paper where he had scribbled the totals from his district. All eyes followed him, looking for clues in his body language, but he stubbornly withheld them.

Jim Flanagan readied his marker and Patsy Delehanty hovered over her calculator.

Bill Diesinger reached the front of the room, looked down at his numbers, then straight into my father's eyes. His voice cracked.

"We won big!" Bill tossed his paper into the air as the pent-up tension of the crowd exploded into joyous screams and wild applause—with only one person remaining in his seat.

Challengers and Sorrentino sisters and luncheonette regulars surged forward, but Mom got there first and kissed Dad. Angelo put his unlit cigar to his mouth and applauded, waiting his turn to pose for more pictures. Judy's tears came from relief as Michael shouted "Yes! Yes!" John almost threw me off balance with a spastic and unexpected embrace.

For a minute, I lost sight of my father but finally wriggled myself into the core of the rabble. And there he was—the first Democrat to be elected mayor of West Long Branch in fifty-six years, and its first paraplegic one ever. Dad and I locked eyes and smirked at each other for one fleeting second. Then I threw my arms around him and burst into tears. I don't think I ever loved my father more than in that moment.

It was nothing short of a miracle that Dad had made it from Christmas Eve 1980 to Election Day 1982, though I couldn't help but wonder which of my own moments of glory never got to see the light of day, or what my life might have been had I been able to stay in New York. I stepped away as more of Dad's supporters rushed in to congratulate him, and walked over to the bar where Vivian and Dolores were reveling.

"You must feel like big shit tonight, huh, *boychick*?" Dolores clinked her glass against mine.

"I can't even describe it!" I raised my drink before filling my big sweet smile with a swig of amaretto sour.

Everyone started calling for Mayor-elect Sorrentino to give a speech. He rolled his wheelchair to the front of the room and did a K-turn in front of the podium, the overhead fixture focused on him like a spotlight. Jim Flanagan handed him the microphone and stood back, still pulling at his beard with one hand and wiping tears from his eyes with the other as my father took center stage. I hadn't seen Dad so exuberant since he had grabbed the microphone three years before at my sister's wedding, handling it like Sinatra and singing "My Way." His voice was now a little raspier, and he couldn't sustain a tone—but even from his wheelchair, he still had the swagger.

"Thank you, thank you." Dad quieted the crowd before continuing. "I don't know if this means anything, but you know"—his pause was contrived—"when I first went into politics, I was five-foot-eight—and now I'm three-foot-ten!"

The burst of laughter and applause that followed suddenly froze into a single blare like Glenn Miller's orchestra sustaining a chord on one of Dad's old records, the moment perfectly registered: Dad had officially entered his heyday.

I was swept up by the joy and excitement in that room, sharing in Dad's victory, but painfully aware just how far off course my own life had gone. I stood back smiling and applauding, slightly blinded by Dad's limelight. For years I had fantasized about a career on the stage, throwing myself into the New York scene, only to wind up back home. And now it was as if my father had made the grandest entrance into a Broadway musical. His illness hadn't robbed him of his eleven-o'clock number, but for me, acute transverse myelitis seemed to have been a showstopper.

Robert Shirvanian and a contingent of the local Republicans eventually made their way through the restaurant and into the Democrats' ballroom to congratulate the mayor-elect as photographers snapped the political adversaries in a friendly handshake.

Dad would wake up the next day to headlines in the *Press* and *Register* that would read SORRENTINO WINS MAYORALTY IN POWER SHIFT and HANDICAP NO OBSTACLE AS SORRENTINO SAILS TO VICTORY.

The *Village Voice* would probably have covered the story with a little more of an edge: SORRENTINO SCORES BIG WHILE SON SCORES PORKROLL.

I was so proud of my father that night, despite the unhappiness that I kept hidden just beneath the surface, but there were others who made no effort to contain their negative feelings.

A few of my father's Republican friends had angrily reported back to him the words of a small contingent of the "Old Gatekeepers" at the opposite end of the restaurant.

Ignorant Old Gatekeeper Man said, "Well, that goes to show ya—you just can't beat a wheelchair!"

Bitter Old Gatekeeper Woman replied, "Yeah, but not to worry—he'll never live out his term anyway!" With that, she buttoned up her cloth coat, unsnapped her leather clutch, and pulled out her car keys, ready to leave the Grand Old Party because she was no longer having fun.

It was jarring to hear Old Gatekeeper Woman's dire prediction amid all the whooping elation of that historic night in West Long Branch—especially since it echoed one of my greatest fears.

32.
SWEARING (IN)

Dad's mayoral term was slated to begin on New Year's Day 1983, adding a heightened sense of excitement and anticipation for my family that holiday season. Still, I found it difficult to get out of bed and go to that goddamn luncheonette on Christmas Eve 1982. But I did.

And while Dolores counted the bills in her Christmas bonus, I began to count my own fucking blessings. *Let's see now.* I had my quiet little bachelor pad near the funeral home—far from all that goddamn noise and life in New York City—*and* I was having an affair with a wonderful man who called me every six or eleven weeks when he could steal away from his wife. Although I sometimes missed his call and had to wait for the next cycle of availability, at least I saw Brent regularly at the luncheonette.

"Merry Christmas, Steve-o!" We had never really discussed our secret code, but I knew that when he stood all shouldery at the counter and said, "I'll have a tuna melt and a Diet Pepsi," he must have really meant, "I love you."

And that night at Christmas Eve dinner, except for one fleeting exchange between Mom and Judy while setting the table, the anniversary of Dad's paraplegia was barely acknowledged. There was much more attention being paid to those first steps that the baby was taking, and the big one that Dad was about to take a week later.

During dessert, I watched the mayor-elect dunk one of Mom's home-made cookies into his coffee, as everyone celebrated the recent election and Dad's stunning comeback in life. I joined in, too, my goddamn smile as icky sweet as the white icing on the homemade *taralle*.

But how could I feel so down when Dad was about to be sworn in as mayor? So what if he was getting more milestones to the gallon than my guzzling old Plymouth Duster? It's not like he was stopping me from taking new steps of my own.

John, Michael, and I, and a few other hands with questionable party affiliation, helped carry Dad up those twelve steps to Borough Hall on New Year's Day 1983. I was still feeling the drumming effects of the kamikazes I'd drunk the night before, but I was proud to watch my father solemnly swear to fulfill his duties as mayor to the best of his ability, so help him, God. Dad was sworn in to resounding applause from fellow councilmen, and all the family and friends who had gathered there at noon. But the Old Gatekeeper couple that would have preferred to see him propped up against a tree had decided to sit this one out, particularly since the new mayor's longevity was doubtful anyway.

Dad's singing voice never did make a comeback, though there were several attempts at a new standard called "The Luncheonette-Is-Yours-If-You-Want-It Rag." I was also struggling with tone and melody those days, but never missed a lyric in the "I'm-Sick-of-This-Place-and-I-Want-to-Get-Back-to-New-York-but-Let's-Talk-About-It-Later Blues." I guess that at some point, Dad had tired of hearing the same old refrain and finally hung out the "For Sale" sign.

It's barely worth mentioning the fact that we sold the luncheonette. I may have been demoted to soda jerk and freed of my managerial responsibilities, but by all appearances, nothing had really changed except for the new proprietor, a cerebral man named Sherman who happened to be part Cherokee.

I'd finally had the opportunity to leave—but I didn't take it. It's as if I was a prisoner and one day the warden said, "You're free to go." I looked around at my familiar surroundings, then at the door to an outside world that now seemed unfamiliar and foreboding. My sheet music and glossies had been stored away in a Pennfield Farms box for almost two years by now, and I only pulled the long black coat out of the closet for holidays and wakes. I had lost touch with my dreams of getting back to New York. My confidence was gone and I was clinging to the luncheonette for dear life.

Sherman was happy that I had decided to stay on, and that the "Mayor on Wheels" spent every lunch hour there, conducting his business and eating American cheese on white with mayo. But maybe it was his Native American heritage that made him wary of the woman who wore heavy pancake on her face like war paint, watching her every move as Dolores whispered to me at the grill, "Goddamn Indian."

There were other staff changes as well. John seemed to have lost his raison d'être when the new management decided to do away with the Sunday papers. I was sorry to see John go. I guess one of the reasons I had picked on him so much was that he reminded me of me. He was devoted to our father as well and always tried to be a good kid. But the resemblance ended in that he was able to see the headlines on the wall and move on from the luncheonette.

Little bastard.

Even Norma was able to walk away from the luncheonette when the time seemed right. The old regulars signed an oversize greeting card on her last day and we gave away free slices of a Mrs. Smith's chocolate cream pie. "I'm weally going to mish her," I said to Dolores with a mouthful as Norma threw in the apron.

"I know, *boychick,* but it's better this way," she reflected.

"Dolores, why are you so hard on her?"

"Oh, don't get me wrong—she's a nice girl—but she don't know how to move her ass."

I, at least, moved my ass out of the closet that year—sort of. Dolores had discovered the world of "adult" films when the new video store opened by the ShopRite. She would sample a few every weekend then report back to me on Monday with her reviews.

"Oh, Steven." She pulled me aside when Sherman and my father were out of earshot. "You gotta rent *Big Daddy Boot Camp IV*. I didn't know men could do all those things to each other!"

"Dolores, you like gay porno?" I whispered my astonishment.

"Sure, *boychick,* don't you?" For almost two years, Dolores had been dropping hints around me like horseshoes. Clearly, she knew my secret, but it was the all-male films that became the real icebreaker on the gay issue. I was now out to two people in town: my heterosexual boyfriend and my sixty-five-year-old fag hag.

Oh, life was good in '83!

"Okay, Sherman, move your ass!" Dolores flipped the switch on the Corey coffee machine as soon as she saw my father waving at the front window. "I'm makin' a fresh pot for the boss!" Almost a year had gone by, yet she still hadn't gotten everyone's titles straight.

Sherman folded his arms and glared at her from his post back in the kitchen. He was thrilled that Mayor Sorrentino had become a fixture at his luncheonette, but the pensive Native American had yet to figure out how to deal with Princess Running Mouth.

"I'll get your dad in." Sherman passed by as I shredded the lettuce, his gray eyes trained on Dolores, who was ringing up Googie the Gizmo's check.

"Hey Steve!" Dad waved as Sherman pulled him up the steps.

"Hi." I grunted back in response.

"Why do you turn into such a grouch when your father gets here?" Dolores said to me once Sherman had gotten him into place at table one, a job that used to be exclusively mine. "Go say hello to your father!"

"I have to set up the Bay Marie for lunch."

"Howdy, Mayor!" Stanley arrived earlier than usual. "Howdy, Mr. Steve— I'll have a ham and Swiss cheese—extra holes."

"I got it!" Dolores said while slamming a Pepsi down in front of him. "I know how ya like your holes!"

"Yep." Stanley took a sip.

Sherman glowered at her as the horn over the firehouse sounded its triple blasts for noon and the counter and tables began to fill up. The lunch rush had begun and Dad was open for business.

"Hello, Mayor, mind if I talk to you for just a moment?" Hoyt Gilman had a quick question about the borough's sanitation services and Mary Owen threw in her two cents about the recycling program. "Thank you, Mayor!" She didn't want to take too much of his time, though Hoyt lingered a minute longer at my father's portable office.

"Well, if it isn't the first son of West Long Branch!" Mrs. White, my seventh-grade science teacher from the Frank Antonides School, had become a regular at lunchtime. Twelve years earlier, she had raved about my ability to grasp the role of endoplasmic reticulum in protein synthesis; now, truth be told, I was just a little bit embarrassed to be wowing her with my tuna-fish sandwiches.

"Hi, Clint!" She waved, sitting down at table three with her colleagues from math and remedial reading.

Everyone greeted my father with salutations both formal and informal, though they were still warming up to the new owner, who spent most of his time back in the kitchen. Sherman nodded from the service window, where he was making pizza, the latest addition to our menu.

"Sherman!" Dolores shouted despite the fact that he preferred having the orders written down. "Gimme two meatball parms for the teachers!" She turned to me. "His balls ain't as good as Angie and Mary's."

"Yep." Stanley hunched over his ham and Swiss.

Dad heard the aside and looked up from his *Daily News* to share the laugh with me, but I looked away.

Angelo had come in the back door and was leaning on the ledge at the end of the counter, watching me make the tuna sandwich for Mrs. White. "Takin' somethin' to go, doll?" Dolores asked, rushing over to him.

"Hold your horses, Dolores. I just want to see what Big Steve is doing here." He pulled the cigar out of his mouth, trying to engage me in some banter, but I didn't even respond when Dolores pinched my ass.

"Leave 'im alone, Angelo, he's workin'. Now go sit the fuck down!"

"Hey, I'd like a little respect if you don't mind. That's my friend the mayor over there."

GUEST RECEIPT

SERVER

SWEARING (IN)

GUESTS
243

TABLE

"Yeahhh, big shit! We'll see what he's gonna do for the poor people."

"He's the mayor now." Angelo puffed on the unlit cigar. "Fuck the poor people!" He walked over to my father and put his arm around him like he was posing for the *Asbury Park Press*. "It's good to be the mayor!"

Dad was trying to catch his breath. His face had turned red but he wasn't looking so good. "Don't make me laugh, Angelo, I have a headache today."

"Okay, *boychick,* let's have a half a number four—extra *gabagool*—for Angelo, and make your father his cheese sandwich." She rushed down to the fountain and started pushing one of the pumps—to no avail. "Shit!" she yelled back into the kitchen. "Sherman! We're outta simple syrup! And gimme two slices to go!" I thought I detected discernible smoke signals coming out of Sherman's ears, but I turned my focus back to my father's lunch order.

"Dad, why don't you eat something healthier?" I lectured him from behind my Formica podium. "You don't take care of yourself!"

"I like my cheese sandwiches," he said sheepishly as Angelo looked down.

"What the fuck is it to you, *boychick*? Let the man have his fuckin' cheese sandwich!"

"Someone's gotta look after him," I mumbled while slapping a couple of slices onto Wonder bread.

"Oh shit!" Dolores tucked a lock of errant hair back under her wig when Sherman seemed to appear out of nowhere.

"Dolores, can I see you for a minute in the kitchen?" Chief Pizza Man looked pissed.

"Sure, bay-bay, you can see me back in the pantry if you want, it's more private."

"Yep." Stanley sucked up the rest of his Pepsi while Dolores was led away like a POW.

I was finishing the dishes a few minutes later when Dolores returned from the kitchen in a righteous huff.

"I told him good! I says, 'Sherman, I been in this business forty-one years—I don't take no shit from no one!' and he tells me, 'Dolores, you gotta tone it down,' and I says, 'I don't need this fuckin' job and I can walk outta here whenever I want to!' Uh-huh. I don't gotta tone it down for no one. Oh no, I told him good!" Her lips continued to move well after she had stopped talking.

"See you tomorrow, Mayor!" The teachers were rushing out the back door to get back to school before the next bell. "So long, First Son!" Mrs. White waved to me as I felt the shame of my unfulfilled potential.

I made myself a milkshake and leaned back against the fountain for a few minutes, watching my father sitting in his wheelchair, eating the cheese sandwich and rubbing his forehead.

Why didn't I leave this fucking place when I had the chance?

Fine Fare was running a special on Morton's chocolate cream pies for only sixty-nine cents—but I had to shop at this particular supermarket with great caution. Each week one of its customers was photographed by a hidden camera and featured in the *Atlanticville* as the "Mystery Shopper." If he or she stepped forward, they were awarded a fifty-dollar gift certificate. Things might have been tough for me, but I still didn't relish opening the local paper and seeing a picture of myself caught in a private moment, sniffing a cantaloupe or something. And even though the Morton's whipped cream topping didn't peak as high as Mrs. Smith's, the bargain price made it well worth the risk.

I put away the rest of my groceries as the pie thawed on the kitchen counter. When it became soft enough to slice, I cut it in two with the intention of limiting myself to half a pie. Before throwing the other half away—as a precaution—I sprinkled a generous amount of salt on it so that I wouldn't be tempted to fish it out of the garbage and eat it later on.

I walked around the apartment eating my pie, taking in my retro surroundings: Mom's stainless-steel canister set from the fifties resting atop the refurbished Hoover hutch in the kitchen, and Dad's shabby old recliner taking up a chunk of space in a living room the size of a cell block. At least the bedroom was large enough to accommodate the distressed chest of drawers from South Broadway, but I would have preferred an adult-size bed to the twin-size mattress and box spring against the wall, a leftover from my boyhood.

It was Thursday, October 20, 1983, a tough day at the luncheonette and a good night for pie. Exhausted from the day and crashing from my sugar fix, I was dead asleep before eleven.

The clock shined one-fifteen when the sound of the ringing phone startled me back to consciousness.

If that's Brent Jamison, tell him I'm too fat tonight and to call back tomorrow!

"Hello?" I cleared my throat. "What?" It was my mother's voice on the other end that I struggled to comprehend, even though the words she spoke were familiar ones.

"There's something wrong with your father."

33.
THE NATURE OF THINGS

The only information my mother had given me over the phone was that my father had gone to bed complaining of a headache. Tylenol had not helped and the pain had progressed so intensely that he was clutching his head and crying. She had never seen him like that. But what had really terrified her was the eerie way in which he had turned to her and articulated his experience: "Something's happening."

I thought I had already seen the worst. Standing at my father's side on Christmas Eve 1980 had been like witnessing an electrocution, watching his legs convulse for several minutes until they finally surrendered to a deathlike stillness. At least Dad had not been in pain. That scene replayed itself over and over in my head as I drove to the hospital, but a new image replaced it when I rushed into the emergency room that night.

There was my father clutching his throbbing head in his hands and thrashing from side to side, moaning.

"Is he okay?" I said to the guy in turquoise scrubs and sneakers.

"This is Dr. Pevner," Mom said as the young man nodded.

Dad barely acknowledged me, but still managed to answer some of the doctor's questions, with Mom filling in the blanks. At one point, Dr. Pevner and my mother turned their attention away from my father and spoke directly to each other. It was the first time since I had entered the room that Dad fixed his attention solely on me. I was frightened by the look of pain on his face and the sounds he was making. I felt awkward in that moment of intimacy and didn't know what to do or say.

That's when the moaning stopped.

Dad's facial expression turned ugly and his head rolled back. He began to stretch his mouth open like a baby bird soundlessly begging for food.

"Look at him!" I nudged the doctor. "He can't speak!"

Dr. Pevner yelled out "Stat!" or "Shit!" or something as a flourish of activity and medical jargon began to whirl around Dad. Mom and I stood back, helpless, like extras in a television drama.

That's when it hit me: I had just witnessed my father having a stroke.

"Can you believe this, Mom?" I asked as we waited in the hallway at one point. "Now he can't even speak."

Her response surprised me. "You know, at first I thought to myself, 'How much more can this man take?' " She looked up like she was seeing heaven through the fluorescent lighting. "And then I just thought, 'Okay, now we'll just deal with this next thing.' "

I wondered where the hell she had found all that courage. She just stood there, calm and resolute, while I hadn't felt such fear since Christmas Eve 1980.

You can be sure that a lot of porkroll-egg-and-cheese was served up the next day at the luncheonette as the old regulars listened to me recount in gestured detail how Mayor Sorrentino had lost his speech.

"Well, I'll be goddamned!" Googie the Gizmo took a bite out of his sandwich.

"Shit," Stanley chimed in. "I'll have coffee with mine."

"Who the fuck is parked in my space?" Dolores burst through the back door to start her shift, ignoring Sherman's previous requests to "tone it down." He glared at her from the service window.

Half Cup Harold sheepishly raised his hand and pulled out his car keys.

"Move it, Howard!" She was about to follow him out to the parking lot when she overheard Martin Leslie Pembrook offering me his condolences.

"I'm so sorry about your father, son," he offered, and went back to his crossword puzzle.

"What?" Dolores's apron must have ridden up on her in the car. She wiggled and pulled to get it back down. I told her what had happened.

"And then his head went back—like *this*—and his face got all contorted and he could no longer speak." For the third or fourth time that morning, I held for someone else's stunned reaction to my story.

"Rrranny bozke!" Dolores made the sign of the cross and wilted onto the end stool like a deflated old weather balloon. "It's just not fair, *boychick*. Fuck!"

I arrived back at Monmouth Medical Center just after noon. The drill was all too familiar: best place to park, use the side entrance, shortcut to ICU, through the automatic doors. Even the sight of my sister walking down the hallway with two cups of cafeteria coffee was a familiar one.

"Judy!" I called to her.

"Can you believe this?" She rolled her eyes.

"Have you been in to see him yet?"

"Oh yeah. He looks great."

Great?

I could hear my mother's voice as we approached. It was like listening to one person's side of the conversation when they are on the phone and you can't hear the responses. "Okay, Clint, do you want another sip? . . . Okay? . . . I'm going to put the bottle of juice on your nightstand . . . Okay? . . . Good . . . You can save it for later . . . Okay?"

Judy walked in ahead of me, handing one of the coffees off to Mom, who was busy rearranging the lunch tray, lowering the volume on the TV, and paying attention to other inconsequential details. And there was Dad, sitting up in bed eating a cheese sandwich. He waved to me with his free hand and smiled without making a peep.

"HOW—ARE—YOU—FEELING—DAD?" I spoke loudly and slowly, the way some people talk to the deaf or foreigners. Dad raised his sandwich into the air as if he were making one of his Christmas Eve toasts, nodded his head in the affirmative, and took another bite out of his sandwich.

"What do the doctors say, Mom?"

She explained to me a little more about the nature of the stroke based on the tests and examinations he had received that morning. Apparently a blood vessel had burst in his brain, affecting the area that controlled speech. The good news was that once the blood had a chance to dissipate, he could expect to start regaining his speech, though there was no guarantee of a full recovery.

I watched Dad gobble down his sandwich. He looked up occasionally, seemingly oblivious to Mom's recap.

The tests that morning may have been able to pinpoint the exact nature of the stroke, but nothing on those high-tech scans could explain to me why this man was still smiling.

How the hell do you do it, Dad?

34.
PARALYZED

Dolores's wig began to lose its elasticity.

The acrylic hair that used to inch its way up her head no longer necessitated a good yank down right in the middle of a rush of Syrians or a scourge of salads. But as the elastic lining began to stretch with age, it became prone to moving sideways with more of a free-floating effect. Although I feared that one day she was going to lose it altogether, I knew in my heart that I was going to be the first to flip my wig.

So much smoke had billowed off that grill and into my face that I barely noticed another year had slipped by. It didn't matter that my father was approaching the midpoint of his four-year mayoral term or that he was speaking in complete sentences again. I was still stuck at that luncheonette for no apparent reason. And who knew why I chose September 25, 1984, to finally snap—but I did.

I guess any number of events had led up to it.

Dolores first suspected that something was up when Pepsi Man restocked the Yoo-Hoo and knuckled up to the cash register with the bill. By the time she grabbed the straight ammonia and ran out to the tables for the rear view, I had already paid the guy and sent him on his way, my mind barely registering an impure thought.

"What's the matter?" She slammed her spray bottle down on the counter and rotated her wig about ten degrees to the left. "You don't wanna play no more?"

Maybe I was just overtired. I had been up late the night before watching Stephen King's *Cujo* on HBO while waiting for a call from the hospital, where my sister was giving birth to her second child. I could still see that rabid dog slamming itself against the car windows while Dee Wallace Stone remained trapped inside, cradling her asthmatic son. She had the choice of staying safely inside where no one could hear her screams—in which case the wheezing child would certainly die—or she could take the risk of venturing out into the world, where a big old pissed-off Saint Bernard foamed at the mouth and waited to pounce.

Or maybe I was still reeling from the message on my Emerson answering machine from the week before.

Beeeeep. "Hey Steve-o. It's about eight-thirty, Wednesday night. You there? Steve-o? Oh well, I only have about an hour. Hmm. Okay. Catch you next time." *Beeeeep.*

I tried talking to an old high school buddy of mine who called me one night to catch up. It was the first time I admitted to anyone how unhappy I had become. "But you've got so much going for you," he said. "You can pull yourself out of anything!"

After hanging up the phone, I rifled through my mental files, looking for anything I could use as a self-affirmation, but all I could come up with was *Hey, look at me—I can make a tuna-fish sandwich!*

"Dasha!" Vivian swept through the back door that day, her silk-lined coat flopping open around a cashmere cowl neck.

"Vwaj, you look goddamn gorgeous!" Dolores ignored Sherman's stern look from the service window.

Spotting an empty slot between Googie the Gizmo and Martin Leslie Pembrook, Vivian hopped up onto a stool.

"How you doin', Steven?" She searched her pocketbook for a compact then looked up and bragged. "Tex is taking me to New York today!"

Oh yeah, I remember that place.

"I'm running out to ShopRite," Sherman said as he came out through the swinging doors and looked at me. "Do you need anything?"

Shopping list: sense of humor, pot, chocolate cream pie, salt.

"We're fine," I answered sullenly.

"Okay, you're in charge, Mr. Sorrentino." He left by the back door.

My mind went fuzzy after that, like I had fallen asleep in front of the TV, jolted awake by a loud commercial for a greatest-hits collection by the Old Regulars:

"Five porkroll-egg-and-cheese—now move your ass!" . . . "Just a half cup—thank you, kind sir!" . . . "I been in this business twenty years, ya-know-wadda-mean?" . . . "A dozen fried eggs, extra greasy!" . . . *Tap. Tap. Tap* . . . "Can't you see the man is busy?" . . . "I putta too mucha shoogah!" . . . "I been in this business thirty years, ya-know-wadda-mean?" . . . "You don't want that ham today, it's all slimy!" . . . "Two regu-lahs! And a bagel with a schmeah!" . . . *Oh yeah, I remember that place* . . . "Steven, go help your father in!" . . . *Lean him back like an appliance on a dolly. Pull the wheelchair up that step* . . . "Howdy, Mayor!" . . . "Fuck the poor people!" . . . "I been in this business forty years, ya-know-wadda-mean!" . . . "Gimme a complimentary knife so I can ssspread my SSSkippy!" . . . *Tap. Tap. Tap* . . . "Can't you see the man is busy?" . . . "Gimme a burger to go for my faggot nephew!" . . . "Thank you, kind sir." . . . "I been in this business two hundred years, ya-know-wadda-mean?" . . . *Lean him back like an appliance* . . . *How the fuck do you do it, Dad?* . . . "Twelve porkroll-egg-and-cheese—no, make that fifty! I'll get the lemonades!" . . . *Why didn't I leave this fucking place when I had the chance?* . . . "Yep."

"Hey, Dasha!" Vivian yelled when the rush started to subside. Dolores's head swiveled a full hundred and eighty degrees, though the wig didn't quite make the complete trip. The part that usually hovered over her left ear shifted around just shy of her eyeball. Vivian started to laugh.

"Dasha, what the hell you got under there anyway?"

"Hair like a *pisdah!*" Dolores shot back, as if she'd been waiting a lifetime for that setup.

Googie the Gizmo and Martin Leslie Pembrook had to lean over side-ways, giving Vivian room for a quick dismount, her convulsive hysterics requiring additional space. She stood about four feet away from the counter, bent over, slapping her hands on her thighs, until cleansing breaths slowly restored her to full posture.

"Oh, oh, I'm tellin' ya!" Vivian carefully dabbed at her eyes so as not to ruin her makeup. "Steven, do you know what she just said?"

"Nope. And I don't think I want to," I responded humorlessly.

"Go 'head, Vwaj, tell 'im!" Dolores dared Vivian.

"I'm not telling him! I don't use language like that!" Vivian got back on her stool, giggling as her mind went to instant replay. "You tell him what the word means."

"Come here, *boychick*." Dolores cupped her hand protectively by her mouth and whispered the translation of *pisdah* in my ear. Googie and Martin leaned forward over their beverages and watched for my response.

More customers walked in as I stubbornly refused to laugh.

That's when it happened.

I was barely keeping up with the toast orders when Big Bobby approached the counter, hard hat in hand, with that same look of reverence I had seen every time he held the door for my father. But this time, the image of this huge man standing before me was like a monument marking the moment I finally lost it.

"What can I get you, Bobby?"

I looked up into that cherubic face as he uttered those fateful words: "I'll have a porkroll-egg-and-cheese."

I can't explain why, but I started to chuckle. Then giggle. I couldn't stop. I nodded politely at him before walking away, even giddier when I passed Dolores coming round the bend. "Bobby needs a porkroll-egg-and-ch—" I pushed through the swinging doors into the kitchen and went back into the dark pantry, where I could hide among the giant cans of Hunt's tomatoes and boxes of Christmas decorations.

And I began to cry. Then sob, uncontrollably, as if someone had died. I'm not sure how long I had been there when I looked up and saw Dolores standing in the doorway—speechless.

"That was pretty funny," I finally said to the woman with the revolving wig and the dirty words. "I'm going to have to write that one down."

Dolores continued to stare at me without saying a word.

"I have to make a phone call," I said, starting to skirt around her. But she grabbed me by the arm and held on for a second, looking me straight in the eyes.

"My *boychick*."

It was a warm and unexpected gesture from the woman who had just taught me how to say *cunt* in Polish.

Brent Jamison was pissed off but he came over that night anyway. I apologized for calling him at the office—that wasn't part of our arrangement—but I was desperate to see him.

"It's okay, Steve-o." He knew his way down the hall to my small living room.

Brent wouldn't look at me at first. I watched him remove his blazer and fold it neatly over the side of the chair. He then loosened his tie and slipped it over his head with the knot still intact as he kicked off his shoes.

"So, you want a glass of wine or something?" I offered.

"No, not tonight." Brent started to pull his shirt out of his pants. "I don't really have much time. One of the babies has a cold and is driving Candy nuts."

Dear, sweet, nutty Candy.

He sat back on the love seat with his long legs splayed outward. "So?"

"I feel like talking."

"Do you have any pot?"

"No!" I sat down next to him and folded my arms.

"So what's up, Steve-o?"

"Nothing." I pouted. "That fucking luncheonette!"

"Steve-o, when are you going to get the hell out of that place? What about going back to school or doing something in New York again?"

"I just don't know." My eyes started to well up. "I'm afraid of everything. It's like I'm always waiting for the next fucked-up thing to happen."

Brent put his arm around my shoulder and pulled me closer to him. At first I resisted, but I finally caved under his weight and fell backward on the couch, my face disappearing into the side of his neck. I could smell the Aramis.

We stayed like that for a few minutes. But when I started to cry, Brent loosened his grip and sat back up and looked at his watch.

"You know, Steve-o, sometimes I really hate myself. And it's definitely not Candy's fault that I sometimes hate her. She's not a strong woman, but that's probably why I picked her. I really don't know what's to become of us—Candy and me, that is."

"Who knows why we stay anywhere." I wiped my eyes dry and tried to move closer, but he had turned slightly. "Brent, I know this doesn't make any sense, but I'm afraid that if I go away, something is going to happen to my father."

"Your father?" He looked at me, incredulous. "Steve-o, he doesn't need you anymore!"

"Fuck you!" I spewed without hesitation, though I immediately regretted it.

"Whoa, Steve-o." Brent raised both his hands like he was trying to stop an oncoming truck.

"I'm sorry, I didn't mean that," I said, surprised that I hadn't driven him away right there and then, but apparently I was yet to leak out the real magic words. I looked into his eyes. "I love you, Brent."

But it was too late to take *that* one back.

"It was *never* supposed to be about that!" he said, jumping up from the couch.

We both began to panic. Brent rambled on something about loving his kids "more than any *thing* or any *one* else in this world." He half tucked his shirttail back into his pants then slipped his tie back over his head and slid the knot up into position.

"I just can't do this anymore," he mumbled while looking down and stepping back into his loafers.

"You just can't do this anymore *tonight,* or anymore *anymore?*"

He wouldn't even look at me. I tried to hug him, desperate to hold on to I-don't-know-what, but felt the pit in my stomach when his arms remained stiffly at his sides.

"I'll see you soon?" I begged.

"Sorry, Steve-o, I think I have to stay away from the luncheonette for a while."

He grabbed his blazer from the chair and rushed out the door.

I don't know how long I stood there after Brent left. It may have been hours or merely minutes, but all I know is that I felt like I had been standing there—unable to move—since Christmas Eve 1980.

35.
EIGHTY-SIX THE KID

The beauty of planning a suicide is that it keeps your mind off your depression.

After Brent left my house that night, I could no longer see straight. It was as if all the disappointment and fear and loss of the past four years had been released in a blurry floodgate. Desperate for relief, I knew I had to find a project to divert my attention. And it worked! Once I'd decided to kill myself, I was able to focus again. Finding a new purpose in life made it much easier to retain some smiley semblance of normalcy so that no one would suspect anything was wrong.

When it came to depression, I was a real closet case.

Normally, I would have been content with a steady supply of chocolate cream pie or Drake's cakes to keep me preoccupied, but I had lost my appetite. Instead, I began the slow and methodical process of getting my affairs in order. I didn't really get the point of that since I wouldn't be around to reap any of the benefits, but just going through the motions was a preferable alternative to actually experiencing the crippling despair.

For the next several weeks, I cleaned up my neglected apartment. There were dishes in the sink, crumpled pie tins falling out of the garbage, and a coating of dust on the furniture. I guess my mother had taught me well: When things get to be too much, get out the Lemon Pledge and run the vacuum.

One night, at the end of October, I went through all my clothes and pulled out everything that was worn or no longer fit. I ran the stuffed bags down to Goodwill, never appreciating the irony of keeping all the good stuff—it was not like I'd be able to take the Sasson jeans with me. Although I had grown out of a lot of things, one item in particular felt way too big for me to fill out anymore. I opened the large bin and dropped in the bag containing my long black coat.

And I can't even begin to explain why I pulled out all of my albums and tapes and compulsively rearranged them by genre and artist, as if the first concern voiced by whoever found my lifeless body would be, "Oh my God! Where are the Streisands?" But at least I'd be leaving my house in order.

The cleaning and organizing took up all my time and energy, but it was the fantasies that diverted my mental attention.

I pictured my wake at Damiano's as if I would actually be there to enjoy it. For weeks, a parade of people filed by the open casket. First, the old regulars from the luncheonette would arrive, shocked and perplexed. "He was sssuch a great kid," Gertie would whisper to Martin. "I just don't understand it—his eggs were perfect," Googie would say, shaking his head as Stanley and Vivian and the rest of the good ones would line up. But Vida and Buddy would block the front door when Herck the Jerk showed up, having gotten explicit instructions in my will to tell him to go fuck himself. When I imagined Dolores approaching the coffin in her daisy-print cocktail dress with the lethal darts, I started to chuckle, but the laughter quickly dissolved into tears as I imagined her grief. It was the same for Uncle Tony and Nonny and Judy and my brothers and my mother—I had to stop. As my family began to arrive at the imaginary service, I became overwhelmed with empathic grief for myself, having to completely shift fantasies before my father arrived.

It did give me pleasure, however, to picture Brent Jamison standing discreetly off to the side, blaming himself for all the pain he had caused, weeping behind dark glasses, and repeating, "If only I had stayed. If only I had stayed!"

In my fantasy, he finally realized how much he loved me. But that's when I realized that none of this had anything to do with him.

In fact, all the fantasies and the cleaning and organizing were becoming tiresome as the true heaviness of the depression returned again in waves. It was the end of November 1984, and I didn't think I could bear to live through another Christmas.

"Sherman! Go let the mayor in!"

Dolores didn't understand why I cringed every day about 11:45 when Dad appeared at the front window, but she remained loyal to me and protective of my father at the same time. "Let the goddamn Indian do it," she'd whisper to me as a gesture that she was on my side, before rushing a cup of coffee over to Dad's table so it would be waiting for him when Sherman rolled him into place.

I was the only one being cold and inattentive to the old regular, though he remained reliably cheery. I couldn't even look Dad in the eye most mornings, afraid of what might be reflected back. I don't know what I feared seeing more: *my* rage or *his* love? The last thing I wanted was a reminder that I might have something to live for.

One day, we played a little eye game. He sat there patiently stroking the ridge of his right ear until he caught me catching a peek. His expression was quizzical. "Hi, Steve?"

"Hi."

Satisfied that he'd made contact, he stirred his two teaspoons of sugar and healthy plop of milk into his coffee as one or two of his spontaneous appointments of the day stopped by his table to discuss random pieces of borough business. I fixed him an American cheese on white with mayo, which he saved off to the side until Angelo joined him later with a pepper-and-egg sandwich.

It had been so long since Dad and I had watched one of our old variety shows together or since he had sung along with Dean Martin or given me one of his instant lectures on some old forties standard. But now I watched him sit there, guests rotating around him like he was Merv Griffin, while I shrank behind the protective confines of the Formica counter and sulked like one of Ted Mack's rejects on the *Amateur Hour,* my music having been cut short in the preliminaries.

The only thing whirling around *me* was the smoke from Stanley's flake steak and the eye-burning mist from Dolores's spray bottle.

"You don't fool me, *boychick,*" Dolores prodded while wiping down the counter in broad sloppy stokes after the rush. "Something's up."

"Dolores. I'm just sick of—oh, I don't know."

"Sick of bein' Mr. Goody Goody Shithouse?"

"Something like that." I looked over at Dad and company lingering at table one. "Everyone around here thinks I'm this wonderful son," I scoffed. "And I smile for them and everything is more wonderful and—shit. Then I go home and—shit. If they only knew."

"I know, doll." Dolores was wadding up paper towels into a clump and spraying straight ammonia across the hood of the Bay Marie when she delivered her latest pearl. "But you know what they say, hon: Behind lace curtains are the biggest holes."

Some people have a certain flare for synthesizing great wisdom into a few well-chosen words. And then there was Dolores.

I was startled one day when I heard an explosion of laughter from table one. I looked up from my grilling just as Dad had delivered the punch line to Angelo and Uncle Tony and whoever else was locked in his captive audience. He saw me watching and raised his head out of the little huddle and looked at me like we were the only two people in the room. It felt like the time I'd caught his eye from the stage of the tiny Quaigh Theater in New York where I was doing a farcical piece called *Ishtar.* I had just pulled off one of the bigger laughs of the evening built around a line about a rutabaga. (Don't ask.) All I remember was how wide Dad's grin was, like he was checking his teeth in a mirror.

Looking into his eyes that day in the luncheonette, I had a momentary recollection of who I was—but I quickly turned away. I guess I saw myself in my father but had become oblivious to all the incredible obstacles he'd overcome and all the goodwill and accomplishment that now surrounded him.

The only thing reflected back to me now was the wheelchair—with spokes that looked more like the bars of a portable prison.

The cleaning and organizing was still somewhat therapeutic, but the fantasies of being laid out at Damiano's fizzled out. It was time to occupy my thoughts with the more practical aspect of plotting my escape. I still hadn't come up with a plan.

One night, while Windexing the bathroom mirror, I began to ponder all the different ways I could end my life. My sparsely stocked medicine cabinet didn't yield much potential unless I honestly thought I could overdose on Excedrin or Ace-bandage myself to death. And when I moved on to the tub, I seriously considered the possibility of slitting my wrists using that little trick of running them under hot water to curtail the pain—or was it cold? Regardless, I knew my thoughts were morose and sometimes ridiculous, but the sheer suicidal ideation kept me preoccupied.

I almost forgot how depressed I was until one night I seriously considered the possibility of running down to the Long Branch Passenger Station and throwing myself in front of a train. But I couldn't imagine that kind of impact. I had to figure out a better way.

In the weeks that followed, I slipped deeper into a well of darkness, my sadness giving way to self-pity. Although the compulsive cleaning had lost most of its appeal, there was still one final project that needed to be completed.

I went into the hall closet, pushed aside the coats and jackets, moved the vacuum cleaner, and there it was: the Pennfield Farms box. I carried it into the kitchen and placed it next to the garbage can and pulled up a chair. Yanking off the strip of tape, I pulled back the flaps of the box and began to sift through the contents not seen since the day I'd moved out of New York City three years before.

The cassette tape from my session with Ernest the Central Park West Psychic sat on top. I could almost hear his spot-on assessment of me—Music, music, music—and his ominous warning of a "crisis" in the family and promises of my growing "very old." Well, everyone has a crisis here and there, the music was dead, and soon I would be, too. "What a crock of shit!" I said out loud as I yanked the tape from the casing and threw it away.

Next, I gathered up the Wildwood matchbooks and scraps of paper containing phone numbers of men I no longer remembered. I guess that George, whose name had been annotated with *the Greek guy who ripped me off,* had moved on to other people's unattended wallets long ago, leaving me with that nagging feeling that stolen cash aside, we had had something special. I released the shreds of George and the other notes and love letters into the garbage bin like funereal ticker tape.

I don't know why the photo of Parris and me in our straw hats didn't make the cut, but I put it aside. The same for my collection of Broadway scores, fake books, and sheet music.

But I destroyed most everything else.

The first page that I tore out of my journal was dated January 22, 1977, and simply stated the excitement of a nineteen-year-old: *Today I moved to New York City.* The pages that followed documented four years of auditions and rejections, colorful neighbors, betrayals and dramas, Bloomingdale's and catering gigs, and sexual escapades. I tore the pages out two or three at a time until I reached the final entry. December 9, 1980. *I found out this morning that John Lennon was murdered last night at the Dakota. I ran over there and stood with the crowd. Many were holding candles and someone was playing a tape of "Imagine."*

There were no entries after that. The rest of the journal was blank. I threw it aside.

If I had poured out my heart into the journal, the next stack of papers contained my soul. I came upon pages of creative writing I had done during my years in New York. A song, short stories, an unfinished play, and countless undeveloped ideas were piled up. Although what I was doing was perfectly within my legal rights, I carefully shredded each page, occasionally looking over my shoulder like I was destroying evidence. But it wasn't a crime I was trying to cover up. It was my life.

I was packing the photo and the music and a few other items back into the Pennfield Farms box when I noticed my figurine of Tevye rolled up in my old sweatshirt and stuffed into one of the corners. I remembered the theatrical pose he struck, and the brightness in the skillfully molded and painted face, like he was dreaming of the future. When my parents gave him to me, I put him up on a shelf and stared at him like he was about to spring to life. But I knew that if I unrolled that sweatshirt and looked him in the face this time, I would have shattered the statue into a thousand pieces. So I left him there, still covered up, and closed the flaps.

The cleanup was complete.

I carried the carton back to the closet, the door of which was still open, and wedged it back into place on the floor next to my mother's green Eureka canister vacuum cleaner with all the original attachments.

That's when the idea came to me.

I waited until late at night when I was sure my downstairs neighbors would be asleep and no one would be on the street. I had detached the green hose from the body of the vacuum cleaner and carried it out to my 1972 blue Plymouth Duster parked out front. Just as I suspected, the nozzle fit over the exhaust pipe, though masking tape would be necessary to hold it securely in place. But there was still a problem. I discovered that the hose was not long enough to stretch around to the top of the car window.

I ran back inside and grabbed the two metal tube attachments. They would add approximately four more feet to the overall length. Something was still missing to complete the plan. I went into the linen closet and perused my stack of towels, grabbed one of the unmatched ones so as not to break up my good set from JC Penney. I ran back out to the car.

I cracked the rear window about two inches—just enough to accommodate the metal tubing that would carry the exhaust from the tailpipe, through the green hose, and into the car. I then stuffed the towel into the open space to provide insulation so that precious carbon monoxide would not escape. My heart raced. I hadn't been this excited since my seventh-grade project on thermal pollution won third prize at the science fair. Mrs. White would be so proud to know that tuna sandwiches aside, I hadn't lost my touch.

Cleanup . . . *check.*

Method . . . *check.*

Time . . . to be determined.

I carried my green hose, metal tubes, and toweling back inside and stuffed them into an Abraham & Straus shopping bag before going to bed.

Okay, Steven, now all that's left is to just do it!

Just do it!

I slept soundly for the first time in months.

The 1984 holiday season was upon us. There was an eerie sense of contentment in knowing that my plan was in place. But once the distraction of all the preparation was behind me, the depression began to weigh more and more heavily, though I still managed to perform my duties at the luncheonette. I even played along with all the old regulars as they counted down shopping days until Christmas, though I was pondering a more fatal event.

Maybe tonight will be the night.

December 8, 1984. The Immaculate Conception. The night Lennon was shot.

No, not tonight.

December 15 . . . 16 . . . 19 . . . 23 . . .

Well, I've waited this long.

Christmas Eve 1984 arrived with its stubborn significance to my family.

My three-year-old niece was picking at the tiny honey-drenched balls with the rainbow sprinkles. *"Strufoli!"* Judy instructed her older daughter while cradling the infant who had been born the night of *Cujo.*

My brother Michael sautéed garlic and fresh parsley for the clam sauce while Mom started the water for the linguine. "You think three pounds will be enough?"

"Four!" Dad hollered from his wheelchair in the other room.

Nonny had started to enjoy Christmas again. She waddled her way from room to room, handing out envelopes from her purse. And Aunt Rosie was her usual jolly self. "I can't stand anything that smells!" she griped when she unwrapped the scented soaps I bought her.

"You're welcome," I said.

"Thank you." She half smiled and gave the top of my hand a little slap.

John and Charles looked at me and laughed while plucking more jumbo shrimp and roasted peppers from trays of antipasto that were placed around the kitchen and den.

"Reggie!" Mom chased our mutt who was yapping and nudging our guests for scraps.

And at the center of this holiday bazaar was Dad, his calibrated urine bag freshly emptied, his speech fully restored, his smile broader than ever, as he locked his arm around the handlebar of his wheelchair so he wouldn't topple over while filling his plate with mozzarella and pepperoni and extra cocktail sauce for the shrimp.

I knew that the anniversary of Dad's paralysis still weighed heavily on everyone's mind, but there was no reference to it until we got to the dinner table.

"Can you believe it?" Judy handed the baby off to Charles and pursed her lips. "Four years ago tonight."

"Christmas!" Mom shuddered the word off like a doomsday prophecy, blowing a storm of air out of her mouth as she and my sister methodically arranged platters of pasta and seafood on the table.

Dad ignored them as he started to fill his dish. Without a trace of regret or even nostalgia, he locked his arm around the handlebar of his wheelchair again and reached precariously to the center of the table for a lobster claw.

And I just sat there trying to understand why the fuck this man still loved Christmas.

I went home that night and looked at the A&S shopping bag containing the green hose and bath towel and masking tape.

No, not tonight.

Not Christmas Eve. That date belongs to him. I want my own.

I honestly believed that I didn't have any options, yet I was stalled by excuses to *not* die, like when I rehashed my plan in my head and couldn't bear the thought of being caught dead in that 1972 blue Plymouth Duster with my mother's green Eureka canister vacuum cleaner with all the original attachments. But once the excuses were to run out, I would have no choice but to follow through on my plan to kill myself—unless, on the flip side, I were to find a reason to live.

December 25, 1984.

Christmas Day. No, I couldn't possibly . . .

December 26 . . .

I want to die. But just not tonight.

On December 27, 1984, I was so depressed that I could barely get out of bed.

The potential for a truly dramatic suicide was slowly slipping away with the holiday season. Any two-bit depressive could kill himself in January or February, but I wanted to get the old vacuum cleaner going before New Year's.

Maybe tonight.

I dragged myself to the luncheonette that morning, wrapped my greasy red apron around my waist, and pulled it tighter than the smile I forced across my face.

Dad never showed up for lunch that day.

When I got home later, I started watching *One Life to Live* until I was lulled to sleep during the premature darkness of the winter afternoon. The television was the only light in the room, flashing at me like a strobe, when the persistent ringing of the phone woke me up a few hours later.

Leave me the fuck alone!

"Hello?" I said politely. "What?"

It was my mother calling with a familiar message.

"There's something wrong with your father."

36.
HEART ATTACKS

When it came to holiday drama, Dad still held the corner on the market—though his stranglehold on the Christmas season was really beginning to piss me off. It wasn't enough that my father had eclipsed my glory days, but now he was really fucking with my martyrdom: Dad had chosen *my* eleventh hour to have a coronary.

I was also pissed off that the woman at the reception desk in the emergency room didn't recognize me at first—clearly no appreciation for the repeat customer. She eventually gave me clearance to cross through the electronic doors and tried to direct me back to the patients' area, but I didn't need her help.

"I know the way."

The symptom this time was grievous facial pain. Apparently the paralysis had masked the warning signs that should have come from Dad's chest, causing them to telegraph to a more available terrain of sensation.

His face was pale and still tight with pain when I got to him. Erratic heartbeats registered across the overhead monitor, but he was smiling nonetheless. Keeping his elbow anchored at his side, Dad raised his forearm when he saw me and waved like he was in a motorcade.

"How are you feeling, Dad?"

"Pretty good," he said weakly.

"Your father!" Mom shook her head, her tone of admonishment signaling that the crisis had passed. She had made the call to the first-aid squad despite protests from the stubborn patient. Now she looked up at the green line that continuously regenerated itself across the monitor, each beep taking on seismic significance. "They seem to be more regular now," she concluded.

"How are *you* doing, Steve?" Dad asked hoarsely.

"Shit. I can't wait to see what Dolores is going to do with this one."

Dad's laugh quickly gave way to a distressed attempt at a cough that was too muffled to register any relief. Mom held his hand just as the doctor arrived to examine him.

"I'll wait outside for a few minutes," I said.

I hated being there. I hated the deceptively clean smell of the hospital. I hated the sounds of life support. I hated the feeling of helplessness. All around me I could sense life in delicate balance, death possible in a heartbeat.

I wandered back out to the waiting area where a scrubbed-up CNN anchor read rehashed news in monotone from the ceiling-mounted television. I paced around the room, unable to stand still, until something on a bulletin board caught my attention. I had skipped over the posting asking for blood donations and the cards about careers in nursing or bus trips to Atlantic City. It was the little box tacked firmly in place with the glossy invitation to TAKE ONE that caught my eye. I pulled out one of the little leaflets containing a phone number and put it in my pocket.

A couple of hours later, Dad settled into his room in the coronary-care unit. Mom and I waited outside as they got him hooked up to the proper apparatuses. The doctor assured us that most of what they were doing was cautionary and routine and that fortunately his heart attack had not been massive. The EKG had been satisfactory, but we really knew Dad was stabilized when he recognized the night nurse from a previous stay. "Hey there, sweetheart!"

"You need your rest, Clint!" Mom finally called an end to the evening. I leaned over and kissed Dad on the forehead. As I walked out of the room, I took one final look back and saw that smirk on my father's face as the green line crisscrossed the overhead monitor and registered each heartbeat.

I loved my father so much in that moment but was too angry to tell him.

"Your father!" Mom turned to me in the car as I drove her home.

"Uhhh!" I responded. "I just know that when I come back tomorrow, that man will be sitting up in bed with that same goddamn smile, eating a sandwich, and he'll ask me if I brought him a cup of coffee! Doesn't he know that he's a fucking cripple! How the hell does he do it?"

"You know—he *never* refers to his own condition." She sighed. "When he first came out of the hospital, I tried to get him to join some kind of group or organization so he could meet other paraplegics, just for information, for moral support. You know. He just said to me 'I'm not hanging around with those people!' *Those* people! I get so angry. But he doesn't."

"I don't understand him, Mom."

"And remember how much he loved to play golf? Loved it! But now he can still sit in that wheelchair on a Saturday afternoon and watch it on television for hours. He *still* loves it. No regrets! He never says 'I wish I could still play golf.' "

"And I've never heard him say, 'I wish I could still sing.' "

"Hmm." She sighed, then looked at me. "Are you all right?"

"Yeah, I'm just tired." I pulled my rusted Plymouth Duster into the driveway.

Reggie had pushed the living-room drapes aside with his snout and was pressing his wet nose against the picture window. "Oh, that poor dog must be dying to get out." Mom leaned over and kissed me goodnight. "Thanks, Steven." She grasped the door handle then hesitated. "Did I ever tell you what your father said that first time in the hospital?"

"I don't think so."

"I've never forgotten it. Dr. Herman had just told him that he would probably never walk again, and your father wants to know if there is any chance that he'd recover and be able to get back to the luncheonette so that *you* could go back to New York."

"I never knew that," I said quietly like I was talking to myself.

"Yeah, your father gets the worst news of his life and he asks, 'What about my son?' Herman had to tell him 'Your son will be all right.' "

"Really?"

"Yeah. It was important for your father to know that." Mom looked me straight in the eye. "And you know what else he said?" She paused. "He said, 'Thank God this happened to *me,* and not to one of my kids.' " She looked away and gulped.

I now knew what it felt like to get hit by a train.

When I got home that night, I flipped on the lights in my apartment and plopped myself down on the love seat. Instead of turning on the television, I just looked around. Everything was so clean and orderly. The only clutter was an A&S shopping bag sitting in the corner of the room.

I dropped my head into my hands and groaned, but I didn't cry. I stayed in that position for several minutes, my thoughts racing through everything that had brought me to that moment. I sat up straight.

Okay, Steven, do it!

I stood up but froze again.

Steven . . . just . . . do it!

And I did.

I reached into my right-hand pocket and pulled out the leaflet I'd taken from the bulletin board at the hospital a few hours earlier. I walked over to the kitchen phone and dialed the number.

"Outreach." The voice on the other end of the phone had a friendly urgency to it. "How can I help you?"

"Well, I know this may sound a little weird—"

"It's okay, go ahead."

"Well, um, first of all, I want you to know that I'm okay and I'm not going to do anything foolish."

"Okay."

"Well, it's just weird. You see, I've been obsessed with committing suicide, but I really don't want to do it. I swear. I'm not going to do it."

"Okay. Are you sure you are going to be all right for tonight?"

"Yes." I started to cry, but put my hand over the receiver so she wouldn't hear.

"Tell me your name."

"My name is Steven Sorrentino." I spelled it out for her.

"Okay, Steven. I want you to come in tomorrow morning at nine o'clock sharp. You have an appointment with Dr. Wayne Goldman. Okay?"

"Okay."

"Are you sure you are going to be all right tonight?"

"Yes." I barely got the syllable out.

"You promise?"

"Yes." I took a deep breath, "I'm going to be all right. I promise."

37.
CHECK, PLEASE!

"Make that two regulahs. A *bank*, you said? That's fantastic!" Isaac shouted to Elliot, who was over by the newspapers. "Did you hear that? Steven is going into banking!"

"Fantastic! And a bagel with a schmeah!"

A bunch of the Syrians rushed over to me with their good wishes and raised-print business cards, lauding my career move like I was going to be managing corporate takeovers. I didn't know how much I was going to like my new part-time job as a teller, but I did know for certain that on April 12, 1985, I was wielding that fucking spatula for the last time.

"Scramble two soft with bacon for Lorraine, two over medium with ham for Carmen, whiskey down for both, and move your ass!"

"Coming right up!" I spooned two orders of home fries onto the cooler side of the grill, peeled three slices of bacon for the hot, cracked two eggs onto the warm side, dropped the rye bread into the toaster, made a quick side trip to the Bay Marie for the ham, cracked two eggs into the stainless bowl, and picked up my whisk despite the fact that Old Man Pascucci wouldn't stop tapping his cup on the counter.

"Can't you see the man is busy!" Martin Leslie Pembrook slapped his folded *Times* down on the counter as Dolores scolded the old man.

"*Rrranny bozke!* Gimme your goddamn cup before I kick your ass all the way back to Nippoli!" Even under duress, she could still talk in tongues.

"It's *Napoli,* and be nice!" I think I surprised the old man when I came to his defense, but Mr. Pascucci's corncob pipe damn near fell out of his mouth when I stole his line. "He put too much sugar—it could happen to anyone!"

"Well, aren't you little Mr. Goody Goody Shithouse this morning!" Dolores held the coffeepot out to the side as she passed by, her Banlon-covered breasts brushing across my back with a startling charge of static electricity.

"My God, those things are sparking!" I recoiled.

"You bet they are, *boychick!*" She grabbed the left one with her free hand and aimed it at me like a stun gun.

"Dolores," Sherman quietly warned from his post back in the kitchen, his folded arms and pensive stare framed perfectly in the service window.

"Look at him," she whispered to Martin. "He looks like he's guarding a fuckin' cigar store."

"I heard that."

"Now how the hell can you hear me from all the way back there!" she yelled toward the kitchen while moving farther down the counter to set up a couple more coffees.

"It's the breed," she whispered in a huddle with Stanley and Googie. "I think he's incensing my vibrations."

"I heard that."

"Christ!"

"Yep." Stanley stirred a plop of milk into his cup and Googie the Gizmo winked at me.

"Dolores," I said with all due respect, "why are you being such a *pisdah* this morning?"

"*Yebotch yeh!*" She was pouring coffee for Half Cup Harold but managed to shoot a finger at me with her free hand.

I won't take that personally. Thank you, Dr. Wayne Goldman.

"Here you go, Howard bay-bay."

"Thank you, kind ma'am." Harold held up his hand to stop her midpour. "So, Steven, when do you start your new job?"

"Monday!" I beamed. "I'm kind of excited about it."

"Congratulations!"

"Yeahhh, Mr. Big Shit Pinstripe Suit Banker. Where the hell are my eggs!"

Half Cup Harold commended my move to Shadow Lawn Savings & Loan just up Monmouth Road, but Dolores was not impressed. "It sounds like you're goin' to work in a fuckin' cemetery!"

"Thanks, Dolores, I'm going to miss you, too." I tried to give her a smooch, but she pushed me away.

"You're full of *goovno!*"

"Today yer last day at the luncheonette?" Stanley looked up from his coffee.

"Sorry to say, old pal, but I've had this place up to *here*," I said, using a familiar gesture for effect.

"Shit." He scratched his head. "I'll have a porkroll-egg-and-cheese."

"Well, I'll be goddamned!" The flesh on Googie's face reconfigured around that downturned smile people get when they're feeling proud, his jowls flopping in affirmation.

"Good luck to you, son." Martin Leslie Pembrook tapped his pen against his crossword puzzle, suddenly at a loss for words.

Up and down the counter, the old regulars nodded their heads and grunted and groaned in agreement.

"Good for you, honey!" Lorraine cheered, waving a bacon strip.

"Big deal!" The grouchy head waitress was having none of it.

Dolores and I each had our own way of dealing with our impending separation, though for a minute I thought we'd share one last hurrah when the Pepsi truck pulled up to the front of the luncheonette. Unfortunately the *hurrah!* turned into a *huh?* when a scrawny little man in a baggy blue uniform walked in the front door.

"Hello?" I approached him cautiously when he came to the cash register with the bill. "Where's the other guy?"

"What other guy?" he honked in a voice that originated from behind his nose.

"You know, the one that looks kind of like that big guy from *C.H.I.P.S.*"

"Oh! You mean Bruce!"

His name was Bruce?

"Oh yeah," he squeaked. "He moved on to Coke. Hih-hih-hih-hih-hih." He laughed at his own double entendre like an old celebrity panelist Dad and I had seen on *Hollywood Squares*. But I didn't find it funny in the least—Erik Estrada had been replaced by Wally Cox!

Dolores hadn't even bothered to run out to table one for a posterior inspection of Pepsi Nerd. Instead she placed the spray bottle back on the shelf, admiring it like it was an Oscar on a mantel. "Shit." Then she winked at me and snapped the elastic waistband of her black stretch pants like she was signaling the end of an era.

On Christmas Eve 1980, I had begun to see life only for what could be taken away—the hope and promises temporarily obscured. Each of Dad's setbacks was bad enough, rattling my confidence as I felt the loss of independence and power. But it was each of his successes that seemed to throw a spotlight on my own failed dreams, until they were depleted like yesterday's lunch special.

Loss. That was all I could talk about in those first few sessions with Dr. Wayne Goldman—until the day he turned the tables on me and asked me what it was my *father* had lost.

"If you saw him in action, Wayne, you'd think he hadn't lost a thing," I heard myself answering. "And he still has so much to give."

"And what do *you* have to offer *him*?" he said as I squirmed around on the couch, replaying the words in my head that Mom told me Dad had said.

"Hope?" My revelation sounded more like a question.

"At least!"

"Hey, I'm making progress, Doc. Not too long ago, my answer would have been 'American cheese on white with mayo.'" I wasn't kidding.

The truth was, I now had more to offer by venturing out into my own world, not hiding in his. It had seemed easier to fancy my dreams dashed and my life over than to take responsibility for my own comeback. Dr. Goldman had thrown around terms like *anxiety* and *post-traumatic stress*, but Dolores had nailed my condition with her own clinical term: *scared shitless*.

It was really just my expectations of how life was *supposed* to be that had been eighty-sixed. I'm sure Dad's life hadn't aligned with his expectations either, but he had shown me that there were plenty of other items on the menu, and as long as the people he loved buzzed around him, safe and sound—then even paraplegia was well worth his while.

I still had trouble getting out of bed some mornings and spent an evening here and there staring at the telephone. I always kept a full saltshaker on hand for those nights when I was teetering on the edge, wavering between Morton's and Mrs. Smith's. "At least you have choices," Dr. Goldman had been quick to remind me a few sessions back.

But one afternoon, I got the impulse to revisit my Pennifield Farms box. I unpacked the Broadway scores and sheet music, and finally unrolled the old sweatshirt and placed my statuette of Tevye the Dairyman back on the shelf—a fond remembrance of days gone by. The meticulously detailed eyes were not unlike Dad's, reminding me that it was okay to wink at the past, just don't stare at it!

I had enrolled in some journalism classes at Baruch College in New York. The prospect of managing a new job around the commute was daunting, but my confidence was slowly returning. I had cocooned myself in that luncheonette long enough and was ready to move on. My father had. After all he had gone through, Dad still rolled up alongside the front window and tapped on the glass at 11:45 with a big goddamn smile on his face.

"He's here!" Dolores replaced the basket of grounds and hit the button to start the Corey coffee machine. "I'm makin' fresh!"

"Pot," Sherman reminded her pointedly from the service window just before the water started to flow onto the empty burner. "I'll get Clint," he said.

"I got 'm," I said, wiping the grease from my hands and tossing the towel aside.

Other than a couple of missed lunches, the heart attack Dad suffered four months before hadn't affected him much, though I was still somewhat rattled. I didn't know whether or not my father would live out his term as mayor of West Long Branch, or what other unexpected turns life might take for him—or me. But as long as he was willing to go along for the ride—no matter what the destination—so was I.

"Lock your arm, Dad." I reminded him to brace himself around the handlebar as Big Bobby dropped his porkroll-egg-and-cheese to rush over and hold the door. "Thanks, Bobby." I leaned Dad way back and pulled him up that single step with one heave.

"Hello, Mayor!" Gertie parked her cigarette before swiveling around and sliding off her stool. She sauntered over to my father and gave him a kiss on the forehead. "We're going to miss that sssonovabitch ssson of yours!" she sprayed, wiping his forehead dry with her fingers, trying not to muss the hair that he had carefully swept over from the left.

"Well, he's not going too far, I hope." Dad smiled as Dolores pushed me aside to get in her own two cents with the old regular, but he beat her to the punch line. "Dolores! Where the hell is my coffee? I've been sitting here for two whole minutes!"

"Jesus Christ, Clint, I was makin' ya fresh!" She took off down the counter with one hand flat on top of her wig like she was holding down a hat in the wind.

Sherman looked at me and shook his head, but Dad just smirked as the front and back doors flew open. The empty chairs at his table filled up faster than the horn at the firehouse could blare its three noon blasts, and the stools at the counter were spinning.

The final lunch rush of my career had begun.

"Gimme a hamburger. And one to go for my faggot nephew."

"No problem!" I threw two patties on the grill for Herck the Jerk then brought him a free refill on his Pepsi.

"Here you go!"

"I didn't ask for that!" he blatted, pushing it away angrily.

I decided to take a chance. Dolores was delivering lemonade to Vivian two stools down when I looked the Jerk straight in the eye and made my move.

"Go fuck yourself, Herck!" I pushed the soda back toward him.

"Ahhh!" Vivian threw up her arms then reached across the counter to grab Dolores. "Dasha! Did you hear this kid? Ah! We're going to miss him. I'm telling you."

Herck didn't bat an eye. He just broke the straw through the end of the paper, put it to his mouth, and blew the wrapper on the floor before dipping in for a sip. He never said a thing. It dawned on me that he was probably used to being treated like that. I suddenly felt sorry for him, that he hadn't been able to put his bad days behind him.

"What are you trying to do, *boychick*, drive away all the customers and then just drop me like a hot tamale?"

"*Potato!* Dolores, why are you wearing all black today? Are you okay? Is there something you want to express?"

"Don't give me any of your psycho shit! I need a pepper-and-egg sub for Angelo and a cheese sandwich for your father—and hold the commentary!"

"Dasha, how much simple syrup did you put in here?" Vivian puckered her lips and squinted after a sip of the lemonade. "I'm telling you, Steven."

"No need to tell me, Vwaj—I already know!" I tried catching Dad's eye to share the laugh, but he was preoccupied.

"Howdy, Mayor!" Stanley's job with the roads department took him past the luncheonette several times a day, but on the noon trip in particular he could bring Dad all the gossip from the borough garage.

And Uncle Tony had barely limped over to the table before Dad mentioned some problem with his shower in the new bathroom, knowing his brother-in law would have it fixed by supper time.

"Here you go, Clint." Dolores went over to refill his cup. "But don't blame me when you start with the palpyootations!" She had given up her battle to get my father to switch over to decaf, but that didn't stop her from issuing the stern warnings. "Take care of that heart, hon. Ya don't wanna get another attack of vagina!"

"I think he just did," I called from my perch behind the counter as Angelo cupped his hands over Dad's ears.

"Dolores! Careful! The man's been sick!"

I watched Dad during my final lunch hour as he sat at table one like the stationary axis of a child's colorful top, his attentive public and adoring family and loyal friends spinning around him in a kaleidoscopic whirl of love and affection.

"It's good to be the mayor!" Angelo raised his unlit cigar to his mouth, his free arm wrapped around my father like he was jockeying for a political appointment. Although Dad's laughter sounded more like respiratory distress, he would be more apt to describe his state as joyous.

★ ★ ★

"Sit down and have a cup of coffee with your father," Sherman prodded me when the lunch rush began to wind down. "You've done enough."

I felt self-conscious, not one to easily surrender old roles, but I untied my apron and took a seat at table one right next to Dad. Sherman brought a cup of coffee over to me as Dolores suspiciously disappeared into the kitchen.

"Oh shit," I said graciously when she emerged through the swinging doors with a huge cake fashioned after an Oreo cookie, leading an off-pitch customer chorus in "For He's a Jolly Good Fellow." There was a white border around the cake with chocolate wording: TO ANOTHER GREAT COOKIE. GOOD LUCK STEVEN.

Dad couldn't join in the singing but he did lead the applause, the first heard in the luncheonette since his return in the wheelchair four years earlier. We looked at each other but there was nothing to be said.

I did, however, have to comment on the giant Oreo.

"That's quite a piece of *cheska* you've got there, Dolores."

She reached behind and pinched my *poyzladki* as we posed for a photo behind the cake like a bride and groom. Gertie and Stanley and Vivian and Angelo and the rest fussed over me like I was embarking on some kind of odyssey. I helped serve the cake and accepted all their best wishes.

But it was time to leave.

"Well, Dolores. I can honestly say that I've been in this business for four years!" I tucked my hair under an imaginary wig and gave it a tug for emphasis. "Thank you."

"You were a good boss, bay-bay, and you really knew how to move your ass!" Dolores's thick lenses magnified the welling in her eyes like a teary prism. "It's a wonderful thing you did here, *boychick*. Your father—" Dolores couldn't finish her sentence. She started to sob.

"Jesus Christ, Dolores." My voice cracked. "I thought we saved this stuff for back in the pantry!" The sparks I felt this time were more heartfelt as she pulled me into a bosomy hug then pushed me away just as fast so that she could run in the back to blow her nose.

"Come on, Dad. I'll get you out of here," I said, wiping my eyes on my shoulders.

Sherman shook my hand. "Good luck, Steven."

"Thanks."

"I'll see you, Clint." He walked over to hold the front door.

"Lock your arm, Dad."

I leaned the wheelchair back and rolled my father down that single step and out onto the sidewalk in front of the luncheonette where his van was parked.

"I'll miss seeing you here." Dad flipped the switches on the external control panel that opened the side door and lowered the lift to the ground.

"Well, tomorrow is Saturday. I'm not working, so let's meet for lunch!"

"Okay. It's a date." He rolled forward onto the hydraulic lift, grabbed the safety bar, and initiated the grinding gears that would elevate him just slightly into the sky. He flipped the switch to swing him into the van, backed off the lift, then rolled forward, locking the wheelchair into the driver's position.

I was watching him through the open window when he looked at me, his hand about to turn the key in the ignition. "Are you going to stop by the house?"

"No, Dad, I'll just be going my way."

I saw his face light up.

"*Going My Way*. Best Picture 1944. Bing Crosby's big hit was 'Swinging on a Star.'" Dad beamed at his own instant reference to one of his old songs.

"How do you do it, Dad?"

He shrugged his shoulders then turned the key. "Lunch. Saturday." He engaged the van's manual accelerator and pulled away from the curb.

I walked around to the parking lot behind the building, fired up my 1976 silver Mazda GLC with manual transmission, shifted into gear, and finally drove away from the luncheonette.

EPILOGUE

AND ALL THE MONKEYS AREN'T IN THE ZOO,
EV'RY DAY YOU MEET QUITE A FEW.
SO YOU SEE IT'S ALL UP TO YOU.
YOU CAN BE BETTER THAN YOU ARE,
YOU COULD BE SWINGING ON A STAR.

—FROM "SWINGING ON A STAR,"
BY JOHNNY BURKE AND JIMMY VAN HEUSEN

LUNCHEONETTE

I met my father for lunch every Saturday for the next nine years.

Sometimes we talked about the classes I was taking in New York or the new elevator for the disabled being installed at Borough Hall. I described in great detail for him my experience seeing *A Chorus Line* on Broadway for the sixth time, and he detailed for me the council's plans to clean up Franklin Lake. Once he told me a story about one of the borough residents who liked to seek him out at lunchtime to complain about her taxes. He saw her for the first time in a while and heard how she had suffered a temporary paralysis because of some medical condition. "You don't know what it's like to not be able to feel your legs!" she had bellyached to Dad as he nodded sympathetically from his wheelchair.

"What!" I blurted. "What did you say to her?"

"What could I say?" He shrugged. "I just told her, 'At least your taxes didn't go up this year.' "

We had a good laugh over that one and a lot of other stories we shared. But I never did tell him the one about how far I had sunk in 1984. I hoped he at least knew how much all his comebacks and successes had contributed to mine. But we didn't talk about that, either. In fact, we never talked about our relationship at all. Sometimes those lunches just consisted of sitting across from Dad and reading all the columns in the *New York Post* while he grappled with the Jumble in the *Daily News,* and did that thing he always did with his ear.

The luncheonette changed hands once again, but this time neither Dolores nor I was part of the deal. "Oh, they wanted me real bad," she bragged on one of the rare occasions that I ran into her. "But I says, 'I don't need this shit,' ya know wadda mean?"

"You mean they fired you?"

"Yeah." She took a drag on her lipstick-stained Pall Mall.

It was traumatic when the new owners gutted the place and converted it into a pizzeria. The day they yanked out the speckled Formica counter and turquoise spinning stools and pulled the porkroll from the menu was like an Anatevkan pogrom. The old regulars were forced to pick up their *Presses,* grab their parkas off the coatrack, and migrate about a half mile down Locust Avenue like displaced villagers, settling finally at the Hungry Hobo, the new luncheonette in town right next to Cost Cutters.

Dad and I went by van.

Old faces mingled with new ones at the counter of the Hungry Homo (as John and I playfully called it), but it wasn't the same, especially without Dolores. I never saw her again. I heard that she mainly stayed close to home. I pictured her retiring the frosted wig to its Styrofoam head and storing away the Banlon shells, her work finally done. *"Rrranny bozke!"* I would have constructed a carefully worded prayer to God, thanking him for sending me that unexpected friendship during that difficult period, but I didn't think I'd be able to butcher the language enough to do her justice.

I finished school and successfully launched a public-relations career in Manhattan. It seemed economical to maintain my apartment near the Damiano Funeral Home and commute daily to the city, though I slowly came to hate the routine. Maybe I still feared the uncertainty of life and clung to my original attachments, but I wouldn't have traded sitting across from Dad on one of those Saturday lunches for a decade's worth of seats at Broadway openings.

Besides, there was still some unfinished business. I may have left the theater, but in a scene about as dramatic as an after-school special, I finally told my parents one night at dinner that I was gay. They tried to feign surprise, but, when pushed, fessed up to suspecting it all along. The whole scene was almost anticlimactic given all the pent-up anxiety from hiding it all those years. But the part most emblazoned in my memory was the very rare occurrence of Dad actually verbalizing a sentiment. "I love you," he let slip out as I was leaving their house that night. I already knew it at that point but was just so shocked to hear him actually say the words. I was speechless when I leaned over and hugged him in the wheelchair.

And there were other times when duty called and I was grateful to be nearby.

On January 5, 1988, Dad was devastated when Angelo Valenzano died suddenly from a stroke. A blizzard had prevented my father from attending his best friend's funeral, so I went in his place. I felt so bad for my father that day, but as always, he moved forward with a smile on his face, even while pining for Angelo the rest of his days.

Our weekly lunches came to an end in 1994 when I moved back to New York, though I still spent holidays with my family in New Jersey. Every Christmas Eve I sat at the other end of the dining-room table, watching Dad eat linguine and clam sauce, admiring a power and strength in him that I had never recognized in his walking days.

Sadly, however, Dad's appetite eventually waned and his overall health began to fail. Surgery to clear a blockage in his abdomen was not successful, though the bigger blow was the necessity of putting him onto a respirator, rendering him speechless for the final five weeks of his life. We knew he wasn't going to make it, but when I saw him hooked up to that machine and heard that old familiar whooshing sound, I realized that I could not remember his last words. I imagined them to have been some little gem or a sentence that I could endow with special meaning. I would have even settled for one final punch line.

But then again, maybe Dad had not yet had his final word.

For weeks, family and friends and councilmen—not to mention some of the old regulars from the luncheonette—paraded by his bed to say their good-byes. Dad just smiled weakly, silently waving to each visitor in his final campaign. That is until Mom, always the stern advocate for his health, laid down the law to conserve what little energy he had left: immediate family only.

Despite all his medical setbacks—the paralysis, the bedsores, the respiratory ailments, the stroke, the heart attack—Dad had still been the one to save me. Somehow he *always* prevailed, whether in the form of a medical comeback, a sandwich and a smile, or an election victory. I stood at his bedside with Mom and Judy and Michael and John for hours at a time in those final weeks, aching to see if he could pull it off just one more time.

I never asked my father what he considered to be his "dream job." He had been a mason, a baker, and a stockbroker. He had owned a card shop, been a comptroller for another man's business, flipped hamburgers, and been elected to public office. But I don't think he ever thought of himself as teacher.

And neither had I.

Had he taught me how to draft? The blueprints I created after stumbling upon Dad's bore the details and artistry of a serious student, though the lectures had consisted of no more than smiles and nods of approval. He was more informative when it came to music, but my deep love of it had to have been passed along some other way. And somehow, I believe Dad taught me how to sing, but there was no methodology there either. The most specific instruction I had ever received from him was how to make a porkroll-egg-and-cheese sandwich, and even that had to be wrung out of him.

But it all started to come into focus for me: Value life, live in the present, and keep the faith during the harshest tests—even if you find yourself gagging on the Holy Eucharist. It was harder to accept that not all dreams come true, but at least I started to understand that new ones could be born amid the worst nightmares.

Dad never had the words to convey any of that, just examples. They were sometimes extreme and his student sometimes dense. Gertie may have called it best when she sloppily stated, "You know, your ssson is a ssstubborn sssonovabitch like you are."

★   ★   ★

My phone rang at six-thirty one morning.

"Okay, Mom. I'll be there as soon as I can."

I brushed my teeth quickly then jumped into the clothes that I had laid out the night before. Picking up the garment bag with my dark suit and pulling out my keys, I did a quick visual check around the room to make sure I hadn't forgotten anything. *Hmm.* The reflection in my mirror had changed quite a bit over the years. My hair had thinned considerably—the last perm having grown out long ago—but the short crop was simpler and drew the inevitable comparison on the rare occasion that I ran into one of the old regulars: "You're looking more and more like your father!" The long black coat had made its way to Goodwill after a cleaning binge in 1984; now a simple sport jacket over a black tee was all the statement I needed. *Life*, I thought as I ran down the four flights of stairs of my West Seventieth Street brownstone apartment to hail a cab to Penn Station.

Dad had lost his eyesight toward the end, but he turned his head slightly in my direction when I took his hand. The respirator was still forcing air into his lungs, though the whooshing sound had increased in frequency, indicating that his breathing had become more distressed. The heart monitor suspended over the bed registered agitated blips with varying frequency, and his blood-pressure reading had bottomed out at 60/30—as if someone were putting on the brakes.

We all gathered around Dad's bed.

Judy, Michael, John, and I had already concurred that December 24, 1980, had been a major turning point for each of us, our lives forever defined in terms of *before* and *after.* Maybe that's when we stopped being the "kids."

And I can't imagine what it had meant for my mother, resolute and focused, standing the closest to him at his right, as she had always done. If Mom had ever questioned her own ability to go on, she never showed it.

My gaze drifted from face to face around the bed. We were all adults now, living our separate lives, linked by a bond that had been strengthened by Dad's life and was about to be cemented by the shared experience of his death. Still, despite all the experiences we'd shared, I realized there was so much I didn't really know about what they had been through. I hoped that I would learn their stories over the years, and knew that one day—I would tell them mine.

I thought back to Election Night 1982 when Dad had looked around for his family just as the polls were closing. I repeated the same words I'd said to him that night: "We're all here, Dad." And I conceded that Old Gatekeeper Woman, who had predicted that he would never live out his term, had been correct—except for one minor detail: He would not live out his *fourth* term as mayor of West Long Branch.

We all began to utter our last words to him. When it was my turn, I knew that I had to stop clinging.

"We're okay, Dad. Go ahead, go be with Angelo."

As Dad entered a torturous stage of respiratory distress, we gave the order to remove him from the respirator with the doctor's assurances that morphine would alleviate any sensation of suffering. A teary-eyed nurse administered the drip and, when she was sure that the drug had taken effect, removed the tube from his throat and plugged the tracheotomy hole with a plastic stopper.

It was like coming out of a wind tunnel when she turned off the respirator and the room went silent for the first time in five weeks—except for the periodic beep of the heart monitor that was sending out the final signals of life.

We stared at that screen and waited for something to happen.

How will you do it this time, Dad?

I looked into his face. He was completely still, with the slightest smile. His final movement was a tiny gulp as the line on the heart monitor went flat.

"He's gone," my mother said quietly.

But just as we deeply inhaled the finality of it all, one rogue blip suddenly raced across the monitor, signifying a single heartbeat. We were so startled by the sound and its implication that the collective sob we had intended to release escaped instead as a shared burst of uncontrollable laughter. And during those few seconds, when the involuntary sounds of joy had filled the room, Dad died.

If death came in a moment, we had missed it. Was it his final punch line, the joke entirely on us? Dad had always hated good-byes, so maybe he had purposely instigated that final burst of laughter to distract us so he could slip away unnoticed. Or maybe he had wanted to prove that he could prevail just one last time, even if in a single heartbeat.

I looked up at the clock and made a mental note: 11:19 A.M. The year was 1996. And the date: September 11.

On the way home from the hospital, we drove through the intersection where Monmouth Road converged crookedly with Cedar and Locust—Clint's Corner, as I will always think of it.

"Look, Mom!" Diagonally across from the building that once housed the luncheonette, I noticed that the flag over the firehouse was lowered to half-mast. Word was out, and the town had already begun to mourn its beloved "Mayor on Wheels."

I thought that I, too, had already begun to mourn the loss of my father way back on Christmas Eve 1980 when his legs had shuddered to a halt. But as we passed the old luncheonette, I realized that the loss I had felt then was really my youth and innocence slipping away from the boy as the man began to take hold. And though I now felt a new depth of sadness with Dad's death, I accepted it as a measure of his value to my life.

When it comes to family business, I have always been a slow learner. But the timing no longer mattered. I didn't need to know everything right away. I'd found that true wisdom is parceled out into short orders, coming from the most surprising places, at the most unexpected times. But at least it was sinking in. With Dad's final heartbeat, I began to truly appreciate the lessons I'd learned at the luncheonette.

ACKNOWLEDGMENTS

This book would not have happened without the richness of inspiration, support, encouragement, and spirit that has surrounded me.

I must start with my family. Very heartfelt thanks to my mother, Marie "Pete" Sorrentino; my sister, Judy Strollo; and my brothers, Michael and John Sorrentino. How wonderful that we were given the privilege of caring for Dad and one another throughout the years. And I know that all the places where you appear in my story are just the tip of the icebergs of your own experiences. I love you all.

Thank you, Judith Regan, for your faith in me, and for recognizing my role shift. When I first announced that I was quitting my job to write this book, you told me that my life was about to begin. Then you handed me a set of rosary beads and said, "You'll be needing these!" Thank you, *paesana*!

I am so grateful to Stuart Krichevsky, my agent. Thanks for giving an untested commodity a shot. My proposal wouldn't have seen the light of the marketplace without your keen editorial eye and guiding hand.

I can't imagine a better editorial experience: the commitment, gentle nudges, blatant disregard for my bad jokes, the thoughtful suggestions, and—despite our notable age difference—I only stumped you on one pop-culture reference! Thank you, Aliza Fogelson.

And thanks to the rest of the team at ReganBooks and HarperCollins: Paul Olsewski (my friend and brilliant PR director), Lynn Grady, Amy Baron, and Daniel Nayeri. Special note to Michelle Ishay and Lynn Buckley—I love that scratchy ink drawing of my father!

I must also acknowledge my friends and professional colleagues who encouraged me and offered editorial guidance way back when I was struggling through the first hundred pages: Josh Behar, Marjorie Braman, Mauro Di Preta, Claire Wachtel, and Ron Bel Bruno.

And thank you (in no particular order) to: Barbara Gordon for practically reinventing this whole memoir genre, and for your friendship and support over the years; Jerry Stahl for yelling at me over lunch one day: "You *must* write this book!"; Degen Pener, my friend and swing expert; Janusz Mrozek, my handyman and consultant on this book's very questionable Polish; Jessica Jonap for your friendship and "faith"; and Perry Ojeda for your bounty of optimism on my behalf, and the enduring friendship.

I can't begin to list all the family, friends, supporters, and spiritual partners to whom I'd like to express my appreciation and gratitude. At the risk of leaving anyone out, I must say, simply, thank you.

Thank you!
Please Call Again

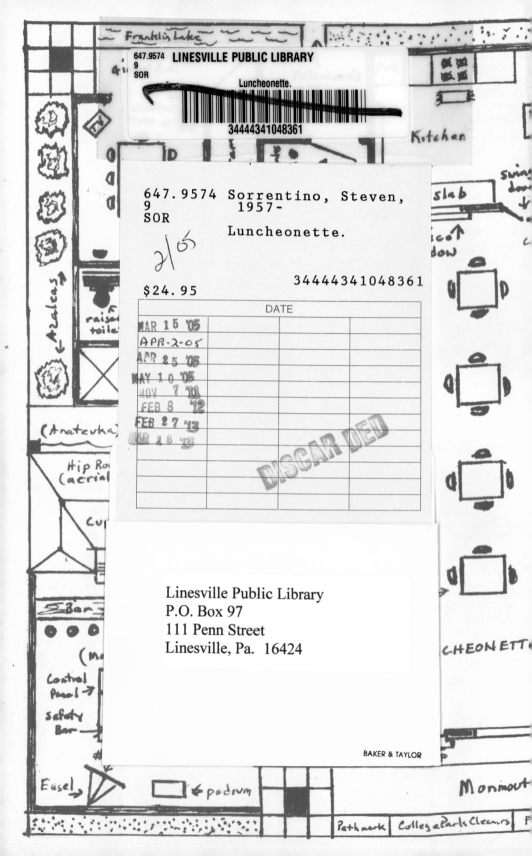